discover
NEW YORK CITY

MICHAEL GROSBERG
GINGER ADAMS OTIS, BETH GREENFIELD, REGIS ST LOUIS

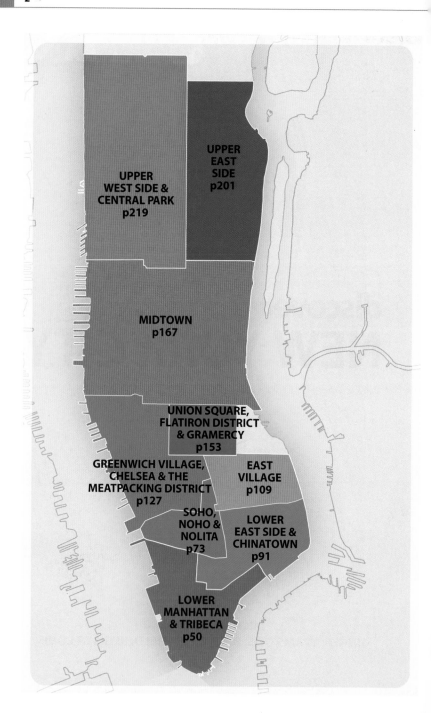

UPPER
EAST
SIDE
p201

UPPER
WEST SIDE &
CENTRAL PARK
p219

MIDTOWN
p167

UNION SQUARE,
FLATIRON DISTRICT
& GRAMERCY
p153

GREENWICH VILLAGE,
CHELSEA & THE
MEATPACKING DISTRICT
p127

EAST
VILLAGE
p109

SOHO,
NOHO &
NOLITA
p73

LOWER
EAST SIDE &
CHINATOWN
p91

LOWER
MANHATTAN
& TRIBECA
p50

DISCOVER NEW YORK CITY

New York City's Top 25 Experiences (p12) The best bits of a great city.

Lower Manhattan & Tribeca (p50) Teeming with iconic images.

SoHo, NoHo & Nolita (p73) Three of the coolest city neighborhoods.

Lower East Side & Chinatown (p91) An enclave for foodies.

East Village (p109) With an electric restaurant and nightlife scene.

Greenwich Village, Chelsea & Meatpacking District (p127) Art, fashion.

Union Square, Flatiron District & Gramercy (p153) A hive of activity.

Midtown (p167) Home to some of the city's most popular sights.

Upper East Side (p201) Museums galore and high-end zip codes.

Upper West Side & Central Park (p219) The city's public playground.

Harlem & Outer Boroughs Excursions (p241) Big on attractions.

New York City in Focus (p248) Information to help you on your way.

⬂CONTENTS

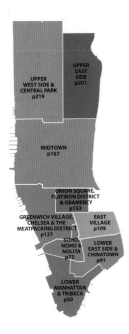

UPPER
EAST
SIDE
p201

UPPER
WEST SIDE &
CENTRAL PARK
p219

MIDTOWN
p167

UNION SQUARE,
FLATIRON DISTRICT
& GRAMERCY
p153

GREENWICH VILLAGE,
CHELSEA & THE
MEATPACKING DISTRICT
p127

EAST
VILLAGE
p109

SOHO,
NOHO &
NOLITA
p73

LOWER
EAST SIDE &
CHINATOWN
p91

LOWER
MANHATTAN
& TRIBECA
p50

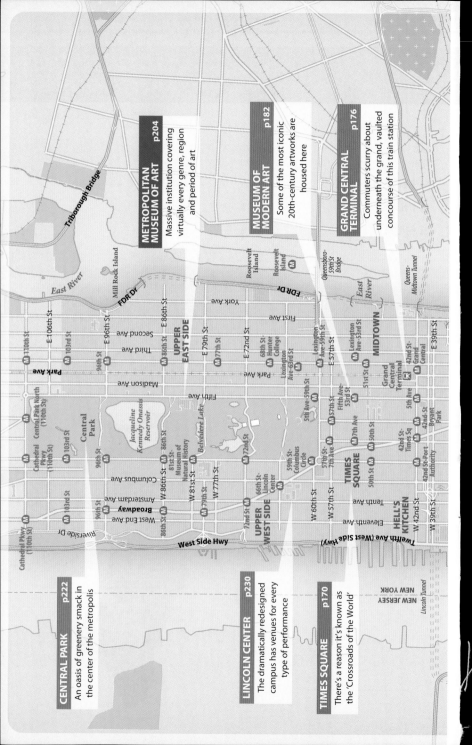

METROPOLITAN MUSEUM OF ART p204

Massive institution covering virtually every genre, region and period of art

MUSEUM OF MODERN ART p182

Some of the most iconic 20th-century artworks are housed here

GRAND CENTRAL TERMINAL p176

Commuters scurry about underneath the grand, vaulted concourse of this train station

CENTRAL PARK p222

An oasis of greenery smack in the center of the metropolis

LINCOLN CENTER p230

The dramatically redesigned campus has venues for every type of performance

TIMES SQUARE p170

There's a reason it's known as the 'Crossroads of the World'

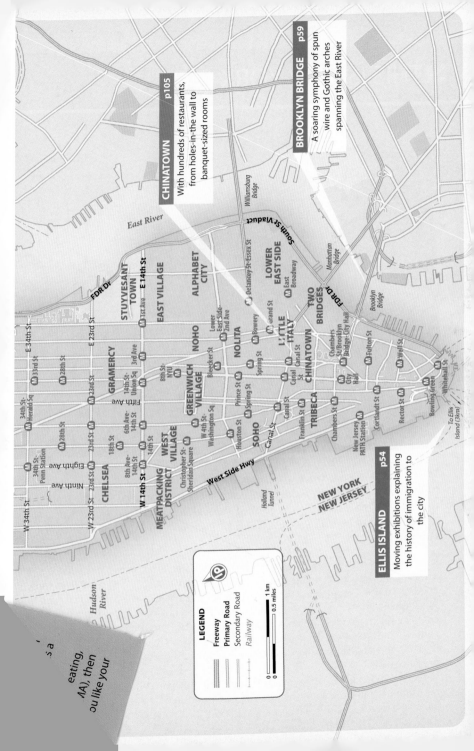

CHINATOWN p105

With hundreds of restaurants, from holes-in-the wall to banquet-sized rooms

BROOKLYN BRIDGE p59

A soaring symphony of spun wire and Gothic arches spanning the East River

ELLIS ISLAND p54

Moving exhibitions explaining the history of immigration to the city

East River

Williamsburg Bridge

South St Viaduct

Manhattan Bridge

FDR Dr

STUYVESANT TOWN

E 14th St

GRAMERCY

EAST VILLAGE

ALPHABET CITY

NOHO

Lower East Side

LOWER EAST SIDE

Delancey-Essex Sts Ⓜ

M East Broadway

FDR Dr

GREENWICH VILLAGE

NOLITA

Grand St Ⓜ

Bowery Ⓜ

LITTLE ITALY

TWO BRIDGES

Brooklyn Bridge

WEST VILLAGE

SOHO

Spring St Ⓜ

Prince St Ⓜ

Spring St Ⓜ

Canal St Ⓜ

CHINATOWN

Chambers St/Brooklyn Bridge–City Hall Ⓜ

Fulton St Ⓜ

MEATPACKING DISTRICT

Canal St Ⓜ

TRIBECA

Canal St Ⓜ

Franklin St Ⓜ

City Hall Ⓜ

West Side Hwy

Chambers St Ⓜ

New Jersey PATH Station

Cortlandt St Ⓜ

Rector St Ⓜ

Wall St Ⓜ

Whitehall St Ⓜ

Bowling Green Ⓜ

NEW YORK
NEW JERSEY

Holland Tunnel

Hudson River

To Ellis Island (3km)

CHELSEA

W 34th St

W 23rd St

Ninth Ave

Eighth Ave

34th St–Penn Station Ⓜ

28th St Ⓜ

23rd St Ⓜ

8th Ave–14th St Ⓜ

14th St Ⓜ

W 14th St

Christopher St–Sheridan Square Ⓜ

18th St Ⓜ

23rd St Ⓜ

28th St Ⓜ

Fifth Ave

Sixth Ave

6th Ave–14th St Ⓜ

W 4th St Ⓜ

Washington Sq

Houston St Ⓜ

Bleecker St

Prince St

Canal St

34th St–Herald Sq Ⓜ

33rd St Ⓜ

28th St Ⓜ

23rd St Ⓜ

Fifth Ave

14th St–Union Sq Ⓜ

8th St–NYU Ⓜ

3rd Ave

1st Ave

E 14th St

E 23rd St

E 28th St

E 33rd St

E 34th St

2nd Ave

LEGEND

Freeway
Primary Road
Secondary Road
Railway

0 —— 1 km
0 —— 0.5 miles

s a

eating,
...A), then
...u like your

↘ THIS IS NEW YORK CITY

Loud, fast and pulsing with energy, New York City (population 8.3 million) is symphonic, exhausting and always evolving. Maybe only a Walt Whitman poem cataloguing typical city scenes – from the humblest hole-in-the wall to grand buildings – could begin to do the city justice.

It remains one of the world centers for fashion, theater, food, music, publishing, advertising and, of course, finance. As Groucho Marx once said, 'When it's 9:30 in New York, it's 1937 in Los Angeles.' Coming to NYC from anywhere else for the first time is like stepping into a movie; one you've probably been unknowingly writing; one that contains all imagined possibilities. From the middle of Times Sq to the most obscure corner of the Bronx, you'll find extremes. From Brooklyn's Russian enclave in Brighto Beach to the mini South America in Queens, almost every country in the world h presence here.

You could decide you'd like your day to be filled with high culture and trend for example, and work your way through the Museum of Modern Art (M watch the New York City Ballet perform at the Lincoln Center. Or perhaps

city to be tougher, and choose to spend an afternoon wandering through the twisting streets of Chinatown and in the art galleries of the Lower East Side. Just don't be too shocked if your day of high culture turns gritty when you come across a gifted jazz singer on the subway platform, or if your bohemian day gets fancy when a trendy boutique seduces you and you're shelling out for the perfect pair of shoes before you know it.

'New York City is constantly in the process of reinventing itself'

Like the successive waves of immigrants who have populated the city, and the striving artists who have pinned their hopes and dreams on making it here, New York City is constantly in the process of reinventing itself. Approach it with an open mind and a loose itinerary and you can experience a little bit of everything.

⬂ NEW YORK CITY'S TOP 25 EXPERIENCES

1

↘ BE A FLANEUR

New York City, down deep, can't be seen until you've hit the sidewalks: the whole place, like Nancy Sinatra's boots, is made for walking. **Broadway** (p225), which runs the length of Manhattan for about 13.5 miles, is as good a place as any to start – every block in the city reflects the character and history of its inhabitants.

↘ METROPOLITAN MUSEUM OF ART

Home to a staggering two million works of art, the **Metropolitan Museum of Art** (Met; p204) hosts some of the city's best-known exhibits and its permanent collection covers every conceivable genre from the last 5000 years. Without a map you'll get lost in the maze of galleries.

↘ CENTRAL PARK

It's hard to believe that verdant grasses, dappled forests, riotous wild-flowers and cool, meandering streams exist in such a cacophonous, car-heavy city, but – praise be – they do. **Central Park** (p222), stretching from Midtown at 59th St to the beautifully restored Harlem Meer at 110th St, serves as the city's collective backyard.

1 Broadway, Lower Manhattan; 2 Metropolitan Museum of Art (p204); 3 Bethesda Fountain (p233), Central Park

⬊ SHOPPING

With upscale and exclusive boutiques along Fifth Ave, hip and stylish stores downtown, and generic chains everywhere in between, a visit to the city will put a dent in your credit card. NYC is still the best American city for shopping (p266) – from Levis to Prada, iPads to Buddhist mala beads, you can find it here.

⬊ CULINARY TOUR

In a city with almost 19,000 restaurants, and new ones opening every day of the year, where are you supposed to begin? Go with whatever your stomach desires, whether it's Italian, French, Israeli, Japanese, South Indian or good ol' American-diner burgers and fries.

↘ RIDE THE SUBWAY

Linking the most disparate neighborhoods in a continually pulsating network, the 100-year-old, round-the clock, 660 mile-long **subway** (p278) is a source of pride, frustration and cohesion, where all walks of life come together. Each line has its own character; every stop is a gateway to another facet of the city's personality.

4 DAN HERRICK; 5 JEAN-PIERRE LESCOURRET; 6 MICHELLE BENNETT

4 Bloomingdale's SoHo (p89); 5 Eating out in a NYC diner; 6 Riding the subway (p278)

⬎ WALK ACROSS THE BROOKLYN BRIDGE

A stroll over the graceful **Brooklyn Bridge** (p59), linking lower Manhattan and Brooklyn, is a rite of passage for New Yorkers and visitors alike, and an inspiration for poets and photographers. Nighttime is especially cinematic when the city lights reflect off the waters below and the bustling streets seem like a distant memory.

7

8

⬎ CATCH A BROADWAY SHOW

Seeing a performance at one of the ornate, lavish (and sometimes over-the-top) early-20th-century **theaters** (p170) surrounding Times Sq is a signature New York experience. Whether the show is a musical spectacular or an Irish family drama, cast members often include well-known movie stars as well as aspiring up-and-comers.

⬎ SKYLINE LOOKOUTS

9

From the observation deck of the **Empire State Building** (p177), the vertical perch where King Kong made his last stand, or the spectacular **Top of the Rock** (p181), where on a clear day you can see far across the Hudson into New Jersey, Midtown offers awe-inspiring views.

7 CHRISTOPHER GROENHOUT; 8 RICHARD I'ANSON; 9 JEAN-PIERRE LESCOURRET

7 Brooklyn Bridge (p59); 8 The Lion King on Broadway (p170); 9 View over Central Park (p232) and Manhattan

10

⬎ NEW YORK HARBOR

Hugging the island's southernmost tip, New York's harbor offers stellar views of Brooklyn's creaky old waterfront to the west, Staten Island to the south, and a nice chunk of the Jersey coast to the east. But the best view of all is of **Lady Liberty** (p54).

⬎ MUSEUM OF MODERN ART

11

The rock star of the modern-art world, the **Museum of Modern Art** (MoMA; p182) offers a broad canvas on which to showcase the visionary works of the past century. Innovative multimedia exhibitions, a sculpture garden, eclectic film screenings and respectable food offerings enhance the artistry.

⤴ WALK THE HIGH LINE

12

Originally constructed in the 1930s to lift dangerous freight trains off Manhattan's streets, the High Line (p130) is now the talk of the town. It's a brilliantly designed elevated space that embraces the old and new, natural and industrial, public and intimate, and extends from the Meatpacking District through west Chelsea.

13

⤴ LINCOLN CENTER

Every top-end genre has a stage at the massive Lincoln Center (p230). It's the showplace of the New York Philharmonic, the Chamber Music Society of Lincoln Center, the New York City Ballet and the New York City Opera. Two theaters present great drama, but the biggest draws are the Metropolitan Opera and American Ballet Theater.

14

↘ RIVER VIEWS

Manhattan is an island and is thus surrounded by water, even if many New Yorkers forget it. The **Roosevelt Island tram** (p213) provides aerial views of the East River, while **Riverside Park** (p229) is the place to go for sunset views of the Hudson River and the Jersey shore.

⤸ DOWNTOWN DRINKS

The city buzzes on an ever-growing list of cocktails, including martinis, cosmopolitans, appletinis, saketinis, mojitos, margaritas and caipirinhas. Old-school dives, hipster bars and posh lounges pop up with ever greater frequency around the nighttime hot spots of the Lower East Side, East Village, Greenwich Village and the Meatpacking District.

15

14 RICHARD CUMMINS; 15 HUW JONES

14 View across East River; 15 White Horse Tavern (p146)

↘ GALLERY HOPPING

The center of the gallery scene still lies in **Chelsea** (p139), which has close to 250 art spaces (it would take about a week to see every one). And while the neighborhood's allure is undeniable, smaller pockets of edgier galleries have popped up in other neighborhoods, mainly the Lower East Side, Williamsburg in Brooklyn and Long Island City in Queens.

16

17

⚓ GRAND CENTRAL TERMINAL

Even if you're not boarding a train to the 'burbs, it's worth exploring the grand, vaulted main concourse at Grand Central Terminal (p176) and gazing up at the restored ceiling, decorated with an image of the night sky. The lower floor houses a truly excellent array of eateries, bringing the idea of 'food court' to grand new levels.

⚓ CHINATOWN

A feast for the senses, Chinatown (p101) is the only place in the city where you can simultaneously see whole roasted pigs hanging in butcher-shop windows, get whiffs of fresh fish, and hear the sounds of Cantonese and Vietnamese rise over the calls of knock-off-Prada-bag hawkers on Canal St.

18

16 DAN HERRICK; 17 CHRISTOPHER GROENHOUT; 18 COREY WISE

NEW YORK CITY'S TOP 25 EXPERIENCES

↘ ICONIC ARCHITECTURE

New York has barely an inch of undeveloped real estate. Between the generic high-rises there are some architectural marvels. Standouts include the **Chrysler Building** (p175), the neo-Gothic **Woolworth Building** (p68), **Grand Central** (p176), the former mansions of Museum Mile, the cast-iron **Singer Building** (p78) and the **New Museum of Contemporary Art** (p100).

19

20

↘ SIDEWALK SITTING

For a city known for its hustle and bustle, where everyone seems to be always on the go, New York offers superlative people-watching opportunities. As soon as the weather warms up, restaurants and cafes commandeer their sidewalk property and parts of the city do their best imitation of Paris.

19 KIM GRANT; 20 JEAN-PIERRE LESCOURRET

21

⬐ BIG-TIME SPORTS

Judging by the 24-hour sports-radio talk shows, New Yorkers live and die by the success of their home teams. Mets fans forever moan their team's inadequacies while the Yankees, fondly known as the Bronx Bombers, give their followers reason to gloat. The NBA Knicks, NHL Rangers and NFL Giants all play to sold-out crowds.

⬐ CITY BEACHES

22

About 50 minutes by subway from Midtown, **Coney Island** (p246) is famous for its sandy beach, amusement rides (recently revamped), hot dogs and carnival games. A five-minute stroll north along the boardwalk brings you to Brighton Beach, where Russian old-timers play chess and locals enjoy *pierogies* (dumplings) and vodka shots in the sun.

⇲ ELDRIDGE STREET SYNAGOGUE 23

The **Eldridge Street Synagogue** (p99), a living monument to the Lower East Side's Jewish history, has been painstakingly restored. Marvel at the Moorish-style stained-glass windows, the chandeliers with vintage glass, 70ft vaulted ceilings and trompe l'oeil murals. Stop in for a serene visit or take advantage of one of the many cultural programs on offer.

⇲ SOLOMON R GUGGENHEIM MUSEUM 24

Architectural icon and heavy hitter in the contemporary art scene, the **Guggenheim** (p212) has a well-respected permanent collection but is better known for its temporary exhibits, which run the gamut from massive retrospectives and large-scale installations to in-depth country surveys.

21 HUW JONES; 22 CHRISTOPHER GROENHOUT; 23 DAN HERRICK; 24 JEAN-PIERRE LESCOURRET

21 Yankee Stadium; 22 Coney Island (p246); 23 Eldridge Street Synagogue (p99); 24 Solomon R Guggenheim Museum (p212)

↘ BROWNSTONE BLOCKS

Strolling along tree-lined brownstone streets admiring the stellar houses – Victorian Gothic, Romanesque, neo-Greco, Italianate – is a lovely afternoon activity. In Manhattan head downtown to the Village, the Upper West and Upper East Sides, as well as Harlem. A few of the classic brownstone neighborhoods of **Brooklyn** (p244) are Brooklyn Heights, Cobble Hill, Park Slope and Fort Greene.

25

25 ANGUS OBURN

25 Brownstone houses, Brooklyn

NEW YORK CITY'S TOP ITINERARIES

ICONS

ICONS

TWO TO THREE DAYS

METROPOLITAN MUSEUM OF ART TO CHINATOWN

Landmarks, highlights, big ticket items: this itinerary will allow you to experience the New York City in everyone's collective imagination. Spend a full day uptown and then another downtown, but allow yourself time to relax and breathe – they'll still be here when you return.

❶ METROPOLITAN MUSEUM OF ART

Start uptown at the **Metropolitan Museum of Art** (Met; p204), the big daddy of museums. You could spend an entire day here but it's best to focus and move on before exhaustion sets in. Check out the Egyptian wing and the European paintings on the 2nd floor. Between exhibits, grab a coffee at one of the on-site restaurants.

❷ CENTRAL PARK

Head outside and turn into **Central Park** (p222), the city's spectacular public backyard. Walk south to the Conservatory Water, where toy boats ply the waters. Continue south and turn slightly west to reach the Mall; follow this tree-lined pathway to its end. From here, you can exit the park to the east and grab a taxi to the next destination or head to Central Park South.

❸ TIMES SQUARE

No matter how you arrive at **Times Sq** (p170), you'll experience sensory overload. Head to the newly formed pedestrian plaza at the southern

Statue of Liberty (p54)

JULIET COOMBE

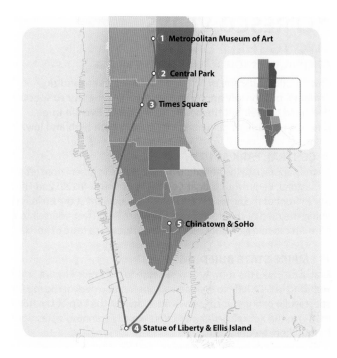

end where you can take in the dazzling tableau. Depending on the time of day, catch a matinee or hang around for an evening performance at one of Broadway's historic theaters.

❹ STATUE OF LIBERTY & ELLIS ISLAND

Head down to Battery Park City in Lower Manhattan. Time your arrival with your ferry's departure (you'll have to make your ferry reservations in advance). Ellis Island (p54) will likely occupy the majority of your visit unless you've arranged a trip to the crown of the Statue of Liberty (p54).

❺ CHINATOWN & SOHO

Take the R train from Rector St to Canal St and Chinatown (p101). No matter the time of day, enjoy a meal at one of the bustling restaurants. To reach SoHo (p81) walk north up one of several streets: Broadway, Mercer, Greene, Wooster or West Broadway. Each will give you a different flavor of the neighborhood.

ALFRESCO VIEWS
TWO TO THREE DAYS
CENTRAL PARK SOUTH TO BROOKLYN BRIDGE

The mythic landscape of NYC is a land of concrete and sky-scrapers, but to truly appreciate what makes the city so special, you need to seek out the breathtaking views. Even in three days it's possible to gain perspective from both high and low.

❶ CENTRAL PARK SOUTH

To truly appreciate the transition from concrete to green, from urban to pastoral, begin your tour at **Central Park South** (p222) and Fifth Ave in front of the historic Plaza Hotel. Gaze upward at the buildings lining the road or the treetops on the other side. Treat yourself to a hansom cab ride along the park's southern area for a taste of fresh air.

❷ EMPIRE STATE BUILDING

Grab a taxi, take the subway or walk south to the iconic **Empire State Building** (p177). Ride to the open-air observation deck at the top for spectacular panoramic city views. Alternatively, the **Top of the Rock** (p181) in the Rockefeller Center offers equally stunning vistas from its multifloor indoor perch.

❸ HIGH LINE

Take a taxi down to the **High Line** (p130), an abandoned railway 30ft above the street, now one of New York's favorite downtown destinations. Enter at 20th St and walk the meandering path for views of the Hudson River and city streets below.

DAN HERRICK

Top of the Rock (p181)

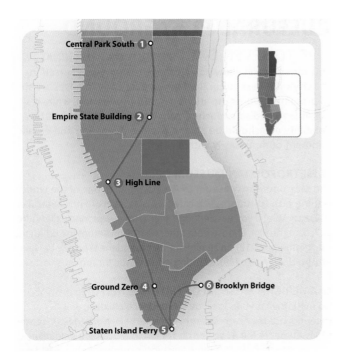

❹ GROUND ZERO

The site of the former World Trade Center, years after the September 11, 2001 attacks, is ever so slowly becoming vertical again. Massive construction equipment surrounds the area and the pit itself. Visit the **WTC Tribute Visitors Center** (p63) for photographs, stories and tours of the perimeter.

❺ STATEN ISLAND FERRY

Take the 1 train to South Ferry and hop on the **Staten Island Ferry** (p62) for the free drive-by tour of the Statue of Liberty. Commuters and tourists alike are afforded postcard-perfect views of downtown and the harbor. Feel free to explore the St George neighborhood of Staten Island or re-board immediately for the return trip.

❻ BROOKLYN BRIDGE

A pathway leads from the ferry terminal (or take the 4 or 5 train to Brooklyn Bridge/City Hall) along the East River to the pedestrian walkway of the **Brooklyn Bridge** (p59). Note that it does involve some street navigation at the end. Join the Brooklynites and hordes of other visitors making this magical pilgrimage on one of the city's most beautiful landmarks.

CULTURAL PLAYGROUND

FIVE TO SEVEN DAYS MUSEUM MILE TO CHINATOWN

This itinerary will allow you a chance to immerse yourself in the city's limitless cultural offerings. Every day involves a visit to prominent sights in various neighborhoods and, while it's possible to dedicate much of your day to these, with a little flexibility you should be able to explore the dining and entertainment options easily within reach.

❶ METROPOLITAN MUSEUM OF ART

The **Metropolitan Museum of Art** (Met; p204), one of the world's leading art institutions, is located on a stretch of Fifth Ave called 'Museum Mile'. If you have enough energy after exploring gallery after gallery at the Met, choose from other nearby museums including the **Guggenheim** (p212), an architectural icon, and the **Whitney Museum of American Art** (p209), a cutting-edge venue for American artists.

❷ AMERICAN MUSEUM OF NATURAL HISTORY

No matter what your age, you'll experience childlike wonder at the exceptional **American Museum of Natural History** (p229). Be sure to save time for the **Rose Center for Earth & Space**, a unique architectural gem in its own right. A few blocks south and then east takes you to the **Bethesda Fountain** (p233), one of the most beautiful spots in Central Park. Rent a rowboat at the nearby boathouse if you're up for some exercise, or take a walk up Broadway from 72nd St to 79th for a typical New York scene; check out the prewar classic buildings.

MICHELLE BENNETT

Metropolitan Museum of Art (p204)

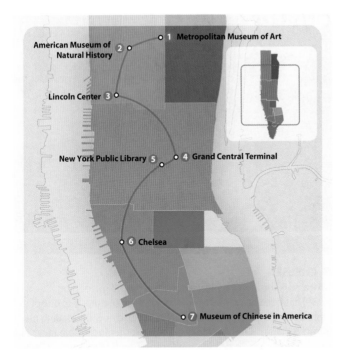

❸ LINCOLN CENTER
The newly redesigned Lincoln Center (p230) campus is a one-stop venue for dance, theater, opera and classical music, while the attached Walter Reade Theater (p238) screens foreign and independent films. Something is always going on here, and there's a nice cafe and public spaces to lounge in while you wait.

❹ GRAND CENTRAL TERMINAL
Even though the commuters running to catch their trains don't have a minute, you should take some time to stroll through the vaulted concourse of the beautiful Grand Central Terminal (p176). Walk east on 42nd St to see the lobby of the Chrysler Building (p175) at Lexington and 42nd St and then past the Ford Foundation to the United Nations (p175), a site not to be missed in NYC.

❺ NEW YORK PUBLIC LIBRARY
One of the best free attractions in the city – a monument to learning, housed in a grand Beaux Arts building – the New York Public Library (p178) has a magnificent Reading Room, a Map Room to get lost in, and Bryant Park (p182) – perfect for a picnic – right at its back door.

DAN HERRICK

Shopping in Chinatown (p108)

❻ CHELSEA

Take a walk through a typical example of New York recyling; **Chelsea** (p139) has been converted from a cookie manufacturer into one of the more delightful shopping areas in NYC. It's also now the leading place for art galleries. **Chelsea Piers** (p140), another incredible recycling example, was once a destination for the *Titanic*, and is now a facility for almost every sport imaginable.

❼ MUSEUM OF CHINESE IN AMERICA

Start the day at the interactive **Museum of Chinese in America** (p82). Afterwards, check out the bustling streets of **Chinatown** (p101), a feast for the senses, and then walk south down Broadway, past the courts and past the **City Hall** (p67) and the park out front. The **Woolworth Building** (p68), once one of the tallest buildings in the US, is not to be missed.

↘ PLANNING YOUR TRIP

NEW YORK CITY'S BEST...

STRESS RELIEF

- **Russian & Turkish Baths** (p124) Alternate between steam rooms, sauna, cold baths and borscht.
- **Chelsea Piers** (p140) Hit the driving range, bowling alley, gym or climbing wall at this sports complex.
- **Boating in Central Park** (p233) Rent a rowboat from the Loeb Boathouse in Central Park.
- **Economy Candy** (p107) Indulge your inner child at this emporium of nostalgic sweets.
- **Winnie's** (p106) Sing your lungs out at this downtown karaoke bar.

DISCOUNT DESIGNER CLOTHES

- **Century 21** (p72) An enormous vault of super-discounted top labels.
- **Filene's Basement** (p166) Endless racks offer fabled rewards for label hunters.

- **Loehmann's** (p151) A Seventh Ave icon with floors of marked-down designer gear.
- **Young Designers Market** (p89) Up-and-coming designers sell their wares at this weekend Nolita market.
- **Clothingline/SSS Sample Sales** (p200) Sharp markdowns on designer labels; stock changes every week.

LIVE-MUSIC SCENES

- **Jazz at Lincoln Center** (p225) Hovering over Central Park, with top acts from Freddy Cole to kd lang.
- **Smoke** (p238) Music pros perform seven days a week in this tiny house of jazz uptown, near Columbia.
- **Joe's Pub** (p88) An intimate supper club with great sightlines and sound.

Lower Manhattan (p50)

JIM WARK

- **Le Poisson Rouge** (p148) Catch wildly diverse acts, from the Winter Jazzfest to Philip Glass.
- **Carnegie Hall** (p194) Gorgeous concert hall for symphonies, orchestras, pianists and solo artists.

FREE SIGHTS

- **Governor's Island** (p60) Take a quick ferry ride to explore this island with priceless views.
- **National Museum of the American Indian** (p63) Fascinating museum housed in a gorgeous former US Customs House.
- **New York Earth Room** (p81) A gallery filled with moist, clean dirt: it's more moving than it sounds.
- **Japan Society** (p185) Rotating exhibits at this intimate gallery are a beautiful draw.
- **New York Public Library** (p178) Experience the stunning Reading Room, as well as diverse, museum-like exhibits.

ROMANTIC STAYS

- **Franklin** (p215) The old-school charm will have you down on one knee proposing in no time.
- **Lafayette House** (p141) Roaring fires, claw-foot bathtubs and big duvets.
- **Gramercy Park Hotel** (p162) Low lighting, impeccable service and plenty of privacy.

- **Inn at Irving Place** (p162) Slip into a huge four-poster bed in one of the idyllic rooms and let love blossom.
- **Inn New York City** (p233) Relax on your private balcony, slide into the hot tub or whip up a candlelight dinner in your suite.

VINTAGE DRINKING HOLES

- **White Horse Tavern** (p146) Dylan Thomas and Jack Kerouac drank at the long oak bar here.
- **Campbell Apartment** (p191) A railroad baron's 1920s-era secret hideaway at Grand Central.
- **King Cole Bar** (p191) Ultra-lux birthplace of the Bloody Mary, in Midtown.
- **McSorley's Old Ale House** (p122) They've been slamming two-for-one mugs in this cobwebby, sawdust-floor East Village dive since 1852.

BRUNCH

- **Balthazar** (p84) Serving sour-cream hazelnut waffles and hang-over drinks such as the potent Ramos Fizz.
- **Café Luxembourg** (p235) A UWS charmer with everything from eggs to full-on bistro meals.
- **Brasserie** (p190) Wake up to some seriously high-gloss design.
- **Spotted Pig** (p143) For something different: spiced-pork hash, pumpkin pancakes and soft-boiled duck eggs.

THINGS YOU NEED TO KNOW

⬆ AT A GLANCE

- **ATMs** On practically every corner.
- **Credit cards** Visa, MasterCard and American Express
- **Currency** US dollar
- **Electricity** 110V to 115V, 60Hz AC. Outlets are made for flat two-prong plugs (which often have a third, rounded prong for grounding).
- **Language** English
- **Smoking** Banned in all enclosed public places including bars and restaurants.
- **Tipping** In restaurants tip at least 15% unless the service is terrible; in taxis around 10%.
- **Visas** Twenty-seven countries have a visa-waiver agreement with the US (see www.cbp.gov); citizens of these countries can enter for stays of 90 days or less (see p275).

⬆ ACCOMMODATION

- **B&Bs & family-style guesthouses** Offer mix-and-match furnishings and some serious savings (if you don't mind some Victorian styles or eating breakfast with strangers).
- **Boutique hotels** Usually have tiny rooms decked out with fantastic amenities and at least one celebrity-filled basement bar, rooftop bar or hip, flashy eatery on-site. Your room might not be spacious, but you'll feel like royalty nonetheless.
- **'Classic' hotels** Typified by old-fashioned, small-scale European grandeur; these usually cost the same as boutiques and aren't always any larger.

- **European-style 'travelers' hotels** Have creaky floors and small but cheap and clean (if chintzily decorated) rooms, often with a shared bathroom.

⬆ BE FOREWARNED

- **Public Restrooms** Few and far between; your best bet is to pop into a Starbucks.
- **Restaurants** Large parties will have trouble getting seated without reservations.
- **Subways** Because of constant track work, weekend schedule changes are confusing.

⬆ INTERNET ACCESS

- **Airports** Only Jet Blue terminal at JFK has free wi-fi; all others charge a fee.
- **Cafes** Many offer free wi-fi, otherwise it's often possible to pick up a surrounding signal.
- **Hotels** Some offer free wi-fi, others charge per hour or 24-hour period.
- **Libraries** Most branches offer free half-hour access on computers.
- **Parks** Free wi-fi at Washington Sq Park, Bryant Park, Union Sq and Madison Square Park.

⬆ EMERGENCY NUMBERS

- **City government and services** (☎ 311)
- **Poison control** (☎ 800-222-1222)
- **Police, fire & ambulance** (☎ 911)

⬊ GETTING AROUND

- **Bus** (p277) Exact change only or use a prepaid Metro Card.
- **Cycling** (p276) Always wear a helmet; pedaling on the sidewalks is illegal.
- **Subway** (p278) Give yourself plenty of time; delays aren't uncommon.
- **Taxi** (p278) Look for one with a lit light on its roof – this means it's available.
- **Walking** Manhattan is divided into east and west sides – the dividing line above Washington Sq Park in the Village is Fifth Ave.

⬊ GETTING THERE & AWAY

- **Air** (p276) Fly into JFK or La Guardia, both in Queens, or Newark in New Jersey.
- **Bus** (p277) Most buses operate out of the Port Authority Terminal in Midtown.

- **Car** Remember that tunnels *into* the city (not out) want money; the George Washington Bridge charges if you're coming in from Jersey.
- **Train** (p278) Penn Station is the main railway hub. Grand Central services upstate and Connecticut.

⬊ WHEN TO GO

- **Spring** (March–May) Blossoming trees; rainy days can feel lovely. The average temperature is 60°F.
- **Summer** (June–August) Free cultural events everywhere. Temperature can be beastly, hovering in the 80°Fs.
- **Fall** (September–November) Leaves change colors; the air is brisk. Average temperature is in the 50°Fs.
- **Winter** (December–February) Buildings are festooned with lights; it's the holiday season. Snow, sleet and cold. Temperature in the 30°Fs.

DAN HERRICK

Commuters at a subway station

GET INSPIRED

⇘ BOOKS

- **Go Tell It on the Mountain** (James Baldwin, 1953) A lyrical novel of a day in the life of a 14-year-old brings readers into Harlem during the Depression.
- **Slaves of New York** (Tama Janowitz, 1986) A real-estate–obsessed collection of deadpan, quirky stories about folks living downtown in the '80s.
- **Bonfire of the Vanities** (Tom Wolfe, 1987) A gripping novel of an uptown investment banker's entanglement with the world of the black South Bronx.
- **Fortress of Solitude** (Jonathan Lethem, 2004) A ballad to the Brooklyn streets and a lyrical journey into race relations and pop culture from the 1970s to the '90s.

- **Lush Life** (Richard Price, 2008) A random shooting on the Lower East Side turns into a pitch-perfect exploration of the conflict between project residents and interloping hipsters.

⇘ FILMS

- **Taxi Driver** (director Martin Scorsese, 1976) Robert De Niro plays a mentally unstable Vietnam-war vet; a reminder of how much grittier this place used to be.
- **Saturday Night Fever** (director John Badham, 1977) John Travolta is the hottest thing in bell-bottoms in this tale of a streetwise Brooklyn kid.
- **Manhattan** (director Woody Allen, 1979) A divorced New Yorker falls for his best friend's mistress in what is essentially a love letter to NYC.

IZZET KERIBAR

Times Sq (p170)

- **American Gangster** (director Ridley Scott, 2007) A Harlem-based drug drama, inspired by a true story.

⇘ MUSIC

- **'Autumn in New York'** (Billie Holiday) Why *does* it seem so inviting?
- **'Empire State of Mind'** (Jay Z) An instant classic – 'These streets will make you feel…'
- **'Chelsea Hotel No 2'** (Leonard Cohen) Sex, grit and bohemia in an NYC landmark.
- **'Lullaby of Broadway'** (*42nd Street* musical-cast recording) A timeless favorite capturing all the hip-hooray and ballyhoo.

- **'New York, New York'** (Frank Sinatra) The ultimate manifesto of NYC exceptionalism.

⇘ WEBSITES

- **Fandango** (www.fandango.com) Breeze past the admissions counter at movie theaters throughout the city for an extra $1.
- **Metropolitan Transportation Authority** (www.mta.info) Subway map, service updates and other transportation information.
- **NYC: The Official Guide** (www.nycgo.com) Comprehensive tourist information site run by the city's official tourism department.
- **Times Square Visitors Center** (www.timessquarenyc.org) Midtown events, deals, news and advice.

PLANNING YOUR TRIP

GET INSPIRED

PLANNING YOUR TRIP

CALENDAR

CALENDAR

| JAN | FEB | MAR | APR |

St Patrick's Day Parade

DIANA MAYFIELD

JANUARY

WINTER RESTAURANT WEEK
One of two official Restaurant Weeks (the other is in July), when nearly 200 expensive, high-profile restaurants offer three-course lunches for around $20 and three-course dinners for $30; see www.nycvisit.com.

FEBRUARY

LUNAR (CHINESE) NEW YEAR FESTIVAL
One of the biggest Chinese New Year celebrations in the country, this display of fireworks and dancing dragons draws mobs into the streets of Chinatown. The date fluctuates from year to year; see www.explorechinatown.com.

MARCH

ST PATRICK'S DAY PARADE
MARCH 17
A massive audience, wobbly from cups of green beer, lines Fifth Ave for this popular parade of bagpipe blowers, sparkly floats and clusters of Irish-lovin' politicians.

APRIL

EASTER PARADE & EASTER BONNET FESTIVAL
This loosely organized tradition brings mobs of well-clad folks to the stretch of Fifth Ave in front of St Patrick's Cathedral on Easter Sunday, where they show off their elaborate bonnets, caps and other headgear; see www.saintpatricks cathedral.org.

⬃ MAY

TRIBECA FILM FESTIVAL
Robert De Niro co-organizes this annual downtown film fest, featuring world and US premieres; see www.tribeca filmfestival.com.

FLEET WEEK
For one week, clusters of uniformed sailors go 'on the town' looking for adventure. The ships they leave behind, docked in the Hudson River, invite the curious to hop aboard for tours; see the **Intrepid Sea, Air & Space Museum** (p184) for more information.

⬃ JUNE

PUERTO RICAN DAY PARADE
The second weekend in June attracts thousands of flag-waving revelers for the annual Puerto Rican pride parade, running up Fifth Ave from 44th to 86th Sts; see www.nationalpuertoricanday parade.org.

JVC JAZZ FESTIVAL
More than 40 jazz shows are performed in clubs around the city for this festival held in mid-June; see www.festival network.com.

GAY PRIDE PARADE
June is Gay Pride Month, and it culminates in a major march – a five-hour spectacle, down Fifth Ave on the last Sunday of the month; see nycpride.org.

MERMAID PARADE
Celebrating the sand, the sea and the beginning of summer is this wonderfully quirky afternoon parade. It's held on the last Saturday of June; see www. coneyisland.com.

⬃ JULY

JULY 4TH FIREWORKS
America's Independence Day is celebrated with fireworks over the East River. Good viewing spots include the waterfronts of the Lower East Side, Williamsburg in Brooklyn, or any high rooftop or east-facing Manhattan apartment.

PAUL HAKIMATA/ALAMY
Gay Pride Parade

CALENDAR

JAN   FEB   MAR   APR

PLANNING YOUR TRIP

CALENDAR

NATHAN'S FAMOUS HOT DOG EATING CONTEST   JULY 4

This bizarre celebration of gluttony brings world-champion food inhalers to Coney Island; see www.nathans famous.com.

PHILHARMONIC IN THE PARK

Free nighttime concerts in the city's parks from the country's premier orchestra are among the most wonderful treats of summer; see www.newyork philharmonic.org.

AUGUST

FRINGE FESTIVAL

This annual mid-August theater festival presents two weeks of performances from companies all over the world. It's the best way to catch the edgiest, wackiest and most creative up-and-comers around; see www.fringenyc.org.

US OPEN TENNIS TOURNAMENT

One of the four Grand Slam tournaments of professional tennis held at the USTA Billie Jean King National Tennis Center, a sort of miniature tennis universe out in Flushing, Queens; see www.usopen.org.

SEPTEMBER

WEST INDIAN AMERICAN DAY CARNIVAL PARADE

Labor Day marks the end of summer, and for two million Caribbean Americans and other fun-loving onlookers it's time to head over to Eastern Pkwy in Brooklyn for the annual Carnival parade featuring delicious Caribbean eats and nonstop music; see www.wiadca.com.

SAN GENNARO FESTIVAL

Rowdy crowds descend on the narrow streets of Little Italy for carnival games,

MICHAEL TAYLOR

Christmas tree at Rockefeller Center (p180)

| MAY | JUN | JUL | AUG | SEP | OCT | NOV | DEC |

Thanksgiving Day Parade

sausage-and-pepper sandwiches and Italian treats; see www.sangennaro.org.

OCTOBER

HALLOWEEN PARADE
OCTOBER 31
The nation's largest public Halloween celebration lures all sorts of freaks and geeks into the streets of Greenwich Village for a wild night of parading; see www.halloween-nyc.com.

NOVEMBER

NEW YORK CITY MARATHON
This 26-mile run through the streets of the city's five boroughs draws thousands of athletes from around the world – and just as many who line the streets to cheer folks on; see www.nyc marathon.org.

ROCKEFELLER CENTER CHRISTMAS TREE LIGHTING CEREMONY
At this traditional event, folks flock around the massive spruce tree at the Rockefeller Center (p180) to watch it light up.

THANKSGIVING DAY PARADE
This famous event parades floats and balloons (watch your head) down Seventh Ave, from 72nd St to Herald Sq; see www.macys.com.

DECEMBER

NEW YEAR'S EVE   DECEMBER 31
In addition to the countdown to midnight and dropping of the Waterford Crystal ball held in Times Sq, the city has plenty of other events; see www. timessquarenyc.org/nye.

Competitors in the New York City Marathon

LOWER MANHATTAN & TRIBECA

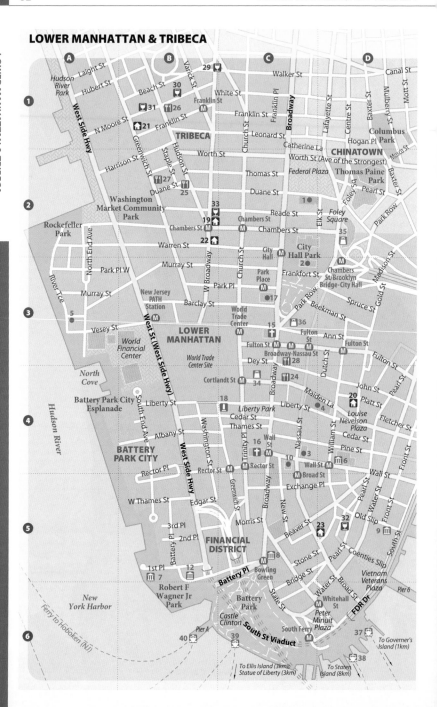

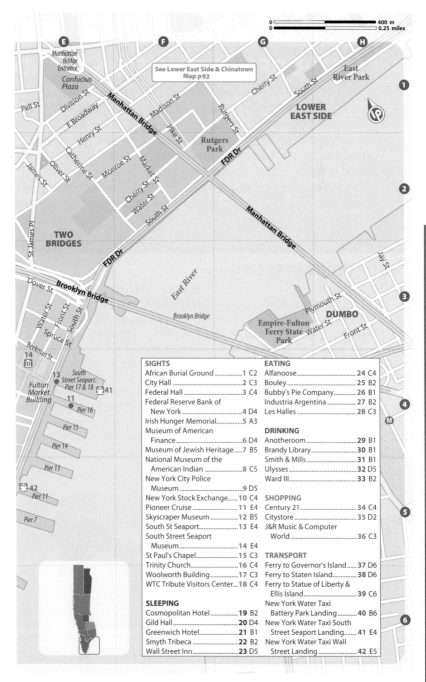

SIGHTS

African Burial Ground	1 C2
City Hall	2 C3
Federal Hall	3 C4
Federal Reserve Bank of New York	4 D4
Irish Hunger Memorial	5 A3
Museum of American Finance	6 D4
Museum of Jewish Heritage	7 B5
National Museum of the American Indian	8 C5
New York City Police Museum	9 D5
New York Stock Exchange	10 C4
Pioneer Cruise	11 E4
Skyscraper Museum	12 B5
South St Seaport	13 E4
South Street Seaport Museum	14 E4
St Paul's Chapel	15 C3
Trinity Church	16 C4
Woolworth Building	17 C3
WTC Tribute Visitors Center	18 C4

SLEEPING

Cosmopolitan Hotel	19 B2
Gild Hall	20 D4
Greenwich Hotel	21 B1
Smyth Tribeca	22 B2
Wall Street Inn	23 D5

EATING

Alfanoose	24 C4
Bouley	25 B2
Bubby's Pie Company	26 B1
Industria Argentina	27 B2
Les Halles	28 C3

DRINKING

Anotheroom	29 B1
Brandy Library	30 B1
Smith & Mills	31 B1
Ulysses	32 D5
Ward III	33 B2

SHOPPING

Century 21	34 C4
Citystore	35 D2
J&R Music & Computer World	36 C3

TRANSPORT

Ferry to Governor's Island	37 D6
Ferry to Staten Island	38 D6
Ferry to Statue of Liberty & Ellis Island	39 C6
New York Water Taxi Battery Park Landing	40 B6
New York Water Taxi South Street Seaport Landing	41 E4
New York Water Taxi Wall Street Landing	42 E5

HIGHLIGHTS

1 STATUE OF LIBERTY & ELLIS ISLAND

The city's earliest immigrants got their first taste of New York at Ellis Island, with the Statue of Liberty in sharp relief nearby. Retracing their footprints is a fine idea. In a city full of American icons, the Statue of Liberty – tall, lean and green, and rising up proudly out of the waters – is magnificent. A tour of Ellis Island and the statue brings you full circle from symbols and mythology to stories of trial and perseverance.

↘ OUR DON'T MISS LIST

❶ THE CROWN

In 2009 Lady Liberty's crown was re-opened to visitors for the first time since September 11, 2001. Folks who reserve in advance can climb the (steep) 354 steps, affording stunning views of the city and the harbor. The bad news: crown access is extremely limited, and the only way in is to reserve your spot in advance – up to a full one-year lead time is allowed.

❷ ELLIS ISLAND IMMIGRATION MUSEUM

The impressive Immigration Museum is housed in a massive, beautifully detailed, red-brick structure. You can explore the history of the island through a series of interactive galleries. Walking through the roomy, light-filled registry today is probably quite a contrast to the reality faced by thousands of newly arrived foreigners back in its heyday.

Clockwise from top: Statue of Liberty; Ellis Isand Immigration Museum; Wall of Honor, Ellis Island Immigration Museum; Statue of Liberty; Ellis Island ferry

CLOCKWISE FROM TOP: MARK NEWMAN; CHRISTOPHER GROENHOUT; DENNIS JOHNSON; ANGUS OBORN; ANGUS OBORN

LOWER MANHATTAN & TRIBECA

HIGHLIGHTS

❸ ELLIS ISLAND TOURS

You can take a free, 45-minute **guided tour** with a park ranger, or a self-guided, 50-minute audio tour of the facility for $6. You can also pick up one of the phones in each display area and listen to the recorded memories of real Ellis Island immigrants, taped in the 1980s.

❹ PASSENGER RECORDS

Resembling the self-check-in kiosk at an airport, the 1st floor of the Immigration Museum has computer terminals where you can type in your family name, year of arrival, port of departure etc and locate the official records of relatives who arrived here.

⬃ THINGS YOU NEED TO KNOW

How to beat the lines Take a ferry from New Jersey's Liberty State Park **Best alternative viewing option** Lady Liberty is visible from the free Staten Island Ferry (p62) **For more on the Statue of Liberty, see p59; for Ellis Island, see p62.**

LOWER MANHATTAN & TRIBECA

HIGHLIGHTS

HIGHLIGHTS

2

⬊ WALKING THE BROOKLYN BRIDGE

The **Brooklyn Bridge** (p59) pedestrian walkway begins just east of City Hall, and affords a wonderful view of lower Manhattan. Observation points offer histories of the waterfront. Take care to stay on the side of the walkway marked for folks on foot – frustrated cyclists, who use it en masse for commuting and pleasure, have been known to get nasty with oblivious tourists.

3

⬊ WALL STREET

Both an actual street and the metaphorical home of US commerce, Wall St is named for the wooden barrier built by Dutch settlers in 1653 to protect Nieuw Amsterdam from Native Americans and the British. Though the **New York Stock Exchange** (p63) has been closed to visitors indefinitely, tourists still gather on the sidewalk to gawk at harried traders who scurry out for cigarettes and food.

⬆ GOVERNOR'S ISLAND

Most New Yorkers have gazed out on this mysterious path of green in the harbor without a clue as to its purpose. Today, after a short ferry ride from downtown, visitors can explore the history of Govenor's Island (p60) as a coast-guard and army base, or laze about its massive lawns and unsurpassed city views.

⬆ FERRIES

It can be easy for ever-distracted New Yorkers to forget that they live on an island, surrounded by water. Join the commuters on the free Staten Island Ferry (p62) and enjoy great glimpses of the skyline. Or hop aboard the free Governor's Island Ferry (p60) for a trip to the smaller Governor's Island off the southern tip of Manhattan.

⬆ GROUND ZERO

Tourists snapping photos, office workers on a break and folks who miss loved ones mill about before the viewing wall that wraps around the ever-changing construction site of the former Twin Towers. The signature building of the site, One World Trade Center, along with the National September 11 Memorial & Museum, is scheduled for completion in 2013.

2 JEFF GREENBERG; 3 KEVIN CLOGSTOUN; 4 JTC/IMAGE BROKER; 5 DAN HERRICK; 6 DAN HERRICK

2 Brooklyn Bridge (p59); 3 New York Stock Exchange (p63); 4 Staten Island Ferry passing Governor's Island (p60); 5 Staten Island Ferry (p62); 6 Site of the World Trade Center

BEST...

⬆ MONUMENTS TO CAPITALISM

- **New York Stock Exchange** (p63) Heart of the beast; frantic buying and selling goes on inside.
- **Museum of American Finance** (p64) Old bank building with exhibits on the financial industry.
- **Federal Reserve Bank of New York** (p65) Tons and tons of gold can be seen on Fed tours.

⬆ DOWNTOWN WATER RIDES

- **Staten Island Ferry** (p62) Free panoramic ride on a commuter ferry.
- **Governor's Island Ferry** (p60) For gorgeous harbor views.
- **Statue of Liberty Ferry** (p59) The only way to get to the statue.
- **Pioneer Cruise** (p66) Old-time sailing tour.

⬆ TRACES OF HISTORY

- **Federal Hall** (p64) Site where George Washington took oath of office as the first US president.
- **Trinity Church** (p64) Originally founded by King William III.
- **St Paul's Chapel** (p65) George Washington worshipped here.
- **City Hall** (p67) Abraham Lincoln's coffin lay in state here for a short time.

⬆ KID-FRIENDLY TIME OUTS

- **Bubby's Pie Company** (p70) Longtime kid pleaser with extensive childrens menu.
- **Hudson River Park** (p62) Playgrounds and dog walkers galore.
- **South Street Seaport** (p66) Food, shops and street performers.

DAN HERRICK

Federal Hall (p64)

DISCOVER LOWER MANHATTAN & TRIBECA

The borough comes to a pencil point at its southern tip, forming the general swath known as Lower Manhattan. Teeming with iconic images that include Wall St, City Hall, the Brooklyn Bridge and, offshore in the near distance, the Statue of Liberty, this is a small region that manages to pack in a diverse wallop of sights.

It has come back to life slowly and surely since being struck a heavy blow on September 11, 2001 (though seriously delayed redevelopment plans have left much of the region still under construction). The whole area, in fact, has gone through a recent renaissance, bringing newness in many forms – museums, hotels and trendy restaurants – that has in turn lured more and more visitors. Add those elements to the area's geographic narrowness – waterfronts and sweeping views are an intimate part of the fabric here – and you've got quite a lively little city corner.

SIGHTS

BROOKLYN BRIDGE

Ⓢ 4, 5, 6 to Brooklyn Bridge-City Hall

A New York icon, the **Brooklyn Bridge** was the world's first steel suspension bridge. When it opened in 1883, the 1596ft span between its two support towers was the longest in history. Although its construction was fraught with disaster, the bridge became a magnificent example of urban design, inspiring poets, writers and painters. Today, the Brooklyn Bridge continues to dazzle – many regard it as the most beautiful bridge in the world.

The Prussian-born engineer John Roebling designed the bridge, which spans the East River from Manhattan to Brooklyn; Roebling was knocked off a pier in Fulton Landing in June 1869 and died of tetanus poisoning before construction of the bridge even began. His son, Washington Roebling, supervised construction of the bridge, which lasted 14 years and managed to survive budget overruns and the deaths of 20 workers.

The younger Roebling himself suffered from the bends while helping to excavate the riverbed for the bridge's western tower and remained bedridden for much of the project; his wife Emily oversaw construction in his stead. There was one final tragedy to come in June 1883, when the bridge opened to pedestrian traffic. Someone in the crowd shouted, perhaps as a joke, that the bridge was collapsing into the river, setting off a mad rush in which 12 people were trampled to death.

The bridge entered its second century as strong and beautiful as ever following an extensive renovation in the early 1980s.

STATUE OF LIBERTY

☎ 877-lady-tix (877-523-9849); www.nps.gov/stli, www.statuecruises.com (ferry info); admission free, ferry (incl Ellis Island) adult/child/senior $12/5/10, with audio tour $17.25/10/12.25, crown tickets (reservations required) additional $3; ⏲ ferries every 15-30min 9am-2pm (from 8:30am in summer), park 8:30am-6pm; Ⓢ 4, 5 to Bowling Green, 1 to South Ferry

LOWER MANHATTAN & TRIBECA

SIGHTS

Governor's Island

DAN HERRICK

GOVERNOR'S ISLAND

For decades, New Yorkers knew **Governor's Island** only as an untouchable patch of green out in the harbor. As of 2003, ownership of the 172-acre island was transferred from the federal government to both the National Park Service and the Governor's Island Preservation and Education Corporation, and both were charged with the job of transforming this well-trod ground into a public parkland. Since then, they've done an excellent job, as today's Governor's Island draws ferries full of folks throughout the summer. Among the highlights are **Picnic Point**, with picnic tables, hammocks and close views of the Statue of Liberty; the **City of Dreams** minigolf course, with nonprofit artist collective Figment delivering a collection of 'holes' from various local artists; **Water Taxi Beach**, a spit of sand that hosts events from dance parties to live concerts; and a 2.2-mile **bicycle path** around the perimeter of the island, which you can pedal with rental bikes from Bike and Roll for $10 per hour (free on Friday).

The island's historic significance is far-reaching: besides serving as a military fort in the Revolutionary War, the Union Army's central recruiting station during the Civil War and the take-off point for Wilbur Wright's 1909 flight around the Statue of Liberty, it's where the 1988 Reagan-Gorbachev summit signaled the beginning of the end of the Cold War. You can visit the spot where that summit took place at the **Admiral's House**, an1843 military residence that's part of the elegant ghost-town area of **Nolan Park**. Other historic spots include **Fort Jay**, fortified in 1776 for what became a failed attempt to prevent the Brits from invading Manhattan; **Colonel's Row**, a collection of 19th-century brick officers' quarters; and the **Castle Williams**. The best way to explore the island is with the National Park Service, whose rangers conduct 90-minute guided tours.

Things you need to know: ☎ 212-514-8285; www.nps.gov/gois, www.govisland.com; admission free; ☀ ferries leave from Battery Maritime Bldg, Slip 7, hourly 10am-3pm Fri & every 30min 10am-5pm Sat & Sun May-Oct; ⊚ 4, 5 to Bowling Green, 1 to South Ferry

One of the most recognizable icons in the world, the Statue of Liberty is a symbol of kinship and freedom formed out of 31 tons of copper and standing 93m from ground to torch-tip. A joint effort between America and France to commemorate the centennial of the Declaration of Independence, it was created by commissioned sculptor Frédéric-Auguste Bartholdi. The artist spent most of 20 years turning his dream – to create the monument and mount it in the New York Harbor – into reality. Along the way it was hindered by serious financial problems, but was helped in part by the fund-raising efforts of newspaper publisher Joseph Pulitzer, as well as poet Emma Lazarus, who in 1883 published a poem called 'The New Colossus' as part of a fund-raising campaign for the statue's pedestal. Her words have long since been associated with the monument and its connection to newly arrived immigrants:

Give me your tired, your poor,
Your huddled masses yearning to
breathe free,
The wretched refuse of your teeming shore.
Send these, the homeless, tempest-
tost to me,
I lift my lamp beside the golden
door!

These famous words were added to the base only in 1903, more than 15 years after the poet's death.

Bartholdi's work on the statue was also delayed by structural challenges – a problem resolved by the metal framework mastery of railway engineer Gustave Eiffel (of, yes, the famous tower). The work of art was finally completed in France in 1884 (eight years after the centennial). It was shipped here as 350 pieces packed in 214 crates, reassembled over a span of four months and placed on a US-made granite pedestal for a spectacular October 1886 dedication.

The statue and Liberty Island were put under the administration of the National Park Service in 1933; in 1984 a restoration began on the Lady's oxidized copper, and the UN placed it on a list of World Heritage Sites.

All visitors will need to undergo a special security screening before their visit, and waiting for that process can take up to 45 minutes. Though reservations to visit the grounds and pedestal are not required (the other option is to buy a Flex Ticket, which lets you enter anytime within a three-day period), they are strongly recommended, as they give you a specific visit time and guarantee you'll

LOWER MANHATTAN & TRIBECA

SIGHTS

ANGUS OBORN

Statue of Liberty

get in. A less crowded approach to the statue is via **Liberty State Park** (☎ 201-435-9499; www.libertystatepark.org), which can be reached by car, taxi or a combination of the PATH train and light rail in New Jersey; call or check the website for details.

Note that in October 2011, the statue will close for nine to 12 months in order to build a second stairwell to improve fire safety.

ELLIS ISLAND

☎ 212-363-3200, www.nps.gov/elis; ☎ 877-lady-tix (877-523-9849), www.statue cruises.com (ferry info); admission free, ferry (incl Statue of Liberty) adult/child/senior $12/5/10; ☺ ferries every 15-30min 9am-2pm; ☺ 4, 5 to Bowling Green, 1 to South Ferry

An icon of mythical proportions for the descendents of those who passed through here, this island and its hulking building served as New York's main immigration station from 1892 until 1954, processing the amazing number of 12,000 individuals daily, from countries including Ireland, England, Germany and Austria. The process involved immigrants getting the once-over by doctors, being assigned new names if their own were too difficult to spell or pronounce, and basically getting the green light to start their new, hopeful and often frighteningly difficult lives here in the teeming city of New York. In its later years, after WWI and during the paranoia of the 'Red Scare' in this country, the immigration center became more of a de facto holding pen for newcomers believed to be radical threats to the US. After admitting its last arrival in 1954 (a Norwegian merchant seaman), the place closed due to changes in immigration law coupled with rising operating costs.

To be sure you get onto a ferry, you should make advance reservations.

However, if you're not one for planning in advance, you can take your chances by going for one of a limited number of time passes available to walk-ups on a first-come-first-served basis. Also, it should be noted that during the especially busy summer months, there is a less crowded approach to Ellis Island, via ferry from New Jersey's **Liberty State Park** (☎ 201-435-9499; www.libertystatepark.org).

STATEN ISLAND FERRY

☎ 311; www.siferry.com; free; ☺ every 30min; ☺ 1 to South Ferry, 4, 5 to Bowling Green

Staten Islanders know the fleet of hulking, dirty-orange ferries as commuter vehicles, while Manhattanites like to think of them as their secret, romantic vessels for a spring-day escape. But that secret is long out, as many a tourist has been clued into the charms of the Staten Island Ferry, which provides one of the most wonderful, free adventures in New York. Today, the ferry service carries more than 19 million passengers each year across the 5.2-mile stretch of the Hudson River that separates downtown Manhattan from the Staten Island neighborhood of St George.

HUDSON RIVER PARK

www.hudsonriverpark.org; Manhattan's west side from Battery Park to 59th St

Encompassing way more than Battery Park (although its beginning is located here) the 5-mile, 550-acre Hudson River Park that runs along the lower western side of Manhattan edges neighborhoods including the West Village, Chelsea and Hell's Kitchen.

Among its charms are a bike/run/skate path snaking along its entire length, community gardens, basketball courts, playgrounds, dog runs, and a collection of renovated piers jutting out into the water that serve as riverfront esplanades, miniature golf courses and alfresco movie theaters and concert venues in summer.

MUSEUM OF JEWISH HERITAGE

☎ 646-437-4200; www.mjhnyc.org; 36 Battery Pl; adult/child/student/senior $12/free/7/10, admission free 4-8pm Wed; ⏱ 10am-5:45pm Sun-Tue & Thu, 10am-8pm Wed, 10am-5pm Fri; ⊕ 4, 5 to Bowling Green

This 30,000-sq-ft waterfront memorial museum, with a six-sided shape and three tiers to symbolize the Star of David and the six million Jews who perished in the Holocaust, explores all aspects of what it means to be Jewish in modern-day NY.

WTC TRIBUTE VISITORS CENTER

☎ 866-737-1184; www.tributewtc.org; 120 Liberty St; admission $10; ⏱ 10am-6pm Mon, Wed-Sat, noon-6pm Tue, noon-5pm Sun; ⊕ E to World Trade Center, R to Cortlandt St (northbound only)

Operated by the nonprofit Families' Association, this center serves as a temporary memorial to the September 11 disaster. It features a gallery of moving images and artifacts, including battered fire-fighting uniforms, and the opportunity to join one-hour tours of the WTC site's perimeter.

NEW YORK STOCK EXCHANGE

☎ 212-656-5168; www.nyse.com; 11 Wall St; ⊕ 2, 3, 4, 5 to Wall St, J, Z to Broad St

Home to the world's best-known stock exchange, Wall Street has become the widely recognized symbol for US capitalism. Before it closed to the public, due to stepped-up security measures, more than 700,000 visitors a year passed behind the portentous Romanesque facade to see where about a billion shares valued at around $44 billion change hands daily.

NATIONAL MUSEUM OF THE AMERICAN INDIAN

☎ 212-514-3700; www.nmai.si.edu; 1 Bowling Green; admission free; ⏱ 10am-5pm Fri-Wed, to 8pm Thu; ⊕ 4, 5 to Bowling Green

This museum, an affiliate of the Smithsonian Institution, is housed in the spectacular former US Customs

RICHARD CUMMINS

National Museum of the American Indian

DAN HERRICK

Museum of American Finance

House (which celebrated its centennial in 2007), near the southernmost point of Manhattan. It's an ironically grand space for the country's leading museum on Native American art, established by oil heir George Gustav Heye in 1916.

MUSEUM OF AMERICAN FINANCE

☎ 212-908-4110; www.financialhistory.org; 48 Wall St; adult/under 6 yr/student & senior $8/ free/5; 🕐 10am-4pm Tue-Sat; ⊙ 2, 3, 4, 5 to Wall St

This stunning museum feels as rich as its subject: comprising 30,000 sq ft in the old Bank of New York headquarters, it's a grand space featuring 30ft ceilings, high, arched windows, a majestic staircase to the mezzanine, glass chandeliers, and murals depicting historic scenes of banking and commerce. Exhibits focus on historic moments in American financial history, and permanent collections include rare 18th-century documents, stock and bond certificates from the Gilded Age, the oldest known photograph of Wall St and a stock ticker from 1867.

FEDERAL HALL

☎ 212-825-6888; www.nps.gov/feha; 26 Wall St; admission free; 🕐 9am-5pm Mon-Fri; ⊙ 2, 3, 4, 5 to Wall St, J, Z to Broad St

Following an extensive renovation, Federal Hall, which contains a museum dedicated to postcolonial New York, features exhibits on George Washington's inauguration and Alexander Hamilton's close relationship with New York City, and a visitor information hall where you can pick up information about downtown cultural happenings.

The building itself, distinguished by a huge statue of George Washington, stands on the site of New York's original City Hall, where the first US Congress convened and Washington took the oath of office as the first US president on April 30, 1789.

TRINITY CHURCH

☎ 212-602-0800; www.trinitywallstreet.org; Broadway at Wall St; 🕐 8am-6pm Mon-Fri, to 4pm Sat, 7am-4pm Sun; ⊙ 2, 3, 4, 5 to Wall St, R to Rector St

This former Anglican parish church was founded by King William III in 1697 and once presided over several constituent chapels, including St Paul's Chapel (below) at the corner of Fulton St and Broadway. The current Trinity Church is the third structure on the site. Designed by English architect Richard Upjohn, this 1846 building helped to launch the picturesque neo-Gothic movement in America. At the time of its construction, its 280ft-high bell tower made it the tallest building in New York City.

The long, dark interior of the church includes a beautiful stained-glass window over the altar, plus a small museum area that hosts rotating art exhibits. Out back, a peaceful, fenced-in cemetery is filled with ancient headstones smoothed by the centuries, and it's a fascinating, serene place to wander.

ST PAUL'S CHAPEL

☎ 212-602-0800; www.saintpaulschapel.org; Broadway at Fulton St; 🕑 10am-6pm Mon-Fri, to 4pm Sat, 7am-6pm Sun; 🚇 4, 5 to Fulton St

George Washington worshipped here after his inauguration in 1789, and that was the biggest claim to fame for this colonial-era chapel (affiliated with Trinity Church, which sits further down Broadway) prior to September 11, 2001. After that fateful day, when the World Trade Center destruction occurred just a block behind this classic revival brownstone, the mighty structure became a spiritual support center for all who needed it. Volunteers worked round the clock, serving meals, setting up beds, doling out massages and counseling rescue workers.

Today a moving interactive exhibit, 'Unwavering Spirit: Hope & Healing at Ground Zero,' sits beneath the elegant cut-glass chandeliers, bringing streams of people who are still searching for healing and understanding.

FEDERAL RESERVE BANK OF NEW YORK

☎ 212-720-6130; www.ny.frb.org; 33 Liberty St at Nassau St; admission free; 🕑 tours hourly 9:30am-2:30pm (except 12:30pm) Mon-Fri; 🚇 J, Z, 2, 3, 4, 5 to Fulton St, A, C to Broadway-Nassau St

The best reason to visit the Federal Reserve Bank is to get a chance to ogle the facility's high-security vault – more than 10,000 tons of gold reserves reside here, 80ft below ground. You'll only see a small part of that fortune, but signing on to a free tour here (the only way in) will also teach you a lot about the US Federal Reserve System. Beware that your passport or other official

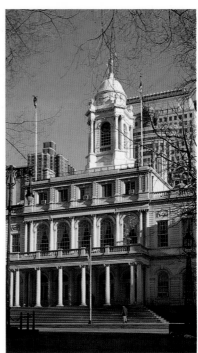

City Hall (p67)

ANGUS OBURN

ID, as well as reservations (which the Fed suggest you make a full month in advance) are required for the comprehensive tour.

SOUTH STREET SEAPORT

☎ 212-732-7678; www.southstseaport.com; ⊕ J, Z, 2, 3, 4, 5 to Fulton St, A, C to Broadway-Nassau St

This 11-block enclave of shops, piers and sights combines the best and worst in historic preservation. It's not on the radar for most New Yorkers, but tourists are drawn to the sea air, the nautical feel, the frequent street performers and the restaurants. **Pier 17**, beyond the elevated FDR Dr, is a waterfront-development project that's home to several floors of shops, restaurants and a rare public bathroom plus

South Street Seaport
ADINA TOVY AMSEL

the permanent creepy-but-fascinating 'Bodies: The Exhibition.' Clustered around the piers are some significant 18th- and 19th-century buildings dating from the heyday of this old East River ferry port, which fell into disuse with the building of the Brooklyn Bridge and the establishment of deep-water jetties on the Hudson River. The pedestrian malls, historic tall ships and riverside locale make the seaport a picturesque destination or detour, and create a lovely backdrop if you happen to be standing in line for discounted Broadway tickets at the TKTS booth.

SOUTH STREET SEAPORT MUSEUM

☎ 212-748-8600; www.southstreetseaport. org; 207 Front St; adult/child/senior & student $12/8/10, 3rd Fri of each month free; ⏰ 8am-6pm Tue-Sun Apr-Oct, 10am-5pm Fri-Mon Nov-Mar; ⊕ J, Z, 2, 3, 4, 5 to Fulton St, A, C to Broadway-Nassau St

Opened in 1967, this museum offers a glimpse of the seaport's history and a survey of the world's great ocean liners, with permanent exhibits and various other sites dotted around the 11-block area. Included in the museum are three galleries, an antique printing shop, a children's center, a maritime crafts center and historic ships: just south of Pier 17 stands a group of tall-masted **sailing ships** – the *Peking, Wavertree, Pioneer, Ambrose* and *Helen McAllister,* among others – and the admission price to the museum includes access to their windswept decks and intimate interiors.

For a special treat, join a sailing tour aboard the gorgeous, iron-hulled **Pioneer** (☎ 212-748-8786; cruise $60), built in 1885 to carry mined sand but today just perfect for holding happy humans transfixed by the views. The two-hour journeys run from late May through mid-September from

DAN HERRICK

Exhibits, New York City Police Museum

⤵ IF YOU LIKE...

If you like gleaning historical knowledge about the city from the South Street Seaport Museum (left), we think you'll like these other museums:

- **African Burial Ground** (☎ 212-637-2019; www.nps.gov/afbg; 290 Broadway btwn Duane & Elk Sts; ⊗ 10am-4pm Tue-Sat; ⊕ 4, 5 to Wall St) This memorial honors the remains of enslaved Africans – an estimated 15,000 – buried here during the 17th and 18th centuries.
- **Irish Hunger Memorial** (290 Vesey St at North End Ave; admission free; ⊕ 2, 3 to Park Place) A labyrinth of low walls and patches of grass, this living sculpture is a metaphor for the famine that led to Irish migration to the US.
- **New York City Police Museum** (☎ 212-480-3100; www.nycpolicemuseum.org; 100 Old Slip; suggested donation adult/child & senior $7/5; ⊗ 10am-5pm Mon-Sat; ⊕ 1 to South Ferry, 2, 3 to Wall St) Chock full of facts and exhibits about New York's finest housed in a building modeled after an Italian palace.
- **Skyscraper Museum** (☎ 212-968-1961; www.skyscraper.org; 39 Battery Pl; adult/senior & student $5/2.50; ⊗ noon-6pm Wed-Sun; ⊕ 4, 5 to Bowling Green) Occupying the ground-floor space of the Ritz-Carlton Hotel, this wonderful ode to skyscrapers the world over features two serene, high-gloss galleries.

Tuesday to Friday evenings and Saturday and Sunday beginning at 1pm; passengers are encouraged to bring snacks and even a bottle of wine for this relaxing, stellar sail.

CITY HALL

☎ 212-788-6865; City Hall Park, Park Row; ⊗ weekday tours by reservation only; ⊕ 4, 5, 6 to Brooklyn Bridge-City Hall, J, Z to Chambers St

This elegant cupola-topped marble hall, located in placid City Hall Park facing the entrance to the Brooklyn Bridge, has been home to New York City's government since 1812. If you take a quick peek into the City Council chambers, you might even see lawmakers of the 51-member body deliberating over issues such as urban development, the budget or civil rights.

Woolworth Building

DAN HERRICK

You can also explore the grand interior of City Hall through free **guided tours** (☎ 311, outside NYC 212-new-york (212-639-9675); tours weekdays by appt only) offered by the Art Commission of the City of New York (call for reservations).

Out front is bustling **City Hall Park**, graced with gas lamps, fountains, lovely landscaping, chess tables and benches, making it a nice place to sit with a sandwich for some prime people-watching.

WOOLWORTH BUILDING
233 Broadway at Park Pl; ◎ 4, 5, 6 to Brooklyn Bridge-City Hall, J, Z to Chambers St

Cass Gilbert's magnificent 60-story Woolworth Building was completed in 1913. At 792ft, it was the tallest building in the city – and the world – until the Chrysler Building surpassed it in 1930. At its dedication, the building was described as a 'cathedral of commerce'; though meant as an insult, FW Woolworth, head of the five-and-dime chain-store empire headquartered there, took the comment as a compliment and began throwing the term around himself. Today the building houses mainly offices, and visitors are not allowed into the building (though you may be able to sneak a peek at the beautifully preserved lobby).

TRIBECA
Taking its moniker from real-estate agents who noted the pocket of land sitting in a 'TRIangle BElow CAnal (St),' this intimate neighborhood is composed of landmark 19th-century buildings as well as massive former warehouses that have been pretty thoroughly converted into luxury condos. Still, local foodies know this as the place to celeb-spot while spending small fortunes on sushi or steak *frites,* and night owls love it for its sultry lounge bars.

SLEEPING
GREENWICH HOTEL   Deluxe Boutique Hotel $$$
☎ 212-941-8900; www.greenwichhotelny.com; 377 Greenwich St btwn N Moore & Franklin Sts; r from $475; ◎ 1 to Franklin St, A, C, E to Canal St; 🖈 💻

Every corner of this hotel – lobby, lounge, rooms and especially the suites – drips with old-world sophistication and that certain type of rustic charm that costs a mint to achieve. Around the inner courtyard there are 88 rooms and suites, each with floor-to-ceiling French doors opening to the flower-filled garden.

GILD HALL
Boutique Hotel $$

☎ 212-232-7700; www.wallstreetdistrict.com; 15 Gold St; r from $289; ☺ 2, 3 to Wall St; ☒ ▣
Step inside the lobby and curl up with a good book and a flute of bubbly; Gild Hall's sensuous entryway leads to a bi-level library and champagne bar. Rooms are part European elegance, part American comfort, with high tin ceilings, glass-walled balconies, Sferra linens and Frette robes, and minibars stocked with Dean & Deluca treats.

SMYTH TRIBECA
Boutique Hotel $$

☎ 212-587-7000; www.thompsonhotels.com; 85 W Broadway; r from $229; ☺ A, C, E, 1, 2, 3 to Chambers St; ☒ ▣
Rooms are decked out with designer soaps, robes and snacks, and everything is as modern and functional as can be in 300-sq-ft rooms. The lobby is decorated with a lot of rich brown leather and tartan rugs; suites are a combo of bright white walls and crisp gray bedding, with vivid red chairs for a splash of color.

WALL STREET INN
Business Boutique Hotel $$

☎ 212-747-1500, 800-695-8284; www.thewall streetinn.com; 9 S William St at Broad St; r from $185; ☺ 2, 3 to Broad St, 4, 5 to Bowling Green; ☒ ▣
The sedate stone exterior of this inn belies its warm, homey Colonial-style interior. Beds are big and plush, and rooms have glossy wood furnishings and long, swooshy drapes. The bathrooms are full of nice touches, such as hot tubs in the deluxe rooms and deep marble tubs in the others.

COSMOPOLITAN HOTEL
Budget Hotel $

☎ 212-566-1900, 888-895-9400; www.cosmo hotel.com; 95 W Broadway at Chambers St; r $149; ☺ 1, 2, 3 to Chambers St; ☒
The 122-room hotel isn't much to brag about – clean, carpeted rooms with private bathrooms, a double bed or two, and IKEA-knock-off furnishings. But it's clean and comfortable, and there are major subway lines at your feet, plus all of Tribeca,

Views across the city

JOHN BORTHWICK

New York Stock Exchange (p63), Wall St

KEVIN CLOGSTOUN

Chinatown and Lower Manhattan in convenient walking distance.

EATING

BOULEY
Classic French $$$

☎ 212-694-2525; www.davidbouley.com; 163 Duane St at Hudson St; ☽ lunch & dinner; ◉ A, C, 1, 2, 3 to Chambers St

The home base of celebrity chef David Bouley attracts an un-flashy crowd of heavyweights who drop small fortunes on sublime takes on classic fare – such as seared halibut with purees of persimmon and cauliflower and a trickle of almond-milk sauce, or tea-smoked organic duckling with vanilla-glazed baby turnips.

LES HALLES
French Brasserie $$$

☎ 212-285-8585; www.leshalles.net; 15 John St btwn Broadway & Nassau St; ☽ lunch & dinner; ◉ J, Z, 2, 3, 4, 5 to Fulton St, A, C to Broadway-Nassau St

Celebrity chef Anthony Bourdain still reigns at this packed and serious brasserie where vegetarians need not apply. Among the elegant light-fixture balls, dark wood paneling and stiff white tablecloths you'll find a buttoned-up, meat-lovin' crowd with deep pockets.

INDUSTRIA ARGENTINA
Argentine Steakhouse $$

☎ 212-965-8560; 329 Greenwich St btwn Duane & Jay Sts; ☽ lunch daily, dinner Mon-Sat; ◉ 1 to Franklin St

It truly feels like a Buenos Aires hot spot in here, where sleek design and masculine details blend to create a solid, confidence-inspiring setting in which to chow down on hearty steaks with chimicurri (Argentian parsley and garlic sauce), mixed grills with lamb chops and sausages and heavenly starters.

BUBBY'S PIE COMPANY
Comfort Food $$

☎ 212-219-0666; 120 Hudson St at N Moore St; ☽ breakfast, lunch & dinner daily, brunch Sun; ◉ 1 to Franklin St

One of the most consistently popular eateries in Tribeca, this low-key standby is a great draw for families with kids,

LOWER MANHATTAN & TRIBECA

who are welcome and easily sated with a kids menu brimming with classics from chicken fingers to buttered spaghetti. Adult draws include the mellow ambience and excellent takes on homey basics.

ALFANOOSE
Middle Eastern $
☎ 212-528-4669; 8 Maiden Lane at Broadway; ⏱ 11:30am-9:30pm Mon-Sat; ⊕ J, Z, 2, 3, 4, 5 to Fulton St, A, C to Broadway-Nassau St

For a break from the big-food fare down in these parts, pop into this unassuming storefront, where you'll find what's been frequently cited by local mags as the best falafel in town.

DRINKING

BRANDY LIBRARY
Cocktail Bar
☎ 212-226-5545; www.brandylibrary.com; 25 N Moore St at Varick St; ⊕ 1 to Franklin St

When sipping means serious business, it's easy to settle into this library, with soothing reading lamps and club chairs facing backlit, floor-to-ceiling, bottle-filled shelves. Go for top-shelf cognac, malt scotch or 90-year-old brandies (prices range from $9 to $298).

SMITH & MILLS
Cocktail Bar
☎ 212-219-8568; 71 N Moore St btwn Hudson & Greenwich Sts; ⊕ 1 to Franklin St

Teensy and stylish, this unmarked bar feels like a kooky professor's lair for kicking back with fellow kooky professors over $12 cocktails. There are a few antiques, plush booths on well-worn wood floors and a few good snack choices.

WARD III
Cocktail Bar
☎ 212-240-9194; 111 Reade St; ⊕ 1, 2, 3, A, C, E to Chambers St

The brainchild of three talented barmen, Ward III aims for old-fashioned jauntiness with its 'bespoke cocktails', elegant

fittings (dark woods, exposed brick, tin ceiling) and gentlemanly house rules (No 3: 'Don't be creepy').

ULYSSES
Irish Pub
☎ 212-482-0400; 95 Pearl St (or 58 Stone St); ⊕ 2, 3 to Wall St

Big with old-school financial types, Ulysses is an Irish/modern hybrid, with a long bar and a kitchen serving oysters and sandwiches; it's best when you're nursing your Harp or Guinness on the wood picnic tables out on cobbled Stone St.

ANOTHEROOM
Lounge
☎ 212-226-1418; 249 W Broadway btwn Beach & N Moore Sts; ⊕ 1 to Franklin St

This industrial-chic, cement-floor place with a sidewalk table or two is the sort

DRINKING

KIM GRANT
Trinity Church (p64)

KEVIN CLOGSTOUN

Century 21

of place you stop for an afternoon drink you hadn't been planning on. It's all beer and wine – no mixed drinks – with chalkboard scrawl advertising the daily catch for mostly middle-aged Tribecans.

SHOPPING

CENTURY 21   Discount Department Store
☎ 212-227-9092; 22 Cortlandt St at Church St; ⏰ 7:45am-9pm Mon-Wed & Fri, 7:45am-9:30pm Thu, 10am-9pm Sat, 11am-8pm Sun; Ⓜ J, Z, 2, 3, 4, 5 to Fulton St, A, C to Broadway-Nassau St
This four-level, marble-floor department store is a favorite New Yorker 'secret.' Problem is, everyone and their mother knows about it. Its popularity is due to its deep discounts on men's and women's designer clothes, accessories, shoes, perfumes and linens (sometimes at less than half the original price).

J&R MUSIC & COMPUTER WORLD
Music & Electronics
☎ 212-238-9000; 15-23 Park Row; ⏰ 9am-7:30pm Mon-Sat, 10:30am-6:30pm Sun; Ⓜ J, Z, 2, 3, 4, 5 to Fulton St, A, C to Broadway–Nassau St
Occupying a full block with J&R shops and their separate entrances, this is considered by many to be the best place in the city to buy a computer of any sort. You can buy any other electronics item here, including cameras, recorders and stereos, as well as DVDs and CDs of every kind.

CITYSTORE   NYC Gifts & Books
☎ 212-669-7452; North Plaza, Municipal Bldg, 1 Centre St; ⏰ 9am-4:30pm Mon-Fri; Ⓜ 4, 5, 6 to Brooklyn Bridge-City Hall, J, Z to Chambers St
This small, little-known City-run shop is the perfect place to find all manner of New York memorabilia, including authentic taxi medallions, manhole coasters, silk ties and baby clothes bearing the official 'City of New York' seal.

↘ SOHO, NOHO & NOLITA

SOHO, NOHO & NOLITA

SOHO, NOHO & NOLITA

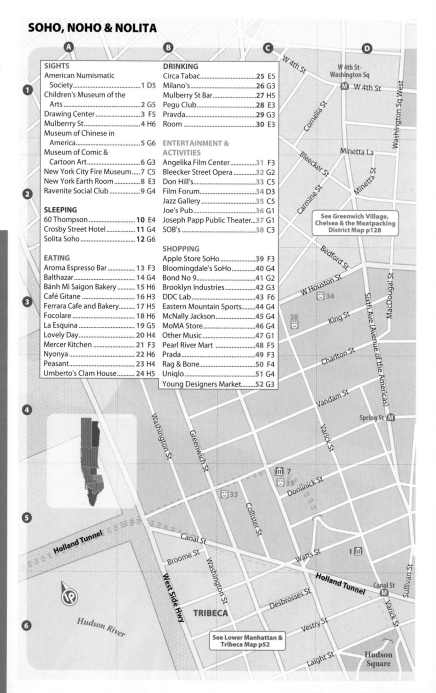

SIGHTS

American Numismatic
  Society...............................1 D5
Children's Museum of the
  Arts....................................2 G5
Drawing Center.......................3 F5
Mulberry St............................4 H6
Museum of Chinese in
  America..............................5 G6
Museum of Comic &
  Cartoon Art.........................6 G3
New York City Fire Museum.....7 C5
New York Earth Room.............8 E3
Ravenite Social Club................9 C4

SLEEPING

60 Thompson.......................10 E4
Crosby Street Hotel..............11 G4
Solita Soho..........................12 G6

EATING

Aroma Espresso Bar.............13 F3
Balthazar.............................14 G4
Bánh Mì Saigon Bakery........15 H6
Café Gitane.........................16 H3
Ferrara Cafe and Bakery.......17 H5
Focolare..............................18 H6
La Esquina..........................19 G5
Lovely Day..........................20 H4
Mercer Kitchen....................21 F3
Nyonya...............................22 H6
Peasant..............................23 H4
Umberto's Clam House.........24 H5

DRINKING

Circa Tabac.........................25 E5
Milano's...............................26 G3
Mulberry St Bar....................27 H5
Pegu Club............................28 E3
Pravda.................................29 G3
Room...................................30 E3

**ENTERTAINMENT &
ACTIVITIES**

Angelika Film Center............31 F3
Bleecker Street Opera...........32 G2
Don Hill's.............................33 C5
Film Forum...........................34 D3
Jazz Gallery.........................35 C5
Joe's Pub.............................36 G1
Joseph Papp Public Theater...37 G1
SOB's..................................38 C3

SHOPPING

Apple Store SoHo................39 F3
Bloomingdale's SoHo............40 G4
Bond No 9............................41 G2
Brooklyn Industries..............42 G3
DDC Lab..............................43 F6
Eastern Mountain Sports.......44 G4
McNally Jackson...................45 G4
MoMA Store.........................46 G4
Other Music.........................47 G1
Pearl River Mart...................48 F5
Prada..................................49 F3
Rag & Bone.........................50 F4
Uniqlo.................................51 G4
Young Designers Market........52 G3

See Greenwich Village,
Chelsea & the Meatpacking
District Map p128

See Lower Manhattan &
Tribeca Map p52

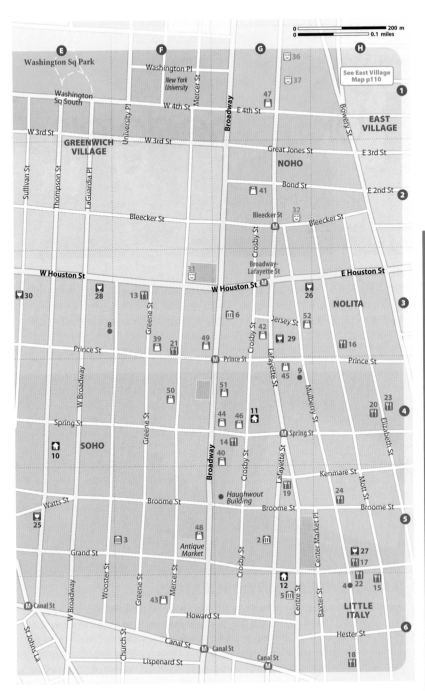

SOHO, NOHO & NOLITA

HIGHLIGHTS

1

⭨ SHOPPING

There are many ways to rack up debt at this major **shopping** (p88) destination.
Broadway is lined with less expensive chain stores. Hidden west along the tree-
lined streets, pricier boutiques sell clothing, shoes, accessories and housewares.
If indie is your thing, continue to Nolita, home to tiny boutiques selling unique
apparel, footwear, accessories and kitschy stuff at marginally lower prices.

2

⭨ INDEPENDENT MOVIE THEATERS

Cinephiles can't beat the selection of classic, avant-garde, foreign and themed
films on offer at the **Film Forum** (p87) on Houston St. Showings are often com-
bined with director talks or other filmic discussions. Listen for the roar of the
subway under your seat at the **Angelika Film Center** (p88), where contemporary
art-house, independent and the occasional Hollywood movies are screened.

⟍ LITTLE ITALY

Once known as a truly authentic pocket of Italian people, culture and eateries, Little Italy today is constantly shrinking (a growing Chinatown keeps moving in). Still, the old-world feels like it's hanging on when you take a nighttime stroll down Mulberry St (p86), past turn-of-the-century tenements where checker-clothed tables are set out on the street.

⟍ JOSEPH PAPP PUBLIC THEATER

One of the best venues in all NYC for top-quality theater, the Joseph Papp Public Theater (p87) has been an important cultural voice for the last half century. Some of the most critically acclaimed off-Broadway productions have been staged here, while the attached Joe's Pub (p88) draws talented musicians.

⟍ SOHO STREETS

To get a sense of the old-school feel of SoHo, amble through the small streets to the west of Broadway after 9pm on a weeknight. You'll be blissfully alone and able to admire the loft buildings and cobblestone streets without the crush of daytime shoppers. The neighborhood's signature cast-iron-facade industrial buildings date from the period just after the Civil War.

1 DAN HERRICK; 2 DAN HERRICK; 3 COREY WISE; 4 DAN HERRICK; 5 COREY WISE

1 Bloomingdale's SoHo (p89); 2 Film Forum (p87); 3 Little Italy; 4 Joseph Papp Public Theater (p87); 5 Mural in SoHo

INSIDE THE ACRONYMS: SOHO, NOHO & NOLITA WALKING TOUR

This walk begins at the Cable Building near the intersection of Broadway and Houston and ends at the New York Earth Room near Prince St. It covers a distance of 1.5 miles and will take between one and two hours.

❶ CABLE BUILDING

Pop out of the B, D, F, V train and get an immediate sense of old-meets-new with NoHo's Beaux Arts **Cable Building** (18 W Houston St), built by famed architects McKim, Mead and White in 1894. Originally used as the power plant for the Broadway Cable Car (the nation's first), it features an oval window and caryatids on its Broadway facade. Today it houses the **Angelika Film Center** (p88), a massive Crate & Barrel store and various offices.

❷ ST PATRICK'S OLD CATHEDRAL

Head east across Houston St and make a right on Lafayette St. Turn left on Prince St and you'll be approaching **St Patrick's Old Cathedral**, dating from 1809 – the original location for the famous Fifth Ave cathedral's congregation. Its ancient, peaceful cemetery is a Nolita haven that's worth a visit.

❸ ELIZABETH STREET GALLERY

Continue along Prince St. If you're hungry, you can stop to fuel up at **Café Gitane** (p84) on Mott St. Otherwise, turn right onto Elizabeth St, where you can pause to admire the fenced-in garden of the curious **Elizabeth Street Gallery** (210 Elizabeth St), part of a fireplace, fountain and garden-ornament shop for the well-off home owner. The biggest attraction in these parts, though, is the simple beauty of the small tangle of streets.

❹ SINGER BUILDING

Turn right on Spring St from Elizabeth St and enjoy the local neighborhood flavor until you hit Broadway. Half a block north is the **Singer Building** (561-563 Broadway), one of the post–Civil War cast-iron buildings that gave this area its 'Cast-Iron District' nickname. The building used to be the main warehouse for the famous sewing-machine company of the same name.

❺ HAUGHWOUT BUILDING

Head south down Broadway and you'll come to a garish Staples store with a fascinating history: it's located in the **Haughwout Building**

SOHO, NOHO & NOLITA WALKING TOUR

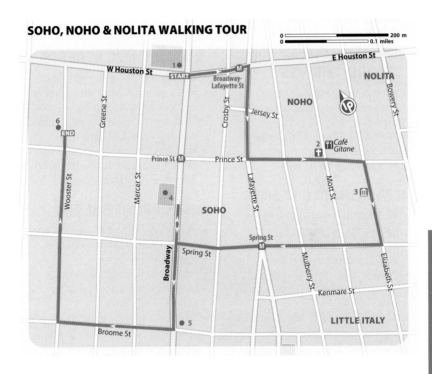

(488 Broadway), the first structure to use the exotic steam elevator developed by Elisha Otis. Known as the 'Parthenon of Cast-Iron Architecture,' the Haughwout (pronounced *how*-out) is considered a rare structure for its two-sided design. Don't miss the iron clock that sits on the Broadway facade.

❻ NEW YORK EARTH ROOM

Cross Broadway at Broome St, walking west, and continue on to Wooster St. Turn right and head up to the **New York Earth Room** (p81), where artist Walter De Maria's gallery filled with cool, moist soil will either thrill you or leave you scratching your head.

BEST...

⬐ PLACES WHERE THE WORD THRIVES

- **Joseph Papp Public Theater** (p87) High-profile, top-quality creative theater.
- **McNally Jackson** (p88) Authors give readings at this quality independent bookstore.

⬐ FASIONABLE SCENES

- **60 Thompson** (p83) One of the hotter, chic SoHo hotels.
- **Café Gitane** (p84) Euro, trendy, with good-looking people.
- **Pravda** (p86) Popular hangout for up-and-coming Russians in all walks of life.
- **Rag & Bone** (p88) Come out looking like a well-groomed, stylish downtowner.

⬐ ICONIC NYC STREETS

- **Broadway** This stretch of one of NYC's most famous thoroughfares is chock full of shopping.
- **Mulberry St** (p86) Picture postcard if touristy block of Little Italy.
- **Houston St** Changes complexion every few blocks, running river to river. Pronounced *house*-ton.

⬐ SHOPPING BREAKS

- **Aroma Espresso Bar** (p84) Strong coffee, healthy sandwiches and buzzy vibe.
- **Ferrara Cafe and Bakery** (p86) Landmark old-school place for pastries and drinks.
- **Mulberry Street Bar** (p86) A classic that's hanging on to the past; good for a strong drink.
- **Balthazar** (p84) Kitchen stays open till 2am from Thursday to Saturday, and weekend brunch is a crowded production.

LEFT: DAN HERRICK; RIGHT: DAN HERRICK

Left: 60 Thompson (p83); Right: Pastries, Ferrara Cafe and Bakery (p86)

DISCOVER SOHO, NOHO & NOLITA

This trio of cutesy acronyms, all named for geographic locales, represents three of the coolest city neighborhoods, known for their tangled thickets of hipness in the form of boutiques, bars and eateries.

Before its current incarnation as an upscale shopping area with a mall-like vibe, SoHo (SOuth of HOuston St) was once the center of the downtown arts scene and before that a manufacturing center.

NoHo (NOrth of HOuston St) is a smaller blend of side streets with quirky offerings, next door to the East Village.

Nolita (NOrth of Little ITAly) is probably the chicest of the three, due to its preponderance of high-fashion shops. Although Little Italy's ethnic character has been largely diluted in the last 50 years, loyal Italian Americans still flock here to gather around red-and-white-checkered tablecloths at a handful of long-time red-sauce restaurants.

SIGHTS

MUSEUM OF COMIC & CARTOON ART

☎ 212-254-3511; www.moccany.org; 594 Broadway btwn Houston & Prince Sts; adult/child $5/free; ⏲ noon-5pm Tue-Sun; ⊕ N, R to Prince St

A heavenly little set of galleries for the cartoon-obsessed among us, the museum's mission is to educate the public about comic and cartoon art, and to help everyone appreciate it in all its forms – comic strips, cartoons, anime, animation, gag cartoons, political illustrations, caricature, graphic novels and more.

DRAWING CENTER

☎ 212-219-2166; www.drawingcenter.org; 35 Wooster St at Grand St; ⏲ noon-6pm Wed, Fri-Sun, to 8pm Thu; ⊕ A, C, E, 1 to Canal St

Here since 1977, this is the only non-profit institute in the country to focus solely on drawings, using work by masters as well as unknowns to show the juxtaposition of various styles. Historical exhibitions have included work by Michelangelo, James Ensor and Marcel Duchamp, while contemporary shows have focused on Richard Serra, Ellsworth Kelly and Richard Tuttle; exhibits can range from the whimsical to the politically controversial.

NEW YORK EARTH ROOM

www.earthroom.org; 141 Wooster St; admission free; ⏲ noon-6pm Wed-Sun, closed 3-3:30pm; ⊕ N, R to Prince St

Since 1980 the oddity of the New York Earth Room, the work of artist Walter De Maria, has been wooing the curious with something not easily found in the city: dirt (250 cu yd, or 280,000lb, of it to be exact). Walking into the small space is a heady experience, as the scent will make you feel like you've entered a wet forest; the sight of such beautiful, pure earth in the midst of this crazy city is surprisingly moving.

DAN HERRICK

Children's Museum of the Arts

↘ IF YOU LIKE...

If you like the quirky subject matter at the **Musuem of Comic & Cartoon Art** (p81), we think you'll like these other sights:

- **American Numismatic Society** (☎ 212-234-3130; www.numismatics.org; 1 Hudson Sq at Varick & Watts Sts; admission free; ⊗ 9am-5pm Mon-Fri; ⊕ 1 to Houston St) The holdings here of more than 800,000 coins, medals and notes are rivaled by only one similar collection in Europe. The items are from all over the map and throughout history.

- **Children's Museum of the Arts** (☎ 212-941-9198; www.cmany.org; 182 Lafayette St; admission $10, pay what you wish 4-6pm Thu; ⊗ noon-5pm Wed & Fri-Sun, to 6pm Thu; ⊕ B, D, F, M to Broadway-Lafayette St) A great place for kids to unleash their inner artist, the small but worthy Children's Museum of the Arts is home to a permanent collection of paintings, drawings and photographs by local school children.

- **New York City Fire Museum** (☎ 212-219-1222; www.nycfiremuseum.org; 278 Spring St btwn Varick & Hudson Sts; suggested donation adult/child under 12/senior & student $5/1/2; ⊗ 10am-5pm Tue-Sat, to 4pm Sun; ⊕ C, E to Spring St) Occupying a grand old fire-house dating from 1904, this museum houses a collection of firefighting artifacts and exhibitions. It's a great place to bring children. The excellent gift shop sells official FDNY clothing, patches and books.

MUSEUM OF CHINESE IN AMERICA

☎ 212-619-4785; www.mocanyc.org; 215 Centre St; adult/senior & student $7/4; ⊗ 11am-5pm Mon & Fri, to 9pm Thu, 10am-5pm Sat & Sun; ⊕ J, Z, N, Q, R, 6 to Canal St

This recently relocated museum, housed in a 12,350-sq-ft space designed by architect Maya Lin (who did the famed Vietnam Memorial in Washington DC), will do to your mind what Canal St can do to your senses. The exhibit galleries, bookstore and visitors lounge, together serving as a national center of information, are chock full of facts about Chinese American life. Browse through interactive multimedia exhibits, maps, timelines, photos, letters, films and artifacts, and catch rotating exhibits. Its anchor exhibit is 'With a Single Step: Stories in the Making of America,' an interactive display touching on subjects including immigration, politics and history.

A new addition to the downtown scene, Solita is great for anyone who wants to soak up the flavor of Chinatown and Little Italy. Part of the Clarion chain, the Solita's got no surprises: a clean, functional lobby accessed through a glass-topped portico on the street, and smallish, slightly octagonal black-and-white rooms with wide beds (plump beige duvets and big pillows), private baths and a tiny desk.

SLEEPING

CROSBY STREET HOTEL
Boutique Hotel $$$

☎ 212-226-6400; www.firmdalehotels.com; 79 Crosby St near Spring St; r from $500; ⓖ 6 to Lafayette St, N, R to Prince St; ⊠ ▯

Step in to Crosby Street for afternoon tea and you'll never want to leave. It's not just the clotted cream and raisiny scones that will grab you, but the fun and upbeat lobby (with mauve sofas and striking artwork), the whimsical striped chairs in the bar and the unique rooms.

60 THOMPSON　　　Boutique Hotel $$
☎ 212-431-0400, 877-431-0400; www.60thompson.com; 60 Thompson St btwn Broome & Spring Sts; r from $300; ⓖ C, E to Spring St; ⊠ ▯

Built from scratch in 2001, the 100-room 60 Thompson is definitely the place to be seen, either in the futurist Thai restaurant, Kittichai, or swirling cocktails on the rooftop Thom Bar. Rooms are small but comfy: beds have goose-down duvets and leather headboards, and you can watch DVDs on the flat-screen TVs from a wing-backed seat or creamy tweed sofa.

SOLITA SOHO　　　　　　Hotel $
☎ 212-925-3600; www.clariohotel.com; 159 Grand St btw Centre & Lafayette Sts; r $129; ⓖ 6 to Canal St; ⊠ ▯

EATING

All three of these foodie destinations will afford you a dose of fabulousness: high ceilings, stylish crowds and excited dins rising over the lovely clatter of clinking wine glasses and forks that dive into fare ranging from French, Italian, Vietnamese, creative American and surprisingly authentic Mexican. Little Italy, with borders increasingly encroached upon by Chinatown and Nolita, has a minuscule culinary scene starring a handful of charming spots that attract mostly tourists.

PEASANT　　　　　Hearty Italian $$$
☎ 212-965-9511; www.peasantnyc.com; 194 Elizabeth St btwn Spring & Prince Sts; ⓥ dinner; ⓖ 6 to Spring St

This homey house of gourmet comfort grub has a vibe of old-fashioned simplicity and quality – due to a warm dining area of bare oak tables structured around a brick hearth and open kitchen, which turns out hearty, pan-Italian, mostly meat-based fare. Peasant has made it onto various best-restaurant lists in town, and always seems to be filled with a crowd of sophisticates.

MERCER KITCHEN　　American Eclectic $$$
☎ 212-966-5454; 99 Prince St at Mercer St; ⓥ breakfast, lunch & dinner; ⓖ N, R to Prince St

Just peering into this soothing gem of a hideaway – part of chef-god Jean-Georges

Vongerichten's top-echelon empire, perched below street level in the endlessly fashionable Mercer Hotel – tells you something special is going on. Favorites, such as baked salmon with fresh-corn pudding, sea scallops and pea-green ravioli, and a dessert of apricot tart with salted-caramel ice cream, reach higher levels thanks to the freshest, most seasonal ingredients.

BALTHAZAR   French Bistro $$$
☎ 212-965-1414; 80 Spring St btwn Broadway & Crosby St; ⏰ breakfast, lunch & dinner daily, brunch Sat & Sun; ◉ 6 to Spring St
Retaining its long-held status as a superstar among the city's glut of French bistros, this bustling (OK, *loud*) spot still pulls in the discriminating mobs. That's thanks to three winning details: the location, which makes it a convenient shopping-spree rest area; the uplifting ambience, shaped by big, mounted mirrors, cozy high-backed booths and airy, high ceilings and wide windows; and, of course, the stellar something-for-everyone menu, which features an outstanding raw bar, steak *frites*, salad *niçoise*, roasted beet salad, and prawn risotto with sage and butternut squash.

FOCOLARE   Italian $$$
☎ 212-993-5858; 115 Mulberry St btwn Canal & Hester Sts; ⏰ lunch & dinner; ◉ J, Z, N, Q, R, 6 to Canal St
If you're bent on a Little Italy dinner experience, this relative newcomer is a fine choice. With a cozy interior warmed by a fireplace in winter (and photos of Frank Sinatra and co all around), the kitchen turns out classics in fine style: homemade pasta, cooked al dente, is an excellent base for various red and cream-based sauces; rice balls ooze with cheese; fried calamari zings with flavor.

LA ESQUINA   Mexican $$
☎ 646-613-1333; 106 Kenmare St; ⏰ 24hr; ◉ 6 to Spring St
This mega-popular and quirky little spot is housed in a former greasy spoon that sits within the neat little triangle formed by Cleveland Pl and Lafayette St. It's three places really: a stand-while-you-eat taco window, a casual Mexican cafe and, downstairs through the taco facade, a cozy, overly hip cave of a dining room.

NYONYA   Malaysian $$
☎ 212-334-3669; 199 Grand St at Mulberry St; ⏰ lunch, dinner; ◉ B, D to Grand St, 6 to Spring St
One of very few Malaysian joints in the city, Nyonya is one of the best. The warm, honey-hued wood and exposed-brick interior is soothing – as are the various noodle soups, casseroles and *roti canai* (crispy pancakes).

CAFÉ GITANE   Moroccan Bistro $
☎ 212-334-9552; 242 Mott St; ⏰ 5:30-11:30pm; ◉ N, R to Prince St
Gitane is the type of place you'd expect to see everywhere in, say, Paris or Lisbon – an ochre-lit space with deep banquettes and warm air, scented by baking bread and garlic hitting a pan. Outside, slouchy, wealthy artist types and high-end-label lovers surrounded by impressive shopping bags are smoking Gauloises, and everyone is drinking coffee.

AROMA ESPRESSO BAR
Israeli Coffeehouse $
☎ 212-533-1094; 145 Greene St at Houston St; ⏰ 7am-11pm; ◉ B, D, F, M to Broadway-Lafayette St
One of the latest, greatest Israeli imports to NYC has been this sleek cafe chain, where you'll find soothing lighting, comfy

and stylish seating and a menu bursting with fresh, tasty, affordable fare.

LOVELY DAY
Pan-Asian $

☎ 212-925-3310; 196 Elizabeth St btwn Prince & Spring Sts; ⏰ lunch & dinner; Ⓜ J, Z to Bowery St, 6 to Spring St

Everything is just precious inside this affordable and funky nook, from the cozy red booths and bedroom-appropriate wallpaper to the lovingly prepared portions of Thai-inflected food. Coconut-rich curries, noodle dishes, papaya salad and spicy tofu squares create a fascinating harmony with the soda-shop-inspired decor.

BÁNH MÌ SAIGON BAKERY
Vietnamese Bánh Mì $

☎ 212-406-2292; 138 Mott St at Grand St; ⏰ 10am-7pm Tue-Sun; Ⓜ J, Z, N, Q, R, 6 to Canal St

This frequently mobbed, no-frills storefront doles out some of the city's best *bánh mì* – Vietnamese roast-pork sandwiches served on fat baguettes with piles of sliced cucumber, pickled carrots, hot sauce and cilantro.

DRINKING

ROOM
Beer & Wine Bar

☎ 212-477-2102; 144 Sullivan St btwn Prince & Houston Sts; Ⓜ C, E to Spring St

The Room is actually two modest rooms, both low-lit, with candles flickering against the exposed brick walls sprinkled with photographs, and a low-key crowd chatting each other up over drinks – which here means wine (two dozen different types) or beer (more than 70 varieties).

CIRCA TABAC
Cigar Bar

☎ 212-941-1781; 32 Watts St btwn Sixth Ave & Thompson St; Ⓜ A, C, E, 1 to Canal St

One of a few bars left in the city where you can still smoke (and are encouraged to do so), this stylish art deco lounge offers more than 150 types of smokes, mainly global cigars. Its specialty drinks include a pucker-inducing Gingersnap

ANGUS OBORN

Balthazar

SOHO, NOHO & NOLITA

DRINKING

DAN HERRICK

Mulberry St

⬎ MULBERRY STREET

Although it feels more like a theme park than an authentic Italian strip, Mulberry St is still the heart of the 'hood. It's the home of landmarks such as **Umberto's Clam House**, where mobster Joey Gallo was shot to death in the 1970s, as well as the old-time **Mulberry Street Bar**, one of the favorite haunts of the late Frank Sinatra. Just a half-block off of Mulberry is the legendary **Ferrara Cafe and Bakery**, brimming with classic Italian pastries and old-school ambience. Take a gander at what was once the **Ravenite Social Club** to see how things have really changed around here, as these days it's host to a rotating roster of legit businesses, including clothing and gift shops. It was once an organized-crime hangout (originally known as the Alto Knights Social Club), where big hitters such as Lucky Luciano and John Gotti (as well as the FBI, who kept raiding the place) logged time.

Things you need to know: Ferrara Cafe and Bakery (195 Grand St); Mulberry Street Bar (☎ 212-226-9345; 176½ Mulberry St btwn Broome & Grand Sts; ☻ B, D to Grand St); Ravenite Social Club (247 Mulberry St, Nolita); Umberto's Clam House (☎ 212-431-7545; 386 Broome St at Mulberry St); ☻ 6 to Spring St

(ginger-infused vodka, crystallized ginger and champagne).

PEGU CLUB
Cocktail Bar

☎ 212-473-7348; 77 W Houston St btwn W Broadway & Wooster Sts; ☻ B, D, F, M to Broadway-Lafayette St

Loosely inspired by a British colonial bar from the Burma days, Pegu is a slick

upstairs cocktail lounge with a touch of Asian wall-dressings, a slightly dressed-up crowd and candlelit booths.

PRAVDA
Cocktail Bar

☎ 212-226-4944; 281 Lafayette St btwn Prince & Houston Sts; ☻ B, D, F, M to Broadway-Lafayette St

This subterranean bar and brasserie lays on the Soviet-era nostalgia with heavy brushstrokes, from the Cyrillic lettering on the walls to the extensive vodka menu, including the caviar martini (vodka with dill, cucumber and a spoonful of you-know-what).

MILANO'S   Dive Bar
☎ 212-226-8844; 51 E Houston St btwn Mulberry & Mott Sts; ⊕ B, D, F, M to Broadway-Lafayette St

For nearly a century, the hole-in-the-wall Milano's has withstood the hipster onslaught of Nolita and stayed true to its divey self (potato chips behind the worn, wooden bar and $3 Pabst Blue Ribbon beers). Grizzled vets and curious youngsters mix it up easily, bonding over pints and a great, stacked jukebox with offerings from everyone from Tony Bennett to the Chieftains.

MULBERRY STREET BAR   Dive Bar
☎ 212-226-9345; 176½ Mulberry St btwn Broome & Grand Sts; ⊕ B, D to Grand St

Frank Sinatra liked this 100-year-old Little Italy hang, which was also used as a backdrop for scenes in the *Sopranos, Godfather III* and *Donnie Brasco*. The gruff, bartenders add to the charm, as does the odd mix of wide-eyed tourists, crusty regulars and the overflow of hipsters.

ENTERTAINMENT & ACTIVITIES

DON HILL'S   Clubbing
☎ 212-334-1390; 511 Greenwich St at Spring St; admission $5-20; ⊕ C, E to Spring St

This ancient club – once swanky, way back in 1991 – wears its scruffy age with pride and has become something of a divey hipster favorite in recent years. Multicolored lights, tattooed walls and stripper poles set the vibe for a raucous young-at-heart party scene.

FILM FORUM   Film & TV
☎ 212-727-8110; www.filmforum.org; 209 W Houston St btwn Varick St & Sixth Ave; ⊕ 1 to Houston St

This three-screen cinema shows an astounding array of independent films, revivals and career retrospectives from greats such as Sidney Lumet. Theaters are small, as are the screens, so get there early for a good viewing spot.

JAZZ GALLERY   Jazz
☎ 212-242-1063; www.jazzgallery.org; 290 Hudson St btwn Dominick & Spring Sts; ⊕ C, E to Spring St

A cultural center rather than your typical jazz club – there's no bar here, folks – the Gallery is for fans who are really serious about their music. The small space with great acoustics hosts several shows per week, often with two sets per night.

SOB'S   Latin
☎ 212-243-4940; www.sobs.com; 204 Varick St btwn King & Houston Sts; ⊕ 1 to Houston St

SOB stands for Sounds of Brazil, but it isn't limited to samba: you can shake it to Afro-Cuban music, salsa, reggae and African pop here, both live and on the turntable. SOB's hosts dinner shows nightly but it doesn't really start jumping until around 2am.

JOSEPH PAPP PUBLIC THEATER
Off-Broadway & Off-Off-Broadway
☎ 212-260-2400; www.publictheater.org; 425 Lafayette St btwn 4th St & Astor Pl; ⊕ 6 to Astor Pl

One of the city's most important cultural centers, the Papp was founded by the late, expansive-minded Joseph Papp, who once returned a massive NEA grant rather than sign its conservative anti-obscenity amendment. The theater has had an almost constant roster of can't-miss productions over the years, and staged world premieres of *Hair, A Chorus Line, Plenty* and *Caroline, or Change,* all of which moved to Broadway. The East Village complex also offers **Joe's Pub** (below) for top-notch musical and cabaret shows, and every summer it presents its famous productions of Shakespeare in the Park at Delacorte Theater, which Papp began back in 1954, before the lovely, open-air theater was even built.

BLEECKER STREET OPERA   Opera
☎ 212-239-6200; www.bleeckerstreetopera
.org; 45 Bleecker St btwn Broadway & Bowery;
◉ B, D, F, M to Broadway-Lafayette St, 6 to
Bleecker St

Another reincarnation of the Amato Opera is this company, which has formed an alliance with the 45 Bleecker theater and is dedicated to offering high-quality, intimate and affordable productions.

JOE'S PUB   Rock & Indie
☎ 212-539-8778; www.joespub.com; Public
Theater, 425 Lafayette St btwn Astor Pl & 4th St;
◉ N, R to 8th St-NYU, 6 to Astor Pl

Part cabaret theater, part rock and new-indie venue, this intimate supper club stages the fringe mainstream (eg folks such as Aimee Mann). It has a nice, long bar, seats cuddled around a corner stage and a bit of a dress-up atmosphere.

ANGELIKA FILM CENTER   Film & TV
☎ 212-995-2000; www.angelikafilmcenter.com;
18 W Houston St at Mercer St; ◉ B, D, F, M to
Broadway-Lafayette St

An old favorite, the Angelika specializes in foreign and independent films. It's often overcrowded – despite the fact that screens can be annoyingly small and you can hear the rumble of the subway going by in the middle of your movie.

SHOPPING

MCNALLY JACKSON   Books
☎ 212-274-1160; www.mcnallyjackson.com;
52 Prince St btwn Lafayette & Mulberry Sts;
◉ 10am-10pm Mon-Sat, 10am-9pm Sun; ◉ N,
R to Prince St

This inviting indie bookshop stocks an excellent selection of magazines and books covering contemporary fiction, food writing, architecture and design, art and history.

PEARL RIVER MART
Chinese Department Store
☎ 212-431-4770; 477 Broadway; ◉ 10am-7pm;
◉ J, Z, N, Q, R, 6 to Canal St

This multifloor emporium is a showcase for all things Asian – including Chinese and Japanese tea pots, dragon-print dresses, paper lanterns, Chinese slippers, jars of Chinese spices and sauces, imported teas, ceramic 'lucky cats,' paper parasols and various Asian instruments.

DDC LAB   Clothing
☎ 212-226-8980; 7 Mercer St; ◉ 11am-7pm
Mon-Sat, noon-6pm Sun; ◉ J, Z, N, Q, R, 6 to
Canal St

A cool boutique for the latest flourishes of urban style, DDC Lab sells a range of nicely designed, slim-fitting wares including sleek limited-edition sneakers, superbly comfortable T-shirts, leather jackets and pea coats, as well as rubbery Nooka belts and other accessories.

RAG & BONE   Clothing
☎ 212-219-2204; 119 Mercer St; ◉ noon-7pm
Mon-Sat, noon-6pm Sun; ◉ N, R to Prince St

DAN HERRICK

Mannequins, Prada

Born in 2002, Rag & Bone has become one of the hot new labels over the years, earning praise for fashionable, versatile basics designed to last.

UNIQLO
Clothing
☎ 917-237-8811; 546 Broadway; ⏱ 10am-9pm Mon-Sat, 11am-8pm Sun; Ⓜ N, R to Prince St
Japan's version of H&M opened its US flagship store in SoHo to much fanfare back in 2006. The enormous three-story emporium owes its popularity to attractive apparel at discount prices.

YOUNG DESIGNERS MARKET
Clothing & Accessories
☎ 212-580-8995; 268 Mulberry St; ⏱ 11am-7pm Sat & Sun; Ⓜ B, D, F, M to Broadway-Lafayette St
This large, colorful market takes over the gym of Old St Patrick's on weekends. As per the name, young and indie designers rule the roost, selling handmade jewelry, unique witty T-shirts and one-of-a-kind stationery, plus dresses, hoodies and lots of other affordable items you won't find elsewhere.

APPLE STORE SOHO
Computers & Electronics
☎ 212-226-3126; 103 Prince St; ⏱ 9am-9pm Mon-Sat, 9am-7pm Sun; Ⓜ N, R to Prince St
Apple's airy flagship location – with translucent stairway and upstairs walkway and fully fledged theater, used for how-to presentations – bustles with SoHo shoppers picking up iPhones, iPods, MacBooks and other items from the iUniverse.

BLOOMINGDALE'S SOHO
Department Store
☎ 212-729-5900; 504 Broadway; ⏱ 10am-9pm Mon-Fri, 10am-8pm Sat, 11am-7pm Sun; Ⓜ N, R to Prince St
The smaller, younger outpost of the Third Ave legend, this Bloomie's sheds housewares and other department-store items for a clear focus on fashion.

PRADA
Designer Clothing
☎ 212-334-8888; 575 Broadway; ⏱ 11am-7pm Mon-Sat, noon-6pm Sun; Ⓜ N, R to Prince St
Transformed from the old Guggenheim SoHo location by Dutch architect Rem Koolhaas, this shop, with sweeping

DAN HERRICK

Bond No 9

wooden floors and tucked-away down-stairs rooms, is a marvel to see.

MOMA STORE
Designer Gadgets

☎ 646-613-1367; 81 Spring St; ◷ 10am-8pm Mon-Sat, 11am-7pm Sun; ◉ N, R to Prince St
This sleek and stylish space carries a huge collection of handsomely designed objects for the home, office and wardrobe.

OTHER MUSIC
Indie Music

☎ 212-477-8150; 15 E 4th St; ◷ noon-9pm Mon-Fri, noon-8pm Sat, noon-7pm Sun; ◉ 6 to Bleecker St
This indie-run CD store has won over a loyal fan base with its informed selection of, well, other types of music: offbeat lounge, psychedelic, electronica, indie rock etc, available new and used.

EASTERN MOUNTAIN SPORTS
Outdoor Gear & Clothing

☎ 212-966-8730; 530 Broadway at Spring St; ◷ 10am-9pm Mon-Sat, 11am-8pm Sun; ◉ N, R to Prince St

In a new, sprawling space on Broadway, this rugged outfitter stocks everything you need to tackle the great outdoors including hiking shoes, jackets, sleeping bags and cool gadgets, plus gear for hikers, snowboarders, rock climbers and cyclists.

BOND NO 9
Perfume

☎ 212-228-1940; www.bondno9.com; 9 Bond St; ◷ 11am-7pm Mon-Sat, noon-6pm Sun; ◉ 6 to Bleecker St
'Making scents of New York' is the motto of this thoroughly unique perfume boutique, where the gimmick is everything NYC.

BROOKLYN INDUSTRIES
Streetwear

☎ 212-219-0862; www.brooklynindustries. com; 290 Lafayette St; ◷ 11am-8pm Mon-Sat, noon-7:30pm Sun; ◉ B, D, F, M to Broadway-Lafayette St
Boasting a smart but decidedly urban aesthetic, Brooklyn Industries is best known for the iconic 'Made in Brooklyn' tees and sweatshirts, though you'll also find sweaters, jackets, jeans, coats, hats, messenger bags and laptop sleeves.

LOWER EAST SIDE & CHINATOWN

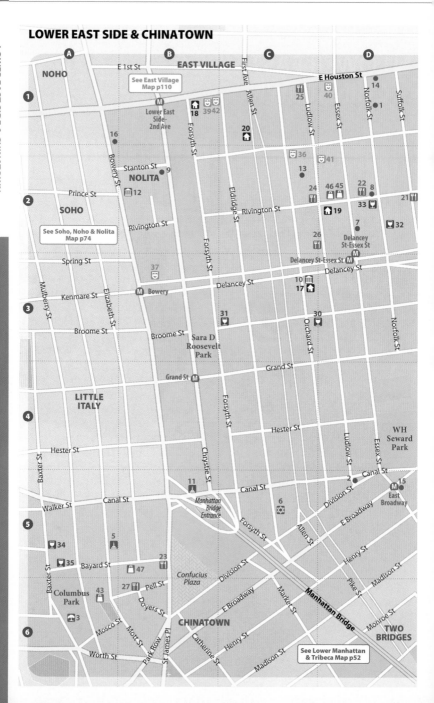

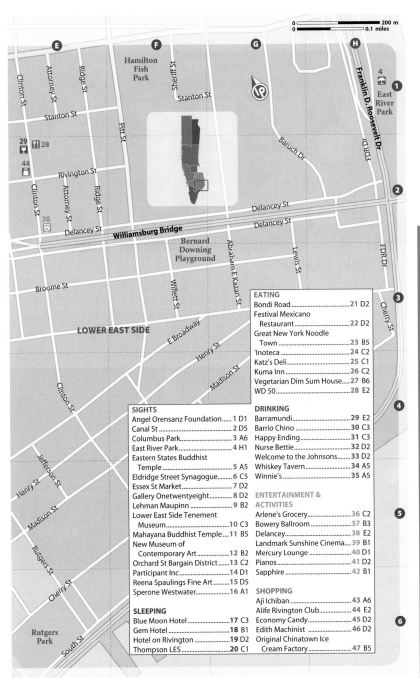

HIGHLIGHTS

↘ CHOW DOWN

Duck into a produce market and check out various oddly shaped and sometimes prickly fruits and vegetables. Buy six cakes of fresh tofu or three luscious turnip cakes for $1 from a street vendor. Sip bubble teas and slurp noodles – with cuisine from Shanghai, Vietnam and Malaysia, from holes-in-the-wall to banquet-sized dining rooms, **Chinatown** (p101, p105) is a true culinary adventure.

↘ OLD JEWISH NEW YORK CITY

In the early 20th century, half a million Jews from Eastern Europe streamed into these parts, lending an ethnic flavor of pickles, knishes and kosher deli foods to the poverty-laden settlement. It was home to Yiddish theaters, synagogues and yeshivas. Twenty years after its renovation began, the **Eldridge Street Synagogue** (p99) is a glorious sanctuary and one of the few remaining survivors of this history.

◥ BAR SCENE

The Lower East Side is hipster central. In a relatively concentrated area there are dozens of pick-up spots and low-key hangouts. Fair or not, in the city's nightlife solar system it has become identified with overly precious, re-created speakeasys, ironically themed dives, and up-towners wanting 'in' on the cool side of town.

◥ ART SPACES

A recent anchor in Manhattan's ever-spinning art world, the stacked-box architecture of the **New Museum of Contemporary Art** (p100) offers a transformative take on the typical gallery experience. A handful of galleries, including **Sperone Westwater** (p101), have also thrown open their doors in the Lower East Side, offering cutting-edge fare.

◥ BOUTIQUE SHOPPING

The downtown fashion crowd looking for that edgy, experimental or old-school hip-hop look head to the Lower East Side to **shop** (p107). Sprinkled throughout are dozens of stores selling vintage apparel, vegan shoes, one-of-a-kind sneakers, old fashioned candy, sex toys, left-wing books and more.

1 KIM GRANT; 2 MARIO TAMA/GETTY IMAGES; 3 ROGER GAESS; 4 DAN HERRICK (ARCHITECTS: SEJIMA + NISHIZAWA/SANAA, 2007); 5 DAN HERRICK

1 Fresh produce, Chinatown (p108); **2** Eldrige Street Synagogue (p99); **3** Arlene's Grocery (p107); **4** New Museum of Contemporary Art (p100); **5** Alife Rivington Club (p107)

CHINESE HERITAGE WALKING TOUR

This walk begins at Chatham Sq and ends with a stop at a Vietnamese restaurant. It covers a distance of 1.5 miles and will take between one and two hours.

❶ CHATHAM SQUARE

Begin your exploration at **Chatham Sq (East Broadway at Bowery)**, where you'll see the **Kim Lau Memorial Arch**, erected in 1962 as a memorial to Chinese Americans who died in WWII. There's also a **statue of Lin Ze Xu**, a Qing-dynasty scholar whose anti-drug-trafficking stance helped lead to the First Opium War in 1839.

❷ DOYERS ST

From the southern point of Chatham Sq head north on Bowery until you come to **Doyers St**. Take a left and stroll along the short, L-shaped lane, home to many barber shops, the local post office and one of the first dim sum restaurants. Legend says the street was constructed with a 90-degree bend to hinder the movement of straight-walking ghosts.

❸ EDWARD MOONEY HOUSE

At the end of Doyers St take a right on Pell St, then a left on Bowery. On your left is the red-brick **Edward Mooney House (18 Bowery)**, New York City's oldest town house, built in 1785 by butcher Edward Mooney. The blend of Georgian-Federal architecture has housed a store, hotel, billiards parlor and Chinese social club; today it's a bank.

❹ MAHAYANA BUDDHIST TEMPLE

Continue walking north on Bowery to Canal St, where you'll see the clogged entrance to the Manhattan Bridge and, just beyond that, the **Mahayana Buddhist Temple** (p102). Head on in to gaze upon the massive golden Buddha and grab a meditative moment.

❺ CANAL ST

Exit the temple and head west on **Canal St**, taking in all the sights and smells and kitschy items for sale from small shops between Bowery and Centre St.

❻ COLUMBUS PARK

Take a left on Mulberry St and walk a block to **Columbus Park** (p102), an active community space since the 1890s filled with mah-jongg and dominos players, tai chi and judo practitioners, and both the old and young (all local residents). An interesting note is that the Five Points neighborhood, home to the city's first tenement slums and the inspiration for Martin Scorsese's *Gangs of New York*, was once located at the foot of where Columbus Park is now. The 'five points' were the five streets that used to converge here; now you'll find the intersection of only Mosco, Worth and Baxter Sts. (Another Columbus Park perk is its public bathroom, making it the perfect place for a pit stop.)

❼ VIETNAMESE RESTAURANTS
From here, head a short block west on Bayard before making a right on Baxter St, known for its many **Vietnamese restaurants**. Stop for a meal, or just take a gander at the varied menus.

CHINESE HERITAGE TOUR

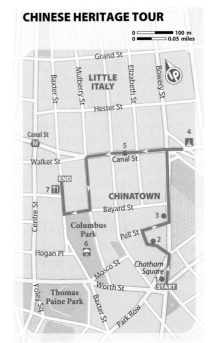

BEST...

⬏ FOOD TREATS

- **Dim Sum** (p105) Point and get served from a constant merry-go-round of carts filled with delicacies.
- **Pastrami sandwich** (p103) Huge helpings of this deli meat made from beef and piled on rye.
- **Dumplings** (p105) Doughy morsels with savory or sweet fillings.
- **Bubble Tea** (p105) Sweetly flavored tea with balls of tapioca or jelly.

⬏ HIPSTER HANGOUTS

- **Welcome to the Johnsons** (p105) A 1970s-era themed bar for the ironic – wash down free Doritos with a Jack and root beer.
- **Winnie's** (p106) Sing your lungs out ($1 per song) before a weird karaoke movie screen playing '80s montages.
- **Arlene's Grocery** (p107) Former bodega, and pioneer of neighborhood music scene.

⬏ STREETS TO WANDER

- **The Bowery** Formerly synonymous with the down-and-out, now houses outposts of the hip and glamorous.
- **Canal Street** (p101) Fake-watch hawkers, knock-off perfumes and everything in between for sale.
- **Rivington** A continuous influx of new bars fuels the nightlife.
- **Mott Street** One of the original core Chinatown streets; loads of groceries, restaurants and shops.

⬏ OLD JEWISH NYC

- **Katz's Deli** (p103) One of the few surviving delis; nostalgic and lively at the same time.
- **Lower East Side Tenement Museum** (p99) Explore the neighborhood's immigration history.
- **Eldridge Street Synagogue** (p99) This house of worship attracted as many as 1000 worshippers for the High Holidays at the turn of the 20th century.

DAN HERRICK

Lower East Side Tenement Museum

DISCOVER LOWER EAST SIDE & CHINATOWN

Originally a settlement for Jews and then Latinos, the Lower East Side (LES) has become the place to be seen. It's either about being cool (by cramming into low-lit lounges and live-music clubs) or about being moneyed (by snagging a table at a pricey restaurant). A bunch of luxury high-rise condominiums and hip boutique hotels coexist with large public housing projects and blocks of tenement-style buildings.

Nearby, more than 150,000 Chinese-speaking residents live in cramped tenements and crowded apartments in Chinatown. It's the largest Chinese community outside of Asia. In the 1990s, the neighborhood also attracted a growing number of Vietnamese immigrants; depending on what street you're on, you'll often notice more of a Vietnamese presence than a Chinese one.

The best reason to visit Chinatown is to experience a feast for the senses – it's the only spot in the city where you can simultaneously see whole roasted pigs hanging in butcher-shop windows, get whiffs of fresh fish and hear the sounds of Cantonese and Vietnamese rise over the calls of knockoff Prada-bag hawkers on Canal St.

SIGHTS
LOWER EAST SIDE
ELDRIDGE STREET SYNAGOGUE
☎ 212-219-0888; www.eldridgestreet.org; 12 Eldridge St btwn Canal & Division Sts; ◉ F to East Broadway

After years of falling into disrepair followed by a long and thorough makeover, this landmark synagogue was recently returned to its original 1887 splendor. A handful of members still worship in a small basement space, but 20 years and $20 million later, the glorious sanctuary has been reopened as a museum. Its Moorish-style stained-glass windows are as sparkly-new as the day it opened. **Tours** (adult/senior & student $10/8; ◷ 10am-4pm Sun-Thu on the half hr, last tour 3pm) of the landmark are also available.

LOWER EAST SIDE TENEMENT MUSEUM
☎ 212-431-0233; www.tenement.org; 108 Orchard St at Delancey; adult/senior & student $20/15; ◷ 10:30am-5pm; ◉ B, D to Grand St, F to Delancey St, J, Z to Essex St

This museum puts the neighborhood's heartbreaking but inspiring heritage on full display in three recreations of turn-of-the-20th-century tenements, including the late-19th-century home and garment shop of the Levine family from Poland, and two immigrant dwellings from the Great Depressions of 1873 and 1929. The visitor center shows a video detailing the difficult life endured by the people who once lived in the surrounding buildings, which more often than not had no running water or electricity. Museum visits are available only as part of scheduled tours, which typically operate daily.

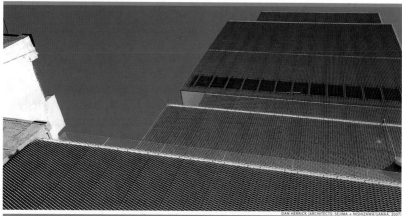

DAN HERRICK (ARCHITECTS: SEJIMA + NISHIZAWA/SANAA, 2007)

New Museum of Contemporary Art

⬊ NEW MUSEUM OF CONTEMPORARY ART

This recent addition to the neighborhood, the New Museum of Contemporary Art is a sight to behold: a seven-story stack of off-kilter, white, ethereal boxes. It was a long-awaited breath of fresh air along what was a completely gritty Bowery strip when it arrived – though since its opening, several glossy new constructions have joined it, quickly transforming this once down-and-out avenue. The thrills don't stop when you step inside, either, as the city's sole museum dedicated to contemporary art has brought a steady menu of edgy works in new forms, such as seemingly random, discarded materials fused together and displayed in the middle of a vast room.

Founded in 1977 by Marcia Tucker and moved to five different locations over the years, the museum's mission statement is simple: 'New art, new ideas.' The institution has given gallery space to artists Keith Haring, Jeff Koons, Joan Jonas, Mary Kelly and Andres Serrano – all at the beginning of their careers – and continues to show contemporary heavy hitters. The museum also houses a small and healthy cafe, and has the added treat of a city viewing platform, which provides a unique perspective on the constantly changing architectural landscape.

Things you need to know: ☎ 212-219-1222; www.newmuseum.org; 235 Bowery btwn Stanton & Rivington Sts; adult/senior/student/under-18 $12/10/8/free; ☽ noon-6pm Wed, Sat & Sun, noon-9pm Thu & Fri; Ⓜ N, R to Prince St, 6 to Spring St

ESSEX STREET MARKET
☎ 212-312-3603; www.essexstreetmarket.com; 120 Essex St btwn Delancey & Rivington Sts; ☽ 8am-7pm Mon-Sat; Ⓜ F to Delancey St, J, Z to Essex St

This 60-year-old historic shopping destination is the local place for produce, seafood, butcher-cut meats, cheeses, Latino grocery items, and even a barber's shop and small art gallery.

LOWER EAST SIDE ART GALLERIES

F to Delancey St, J, Z to Essex St

Though Chelsea may be the heavy hitter when it comes to the New York art gallery scene, the LES has its very own collection of about a dozen quality showplaces, thank you very much. Some have actually relocated here from Chelsea in recent years, and all are now anchored by the **New Museum of Contemporary Art** (left). **Participant Inc** (212-254-4334; www.participantinc.org; 253 E Houston St btwn Norfolk & Suffolk Sts), showcasing emerging talent and hosting varied performances, was one of the places hailed as jump-starting the gallery trend here when it opened several years ago. Other popular, contemporary spaces include **Gallery Onetwentyeight** (212-674-0244; www.galleryonetwentyeight.org; 128 Rivington St), **Reena Spaulings Fine Art** (212-477-5006; www.reenaspaulings.com; 165 East Broadway), **Lehmann Maupin** (212-254-0054; www.lehmannmaupin.com; 201 Chrystie St) and the new **Angel Orensanz Foundation** (212-529-7194; www.orensanz.org; 172 Norfolk St) gallery, housed in a soaring, gorgeous former synagogue that also hosts a slew of special events. But the biggest news of late is that of the new **Sperone Westwater** (www.speronewestwater.com; 257 Bowery) gallery, relocated from the West Village to the Bowery, right near the New Museum, in what was promising to be, at the time of writing, a startling, eight-story sliver sheathed in milled glass, with bright-red elevator doors and entire exhibits visible from out on the street.

ORCHARD STREET BARGAIN DISTRICT

Orchard, Ludlow & Essex Sts btwn Houston & Delancey Sts; Sun-Fri; F to Delancey St, J, Z to Essex St

When the LES was still a largely Jewish neighborhood, Eastern European merchants set up pushcarts to sell their wares here. While it's no longer as quaint as that, the **Lower East Side Business Improvement District** (www.lowereastsideny.com) has made it a goal to bring more shoppers to this area, which sometimes gets forgotten in the trend-seeking rush. Rather than searching high and low for designer label knockoffs – better found at bargain chains elsewhere, such as **Century 21** (p72) and **Filene's Basement** (p166) – know that this is more the type of place for scoring cheap basics such as bras, shoes, army-navy bags and leather jackets. While the businesses are not exclusively owned by Orthodox Jews, they still close early on Friday afternoon and remain closed on Saturday in observance of the Sabbath.

EAST RIVER PARK

Flanked by a looming housing project and the clogged FDR Dr on one side and the less-than-pure East River on the other, you might wonder what the draw is here. But take one visit – especially if it's during spring or summer – and you'll understand. In addition to the great ballparks, running and biking paths, 5000-seat amphitheater for concerts and expansive patches of green, it's got cool, natural breezes and stunning views of the Williamsburg, Manhattan and Brooklyn Bridges.

CHINATOWN

CANAL STREET

J, Z, N, Q, R, 6 to Canal St

While the hidden treasures of Chinatown are found on its tiny side streets, this wide avenue is the area's pulsing artery, and a walk along it will be an exercise not only in frustration – the crowds will leave you at constant impasses – but also in excitement. You'll pass open, stinky seafood markets hawking bloodied, slippery fish; mysterious little herb shops displaying all manner of roots and potions; storefront bakeries with steamed-up windows and the tastiest 50¢ pork buns you've ever had; restaurants with whole roasted ducks and pigs hanging by their skinny necks in the windows; produce markets piled high with fresh lychee nuts, bok choy and Asian pears; and street vendors selling tiny, illegal turtles, as well as endless forms of knockoffs, from Gucci sunglasses and Rolex watches to faux Prada bags.

BUDDHIST TEMPLES

Chinatown is home to Buddhist temples large and small, public and obscure. They are easily stumbled upon during a full-on stroll of the neighborhood, and at least two such temples are considered landmarks. The **Eastern States Buddhist Temple** (64 Mott St btwn Bayard & Canal Sts; J, Z, 6 to Canal St) is filled with hundreds of Buddhas, while the **Mahayana Buddhist Temple** (133 Canal St at Manhattan Bridge Plaza; B, D to Grand St) holds one golden, 16ft-high Buddha, sitting on a lotus and edged with offerings of fresh oranges, apples and flowers.

COLUMBUS PARK

Mulberry & Bayard Sts; J, Z, 6 to Canal St

This is where outdoor mah-jongg and domino games take place at bridge tables while tai chi practitioners move through lyrical, slow-motion poses under shady trees. Judo-sparring folks and relaxing families are also common sights in this active communal space that was originally created in the 1890s and is still popular with local residents today.

SLEEPING

HOTEL ON RIVINGTON

Boutique Hotel $$

☎ 212-475-2600, 800-915-1537; www.hotel onrivington.com; 107 Rivington St btwn Essex & Ludlow Sts; r from $279; F, J, Z to Delancey-Essex Sts;

Opened in 2005, the 20-floor THOR (that's the hotel acronym, not the viking) looks like a shimmering new-Shanghai building towering over 19th-century tenements. The 'unique' rooms have all-glass rooms with enviable views over the East River and downtown's sprawl, along with hanging flat-screen TVs. The standard rooms have one glass wall with a view (instead of three) and are a tighter squeeze.

BLUE MOON HOTEL   Boutique Hotel $$

☎ 212-533-9080; www.bluemoon-nyc.com; 100 Orchard St; r from $250; F to Lower East Side-2nd Ave;

You'd never guess that this quaint, welcoming brick guesthouse – full of festive yellows, blues and greens – was once a foul tenement back in the day (the day being 1879). Except for a few ornate touches, such as original wood shutters, wrought-iron bed frames and detailed molding, Blue Moon's clean, spare rooms are entirely modern and comfortable, with big beds, great views from large windows and elegant marble baths.

THOMPSON LES   Boutique Hotel $$

☎ 212-204-6485; http://thompsonles.com; 190 Allen St near Stanton St; r from $249; F to Lower East Side-2nd Ave;

Another high-end offering from the brains trust behind boutique beauties Gild Hall and 6 Columbus, Thompson LES has 18 floors of industrial, loftlike rooms with exposed concrete walls, beds with lightboxes for headboards and a 'sensuality kit' in the honor bar. Views from the rooms are fantastic, but nothing beats the scenic sweep from the rooftop bar (for guests only).

GEM HOTEL
Budget Hotel $

☎ 212-358-8844; www.thegemhotel.com; 135 E Houston St at Forsyth St; r from $149; ⊕ F to Lower East Side-2nd Ave; ✖ ▢

Renovated from a former Howard Johnson's hotel, the Gem still has the plain, boxy exterior of the well-known chain, but it's done away with the bland inside, replacing it with cheery white linens, colorful comforters and tiny desks. Rooms are small, each with a private bath, and you'll get nice Gilchrist & Soames amenities, but expect some noise to filter up from the street outside.

EATING
LOWER EAST SIDE

It's impossible to keep up with the offerings in these parts, as slinky lounges with elaborate nouveau-fusion menus and instant A-list crowds seem to pop up and replace 'old' places on a weekly basis. Though visitors won't find many remnants of the classic, old-world-Jewish LES dining scene, there are a few stellar holdouts, among them the famous **Katz's Deli** (☎ 212-254-2246; 205 E Houston St at Ludlow St; ⊙ breakfast, lunch & dinner; ⊕ F to Lower East Side-2nd Ave), where Meg Ryan famously faked her orgasm in the 1989 Hollywood flick *When Harry Met Sally*, and where, if you love classic deli grub such as pastrami and salami on rye, it just might have the same effect on you.

WD 50
American Creative $$$

☎ 212-477-2900; 50 Clinton St at Stanton St; ⊙ dinner Mon-Sat; ⊕ F, J, Z to Delancey-Essex Sts

This early leader in chef Wylie Dufresne's empire, a sleek space with bamboo floors, exposed wood beams and a fireplace, has held strong with thrill-seekers for more than five years. Now that the frenzy has slowed a bit, you'll have a better chance of getting in to savor the cutesy-clever-complicated fare: ocean trout, black beans and forbidden rice in root-beer-and-date

DAN HERRICK

Mahayana Buddhist Temple

sauce, or a slab of Wagyu beef served with coffee gnocchi, for example.

BONDI ROAD
Australian Seafood $$

☎ 212-253-5311; 153 Rivington St at Suffolk St; ☾ dinner Mon-Fri, brunch & dinner Sat & Sun; ⊙ F, J, Z to Delancey-Essex Sts

A fun, warming, summery choice, no matter what the season, is this casual Aussie hang, where photos of Sydney's Bondi Beach and projected images of surfers serve as the eye candy. The tasty treats are pretty much fish focused – raw bar, tuna tartar, salt-and-pepper squid, garlic prawns. Add an Australian or New Zealand brewski and you're set.

'INOTECA
Italian Small Plates $$

☎ 212-614-0473; 98 Rivington St at Ludlow St; ☾ lunch & dinner daily, brunch Sat & Sub; ⊙ F to Lower East Side-2nd Ave

Join the crowd waiting at the cramped bar (it's worth it) at this airy, dark-wood-paneled corner haven to choose from *tramezzini* (small sandwiches on white or whole-wheat bread), panini (pressed

sandwiches) and bruschetta options, all delicious and moderately priced.

KUMA INN
Pan-Asian Small Plates $$

☎ 212-353-8866; 113 Ludlow St btwn Delancey & Rivington; ☾ dinner Tue-Sun; ⊙ F, J, Z to Delancey-Essex Sts

Reservations are a must at this strikingly popular spot, in a secretive 2nd-floor location that feels like a reconfigured apartment. The Filipino- and Thai-inspired tapas run the gamut, from vegetarian summer rolls (with the unique addition of chayote) and edamame drizzled with basil-lime oil to an oyster omelet and grilled salmon with mung beans and pickled onions.

FESTIVAL MEXICANO RESTAURANT
Mexican $

☎ 212-995-0154; 120 Rivington St at Essex St; ☾ lunch & dinner; ⊙ F, J, Z to Delancey-Essex Sts

You'll find some of the most authentic South of the Border cuisine in the city at this unadorned, rustic, high-ceilinged

BRENT WINEBRENNER

Dim sum restaurant, Chinatown

gem. Enjoy tacos (chicken, pork, beef, lamb or veg), rich soups and fresh-fruit *licuados* (shakes), along with a mellow and appreciative audience.

CHINATOWN

In addition to being a long-time haven for authentically Chinese bargain meals – and for the mobs of visitors who seek them – Chinatown has also evolved into a spot for all sorts of pan-Asian fare that is, for the most part, incredibly cheap. Find a true culinary adventure by leaving the guidebook in your bag and strolling the crammed and winding streets south of Canal, stopping in to eat at any place that tickles your fancy, including dessert-rich bubble-tea lounges or sweet Chinese bakeries.

VEGETARIAN DIM SUM HOUSE
Vegetarian Chinese $
☎ 212-577-7176; 24 Pell St btwn Bowery & Mott Sts; ⏱ 10:30am-10:30pm; ⊜ J, Z, N, Q, R, 6 to Canal St

Get mocked all day long with dead-ringer takes on classic Chinatown specialties: fake 'shrimp' dumplings, spicy 'spare ribs,' sweet-and-sour 'chicken' and Hunan 'pork' are realistically created with ingredients such as soy, wheat gluten and yams.

GREAT NEW YORK NOODLE TOWN
Chinese $
☎ 212-349-0923; 28 Bowery St at Bayard St; ⏱ 9am-4am; ⊜ J, Z, N, Q, R, 6 to Canal St

The name of this Chinatown stalwart says it all, as the specialties here are endless incarnations of the long and slippery strands, offered up through an easy-to-decipher picture menu. What the no-frills spot lacks in ambience it makes up for in characters – especially once 2am or 3am rolls around.

DRINKING
LOWER EAST SIDE

BARRIO CHINO
Cocktail Bar
☎ 212-228-6710; 253 Broome St btwn Ludlow & Orchard Sts; ⊜ F, J, Z to Delancey-Essex Sts

An eatery that spills easily into a party scene, with an airy Havana-meets-Beijing vibe and a focus on fine sipping tequilas (the menu offers 50, some breaking $25 per shot).

HAPPY ENDING
Cocktail Bar
☎ 212-334-9676; www.happyendinglounge. com; 302 Broome St btwn Forsythe & Eldridge Sts; ⊜ B, D to Grand St

On a forlorn stretch of Broome, Happy Ending is a dark, two-level bar with a smattering of relics left over from its sleazy massage parlor days. High red velvet booths and candlelit tables compose floor one, while down below is the dance floor (which sees action on weekends) and original tiled nooks (former shower stalls), along with the 'swan and naked lady' mirror.

NURSE BETTIE
Cocktail Bar
☎ 917-434-9072; www.nursebetties.com; 106 Norfolk St btwn Delancey & Rivington Sts; ⊜ F, J, Z to Delancey-Essex Sts

Something novel is afoot at this pint-sized charmer: plenty of roaming space between slick modern lounges and 1950s-style ice-cream-shop stools and painted pin-ups on the brick walls. Cocktails get freaky: everything from fruity vodka to brandies. You can bring food in, as many won-over locals do.

WELCOME TO THE JOHNSONS
Dive Bar
☎ 212-420-9911; 123 Rivington St btwn Essex & Norfolk Sts; ⊜ F, J, Z to Delancey-Essex Sts

Set up like a 1970s game room – a bit sleazier than the one on *That '70s Show* –

Essex Street Market (p100)

DAN HERRICK

the Johnsons' irony still hasn't worn off for the devoted 20-something crowd. It could have something to do with the $2 Buds till 9pm, the pool table, the blasting garage-rock jukebox or the plastic-covered sofas.

BARRAMUNDI — Lounge

☎ 212-529-6999; 67 Clinton St btwn Stanton & Rivington Sts; ⊕ F, J, Z to Delancey-Essex Sts

This Australian-owned arty place fills an old tenement building with convivial booths, reasonably priced drinks (including some Aussie imports) and some cool tree-trunk tables. Happy hour runs from 6pm to 9pm.

CHINATOWN

WHISKEY TAVERN — Cocktail Bar

☎ 212-374-9119; 79 Baxter St btwn Bayard & Walker Sts; ⊕ J, Z, N, Q, R, 6 to Canal St

An odd interloper in the Chinatown scene, Whiskey Tavern nevertheless has earned many fans for its uberfriendly bartenders, casual ambience free of pretension, reasonably priced drinks and outdoor rear patio in warm weather.

WINNIE'S — Karaoke

☎ 212-732-2384; 104 Bayard St btwn Baxter & Mulberry Sts; ⊕ J, Z, N, Q, R, 6 to Canal St

Performing drunken, embarrassing karaoke at this tiny Chinatown dive is a rite of passage for New Yorkers. The red booths are always packed, and the disgusting cocktails are ever potent (eg the Abortion, a mixture of Sambuca and Bailey's).

ENTERTAINMENT & ACTIVITIES

SAPPHIRE — Clubbing

☎ 212-777-5153; www.sapphirenyc.com; 249 Eldridge St at E Houston St; admission $5; ⊕ F to Lower East Side-2nd Ave

This tiny, hoppin' venue has survived the crowds of the mid-1990s Ludlow St boom with its hip factor intact, and its $5 cover keeps snootiness at a minimum. The tightly packed dance floor gets lit with a mix of R&B, rap, disco and funk.

LANDMARK SUNSHINE CINEMA
Film & TV

☎ 212-358-7709; www.landmarktheatres.com; 143 E Houston St at Forsyth St; ⊕ F to Lower East Side-2nd Ave

A renovated Yiddish theater, the wonderful Landmark shows foreign and first-run mainstream art films on massive screens.

ARLENE'S GROCERY
Rock & Indie

☎ 212-995-1652; www.arlenesgrocery.net; 95 Stanton St at Orchard St; ⊕ F to Lower East Side-2nd Ave

This club was just pre-curve enough of the LES' 1990s explosion to entitle it to a bit of a self-righteous vibe. The one-room hothouse incubates local talent with live rock 'n' roll karaoke (10pm Monday) and free live shows every night.

BOWERY BALLROOM
Rock & Indie

☎ 212-533-2111; www.boweryballroom.com; 6 Delancey St at Bowery; ⊕ J, Z to Bowery

This terrific, medium-sized venue has the perfect sound and feel for more blown-up indie-rock acts (The Shins, Stephen Malkmus, Patti Smith).

DELANCEY
Rock & Indie

☎ 212-254-9920; www.thedelancey.com; 168 Delancey St at Clinton St; ⊕ F, J, Z to Delancey-Essex Sts

Surprisingly stylish for the Lower East Side, the Delancey hosts some popular indie bands such as Clap Your Hands Say Yeah for doting indie-rock crowds. A good early-evening spot to drink too, particularly from the airy 2nd-floor patio deck.

MERCURY LOUNGE
Rock & Indie

☎ 212-260-4700; www.mercuryloungenyc.com; 217 E Houston St btwn Essex & Ludlow Sts; ⊕ F to Lower East Side-2nd Ave

The Mercury dependably pulls in a cool new or cool comeback band everyone downtown wants to see – such as Dengue Fever or the Slits. The sound is good, with an intimate seating area and dance space.

PIANOS
Rock & Indie

☎ 212-505-3733; www.pianosnyc.com; 158 Ludlow St at Stanton St; ⊕ F to Lower East Side-2nd Ave

This is an old two-level piano shop turned hipster's musical haven, serving mixed-genre bills (DJs, hip-hop, cowpunk, electronica, bad karaoke) and pouring plenty of Rheingold for a large and appreciative Lower East Side crowd.

SHOPPING
LOWER EAST SIDE

Before the neighborhood's recent hipster makeover, shopping here was generally limited to Orchard St's leather jackets and old-school lingerie and Judaica shops on Essex St, between Grand and Canal Sts. They're still there today, and can be fun to browse in, as can the few lingering pickle and bagel shops and Jewish delis sprinkled around the area.

ECONOMY CANDY
Candy

☎ 212-254-1531; 108 Rivington St at Essex St; ☽ 9am-6pm Mon-Fri, 10am-5pm Sat; ⊕ F, J, Z to Delancey-Essex Sts

Bringing sweetness to the 'hood since 1937, this candy shop is stocked with floor-to-ceiling goods in package and bulk, and is home to some beautiful antique gum machines.

ALIFE RIVINGTON CLUB
Sneakers

☎ 212-375-8128; 158 Rivington St; ☽ noon-7pm Mon-Sat, noon-6pm Sun; ⊕ F, J, Z to Delancey-Essex Sts

Concealed behind an unmarked entrance (ring the buzzer), ARC feels more like the VIP lounge of a nightclub than a shoe store. You'll find royal-hued carpeting, a long leather couch and a handsome display case of rare, limited-edition sneakers. Stocks of those coveted Nikes and Adidas change often and sell out fast, so don't dawdle if you see something you like.

EDITH MACHINIST Vintage Clothing
☎ 212-979-9992; 104 Rivington St at Essex St; ☽ 1-8pm; ◉ F, J, Z to Delancey-Essex Sts
To properly strut about the Lower East Side, you've got to dress the part. Edith Machinist can help you get that rumpled but stylish look in a hurry – a bit of vintage glam via knee-high soft suede boots, 1930s silk dresses and ballet-style flats, with military jackets and weather-beaten leather satchels for the gents.

CHINATOWN
Chinatown is a great place for wandering, particularly if you're in the market for some aromatic herbs, exotic Eastern fruits (such as lychees and durians in season), fresh noodles or delicious bakery goodies. Canal St is the major thoroughfare, with lots of touristy merchandise and knockoff designer gear spilling onto the sidewalks. The backstreets are the real joy, however,

with bubble-tea cafes, perfumeries, video arcades, plant shops and fishmongers all hawking their wares.

AJI ICHIBAN Candy
☎ 212-233-7650; 37 Mott St; ☽ 10am-8:30pm; ◉ J, Z, N, Q, R, 6 to Canal St
This Hong Kong-based chain, the name of which means 'awesome' in Japanese, is a ubiquitous sight in Chinatown, as this is just one of five locations here. Here's where you'll find sesame-flavored marshmallows, Thai durian milk candy, preserved plums, mandarin peel, blackcurrant gummies and dried guava, as well as savory snacks such as crispy spicy cod fish, crab chips, wasabi peas and dried anchovies with peanuts.

ORIGINAL CHINATOWN ICE CREAM FACTORY Ice Cream & T-Shirts
☎ 212-608-4170; 65 Bayard St; ☽ 11am-10pm; ◉ J, Z, N, Q, R, 6 to Canal St
Totally overshadowing the nearby Häagen-Dazs is this busy ice-cream shop, where you can savor scoops of green tea, ginger, passion fruit and lychee sorbet among dozens of flavors.

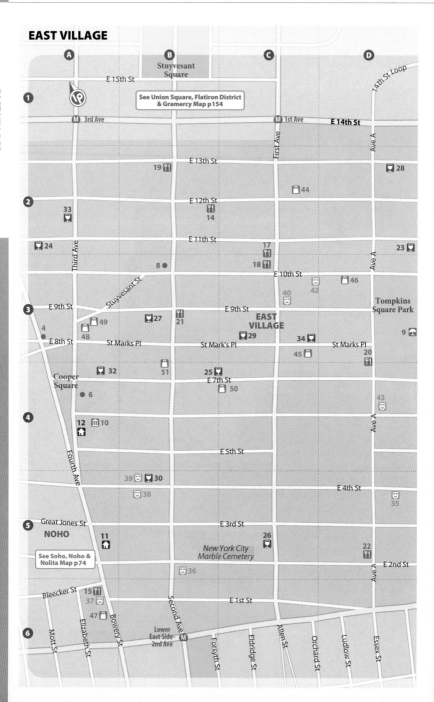

EAST VILLAGE

EAST VILLAGE

Stuyvesant Square

E 15th St

See Union Square, Flatiron District & Gramercy Map p154

3rd Ave

1st Ave

E 14th St

14th St Loop

First Ave

Ave A

E 13th St

19

28

44

E 12th St

14

33

24

E 11th St

17

18

23

8

E 10th St

40

42

46

Stuyvesant St

E 9th St

49

27

21

E 9th St

EAST VILLAGE

29

34

Tompkins Square Park

9

Third Ave

48

4

E 8th St

St Marks Pl

St Mark's Pl

45

St Marks Pl

20

32

51

25

E 7th St

50

Cooper Square

6

12

10

43

Ave A

Fourth Ave

E 5th St

39

30

38

E 4th St

35

Great Jones St

NOHO

11

See Soho, Noho & Nolita Map p74

E 3rd St

26

New York City Marble Cemetery

22

E 2nd St

Ave A

36

Bleecker St

15

37

47

E 1st St

Mott St

Elizabeth St

Bowery St

Lower East Side-2nd Ave

Second Ave

Forsyth St

Eldridge St

Allen St

Orchard St

Ludlow St

Essex St

EAST VILLAGE

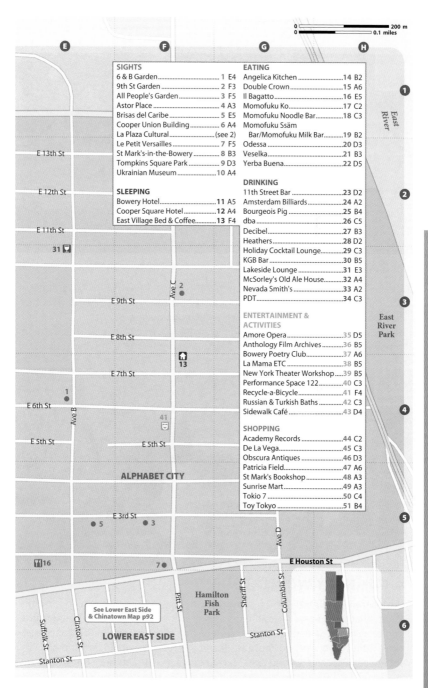

0   200 m
0   0.1 miles

SIGHTS
6 & B Garden...............................1 E4
9th St Garden.............................2 F3
All People's Garden....................3 F5
Astor Place..................................4 A3
Brisas del Caribe.........................5 E5
Cooper Union Building...............6 A4
La Plaza Cultural....................(see 2)
Le Petit Versailles......................7 F5
St Mark's-in-the-Bowery...........8 B3
Tompkins Square Park...............9 D3
Ukrainian Museum...................10 A4

SLEEPING
Bowery Hotel............................11 A5
Cooper Square Hotel................12 A4
East Village Bed & Coffee........13 F4

EATING
Angelica Kitchen......................14 B2
Double Crown...........................15 A6
Il Bagatto..................................16 E5
Momofuku Ko...........................17 C2
Momofuku Noodle Bar.............18 C3
Momofuku Ssäm
   Bar/Momofuku Milk Bar........19 B2
Odessa.......................................20 D3
Veselka......................................21 B3
Yerba Buena..............................22 D5

DRINKING
11th Street Bar.........................23 D2
Amsterdam Billiards.................24 A2
Bourgeois Pig...........................25 B4
dba..26 C5
Decibel......................................27 B3
Heathers....................................28 D2
Holiday Cocktail Lounge...........29 C3
KGB Bar.....................................30 B5
Lakeside Lounge.......................31 E3
McSorley's Old Ale House.........32 A4
Nevada Smith's.........................33 A2
PDT..34 C3

ENTERTAINMENT & ACTIVITIES
Amore Opera.............................35 D5
Anthology Film Archives..........36 B5
Bowery Poetry Club..................37 A6
La Mama ETC............................38 B5
New York Theater Workshop....39 B5
Performance Space 122............40 C3
Recycle-a-Bicycle.....................41 F4
Russian & Turkish Baths...........42 C3
Sidewalk Café...........................43 D4

SHOPPING
Academy Records......................44 C2
De La Vega................................45 C3
Obscura Antiques.....................46 D3
Patricia Field.............................47 A6
St Mark's Bookshop..................48 A3
Sunrise Mart.............................49 A3
Tokio 7......................................50 C4
Toy Tokyo..................................51 B4

East River

East River Park

E 13th St
E 12th St
E 11th St
E 9th St
E 8th St
E 7th St
E 6th St
E 5th St
E 5th St
E 3rd St

Ave C
Ave B
Ave D

ALPHABET CITY

E Houston St

Hamilton Fish Park

Pitt St
Sheriff St
Columbia St
Suffolk St
Clinton St

See Lower East Side & Chinatown Map p92

LOWER EAST SIDE

Stanton St

HIGHLIGHTS

1 ⬎ BAR CRAWL

The further east you go – away from gentrifying Third Ave – the looser it gets. You can't walk a block without happening on a dirty dive filled with NYU students or postgrads with lofty goals, or lounges pulling in outsiders wanting booze in NY punk rock's old HQ. From cocktail bars to dive bars and everything in between, the East Village is the ideal neighborhood for a tippling tour.

2 ⬎ CULINARY WORLD TOUR

The epitome of NY's dining scene (p120), the East Village has a mind-blowing variety that covers several continents as well as the whole gamut of budgets in a single city block. St Marks Place and around, from Third to Second Ave, has turned into a little Tokyo, with Japanese sushi and grill restaurants. On the strip of E 6th St between First and Second Aves, decent Indian restaurants are a dime a dozen.

◥ DOWNTOWN THEATER

With its scruffy theaters – incubators for young talent and venues for established artists – theatergoing in the East Village can be a hit-or-miss experience. Expect everything from 'interdisciplinary' pieces with life-sized gorilla puppets to more traditional updates of Greek classics.

◥ VINTAGE SHOPPING

You'll still find urban and outsider fashion in the East Village, but new local designers, sleeker shops and even chain stores have moved in, blunting the neighborhood's former edginess. Still, there's more than a whiff of those rockin' 1980s days at punk-rock T-shirt shops, tattoo parlors and dusty stores selling furniture and vintage clothing.

◥ TOMPKINS SQUARE PARK

It was once an Eastern European immigrant area, and while you'll still see older Ukrainians and Poles hanging out in Tompkins Square Park (p119), they will be alongside punks, students, panhandlers and a slew of dog-walking yuppies. Every corner of the park has a different profile.

1 DAN HERRICK; 2 ANGUS OBORN; 3 ANGUS OBORN; 4 DAN HERRICK; 5 DAN HERRICK

1 Bar at Bowery Hotel (p118); 2 Food mural; 3 Performance Space 122 (p124); 4 Stalls, St Mark's Place (p114); 5 Practicing yoga, Tompkins Square Park (p119)

EAST VILLAGE NOSTALGIA WALKING TOUR

This walk begins at the former CBGB near Bleecker St and ends at the Bowery Hotel, also on Bleecker. It covers two miles and should take between 1½ and 2½ hours.

❶ FORMER CBGB/JOHN VARVATOS

From the Bleecker St subway station, head east along Bleecker St for a few blocks, where you can see what's become of CBGB (315 Bowery btwn 1st & 2nd Sts), the famous music venue that opened in 1973 and was shuttered in 2006, and launched punk rock via the Ramones. Today it's a John Varvatos boutique.

❷ JOEY RAMONE PLACE

The corner just north of here marks the block-long Joey Ramone Place, named after the Ramones' singer, who succumbed to cancer in 2001.

❸ COOPER UNION

Head north on the Bowery to Astor Pl. Turn right and head east through the square to Cooper Union (p118) where, in 1860, presidential hopeful Abraham Lincoln gave a rousing antislavery speech.

❹ ST MARK'S PLACE

Continue east on St Mark's Place, a block chock-full of tattoo parlors, cheap eateries and classic T-shirt shops. Poke your head into Trash & Vaudeville (4 St Mark's Pl), a landmark goth-and-punk shop where Yoko Ono (pre-John) staged happenings in the 1960s.

❺ FILLMORE EAST

Continue south down Second Ave to the site of the long-defunct Fillmore East (105 Second Ave), a seriously big-time, 2000-seat live-music venue where the Who premiered their rock opera *Tommy*.

❻ PHYSICAL GRAFFITI ALBUM COVER

Cross Second Ave at 6th St and head down the block-long strip of Indian restaurants. At First Ave, turn left, rejoin St Marks Place and turn right. The row of tenements is the site where Led Zeppelin's Physical Graffiti album cover (96-98 St Marks Pl) was taken.

❼ TOMPKINS SQUARE PARK

The trees looming ahead belong to the infamous Tompkins Square Park (p119), where drag queens started the Wigstock summer festival at the band shell where Jimi Hendrix played in the 1960s, and where riots broke out in 1988 when police kicked out squatters.

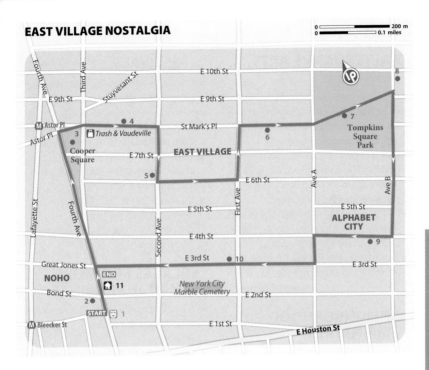

❽ CHARLIE PARKER'S HOME

Facing the park is jazz-sax great **Charlie Parker's home** (151 Ave B). He died at age 34 in 1955 and is remembered today through the Charlie Parker Jazz Festival.

❾ MADONNA'S FIRST NEW YORK HOME

From the park, head south on Ave B, turning right on 4th for a worthy detour to see **Madonna's first New York home** (230 E 4th St), which housed the up-and-comer in 1978.

❿ HELL'S ANGELS MOTORCYCLE CLUB

Continue west on 4th until Ave A, then make a left. Then turn right on 3rd St and just past First Ave you'll see the mass of Harleys lined up outside the New York chapter of the **Hell's Angels Motorcycle Club** (77 E 3rd St).

⓫ BOWERY HOTEL

Continue along 3rd St to the Bowery and take a left to see where rock, jazz and pop stars of today's world stay when they blow through the East Village: at the upscale **Bowery Hotel** (p118), with a see-and-be-seen restaurant that the gossip pages love.

EAST VILLAGE

BEST...

BEST...

ALTERNATIVE ARTS SPACES

- **Performance Space 122** (PS 122; p124) Interdisciplinary pieces from accomplished award winners to young up-and-comers.
- **Ontological Hysteric Theater** (p117) Thought-provoking and weird from Richard Foreman, a pioneer of the avant-garde.
- **KGB Bar** (p122) Theme nights with lineups of journalists, poets, crime authors and fantasy writers.
- **Amore Opera** (p124) Humble and committed performances such as *La Bohème* and *The Merry Widow*.

NEIGHBORHOOD MAINSTAYS

- **Russian & Turkish Baths** (p124) Work out your stress.
- **Veselka** (p117) Bustling 24 hours with tablefuls nursing hangovers.
- **Holiday Cocktail Lounge** (p121) For hardcore daytime drinkers.

FESTIVALS

- **Fringe Festival** (p48) Two weeks of edgy, wacky theater in August.
- **Howl! Festival** (www.howl festival.com) Week-long celebration, named for Beat writer Allen Ginsberg's famous poem, brings visual art, theater, dance, film and literature to Tompkins Sq Park.
- **Charlie Parker Jazz Festival** (www.summerstage.org) Free concerts in Tompkins Sq Park with fine musicians.

PLACES FOR MORE THAN JUST DRINKS

- **Bowery Hotel** (p118) The Bowery Hotel's opulent lobby bar has great scenery.
- **KGB Bar** (p122) Literary types come here for readings.
- **Sidewalk Café** (p123) Streetside seating, burgers and music makes for a mellow combination.

Literary reading, KGB Bar (p122)

DAN HERRICK

DISCOVER EAST VILLAGE

Welcome to the new East Village, folks. Though its image as an edgy, radical, be-yourself kind of place has been pretty unshakable for the better part of four decades, things have taken quite a turn in the past few years, pushing that image squarely in the 'nostalgic fantasy' category.

Sure, it's still very cool – filled with endless boutiques, bars, restaurants and characters of the scruffiest, edgiest order. And it'll always have its history: this neighborhood was the inspiration for many cultural contributions, including the musical-turned-movie 'Rent' and Led Zeppelin's 'Physical Graffiti' album cover (the building in the photograph still stands at 98 St Marks Pl). The NYC drug scene was headquartered here for much of the 1970s, and the '80s ushered in a major art scene. A quick look around today proves that the moneyed residents and frantic developers are now the only ones truly shaping the neighborhood – especially along the Bowery, a formerly (and famously) scruffy strip that's now an aisle of luxury condo towers and hotels.

SIGHTS

ST MARK'S-IN-THE-BOWERY

☎ 212-674-6377; www.stmarkschurchbowery. org; 131 E 10th St at Second Ave; ⓧ 10am-6pm Mon-Fri; ⓔ L to 3rd Ave, 6 to Astor Pl

Though it's most popular with East Village locals for its cultural offerings – such as poetry readings hosted by the **Poetry Project** (☎ 212-674-0910; www.poetryproject. com) or cutting-edge dance performances from **Danspace** (☎ 212-674-8194; www. danspaceproject.org) and the **Ontological Hysteric Theater** (www.ontological.com) – this is also a historic site. This Episcopal church stands on the site of the farm, or *bouwerie,* owned by Dutch governor Peter Stuyvesant, whose crypt lies under the grounds.

UKRAINIAN MUSEUM

☎ 212-228-0110; www.ukrainianmuseum. org; 222 E 6th St btwn Second & Third Aves; adult/under 12yr/senior & student $8/free/6;

ⓧ 11:30am-5pm Wed-Sun; ⓔ F to Lower East Side-2nd Ave, L to 1st Ave

Ukrainians have a long history and still a strong presence here, hence the existence of several (though rapidly disappearing) pierogi &dumling) joints – including the famous **Odessa** (☎ 212-253-1482; 119 Ave A btwn 7th St & St Mark's Pl) and **Veselka** (p120) – and this interesting museum, which moved into its sleek and expansive headquarters several years ago. Its collection of folk art includes richly woven textiles, ceramics, metalwork and traditional Ukrainian Easter eggs, as well as the research tools needed for visitors to trace their own Ukrainian roots

ASTOR PLACE

8th St btwn Third & Fourth Aves; ⓔ N, R to 8th St-NYU, 6 to Astor Pl

This square and street is named after the Astor family, who built an early New York fortune on beaver pelts (check out the tiles in the wall of the Astor Pl

EAST VILLAGE

6th & B Garden

DAN HERRICK

➥ IF YOU LIKE...

If you like **Tompkins Square Park** (right), we think you'll like exploring these community gardens:

- **6th & B Garden** (www.6bgarden. org; 6th St at Ave B) A well-organized space that hosts free music events, workshops and yoga sessions.
- **9th Street Garden** and **La Plaza Cultural** (www.laplazacultural.org; E 9th St at Ave C) Three dramatic weeping willows, an odd sight in the city, grace these twin plots.
- **All People's Garden** (E 3rd St btwn Aves B & C)
- **Brisas del Caribe** (237 E 3rd St) Easily located thanks to its surrounding white-picket fence.
- **Le Petit Versailles** (346 E Houston St at Ave C) A unique marriage of a verdant oasis and an electrifying arts organization, offering a range of quirky performances and screenings to the public.

SLEEPING

subway platform) and lived on **Colonnade Row** (429-434 Lafayette St), just south of the square; four of the original nine marble-faced, Greek Revival residences on Lafayette St still exist. The large, brownstone **Cooper Union building**, the public college founded in 1859 by glue millionaire Peter Cooper, dominates the square –

now more than ever – as the school has just constructed its first new academic building in 50 years, a striking, twisting, nine-story sculpture of glazed glass wrapped in perforated stainless steel (and LEED-certified, too) by architect Thom Mayne of Morphosis. Still, the **Alamo** cube sculpture, which sits in the middle of the square, remains a popular spot for skateboarding teens and liquored-up NYU students to hang out under.

SLEEPING
BOWERY HOTEL

Deluxe Boutique Hotel $$$

☎ 212-505-9100; www.theboweryhotel.com; 335 Bowery; r from $350; ⊕ B, D, F, M to Broadway-Lafayette St, 6 to Bleecker St; ✗ ▯ Pick up your old-fashioned gold room key with its red tassel in the dark, hushed lobby – filled with antique velvet chairs and Persian rugs – then follow the mosaic floors to your room. There you can dock your iPod, use the wi-fi, check out the plasma, watch some DVDs or raid your bathroom goodies (courtesy of CO Bigelow, the Greenwich Village apothecary). Rooms have huge factory windows with unobstructed views, simple white spreads and elegant four-poster beds.

COOPER SQUARE HOTEL

Indie Boutique Hotel $$$

☎ 212-475-5700; www.thecoopersquarehotel. com; 25 Cooper Sq; r from $329; ⊕ 6 to Astor Pl; ✗ ▯ Rising above the East Village like an unfurled sail, Cooper Square's gleaming, white structure has caused controversy since day one. Visitors are entranced by the futuristic, white-walled rooms with sweeping East Village views (and either love or hate the dark hallways and chic lobby with greenish glass walls).

EAST VILLAGE BED & COFFEE B&B $

☎ 917-816-0071; www.bedandcoffee.com;
110 Ave C at E 7th St; r $120; ◉ F to Lower East
Side-2nd Ave, 6 to Astor Pl; ⚇ ▢

Owner Anne has turned her family home into a quirky, arty, offbeat B&B with color-ful, themed private rooms (one shared bathroom per floor) and great ameni-ties, such as free bikes, free wi-fi, and wonderful insider tips on the best the East Village has to offer. Each floor has shared common and kitchen space, and

Dog run, Tompkins Square Park

↘ TOMPKINS SQUARE PARK

This 10.5-acre park honors Daniel Tompkins, who served as governor of New York from 1807 to 1817 (and as the nation's vice president after that, under James Monroe). It's like a friendly town square for locals, who gather for chess at concrete tables, picnics on the lawn on warm days and spontaneous guitar or drum jams on various grassy knolls. It's also the site of basketball courts, a fun-to-watch dog run (a fenced-in area where humans can unleash their canines), frequent summer concerts and an always-lively kids playground.

The park, which recently underwent a facelift, wasn't always a place for such clean fun, however. In the 1980s, it was a dirty, needle-strewn homeless en-campment, unusable for folks wanting a place to stroll or picnic. A contentious turning point came when police razed the band shell (where the legendary and now-defunct Wigstock dragfest was founded by Lady Bunny and cohorts) and evicted more than 100 squatters living in a tent city in the park in 1988 (and again in 1991). That first eviction turned violent; the Tompkins Square Riot, as it came to be known, ushered in the first wave of yuppies in the dog run, fashionistas lolling in the grass and undercover narcotics agents trying to pass as druggie punk kids.

Things you need to know: btwn 7th & 10th Sts & Aves A & B; ◉ F to Lower East Side-2nd Ave, L to 1st Ave

Double Crown

DAN HERRICK

guests get keys so they can come and go (no curfew).

EATING

The neighborhood's roots lie with Ukrainian traditions, and you can still find some low-key pierogi (dumpling) palaces hanging on, such as the classic and uber-popular **Veselka** (☎ 212-228-9682; 144 Second Ave at 9th St; 🕒 24hr; 🚇 6 to Astor Pl, L to 3rd Ave).

YERBA BUENA   Pan-Latin $$$
☎ 212-529-2919; 23 Ave A at 2nd St; 🕒 dinner Mon-Fri, brunch & dinner Sat & Sun; 🚇 F to Lower East Side-2nd Ave

One of the newest additions to ever-evolving Ave A is this shrine to Latin flavors, where chef Julian Medina pays homage to Cuba, Mexico, Argentina, Chile and Peru in his bustling open kitchen. Some standouts include Peruvian shrimp soup, sweet plantains with truffle cream, Baja-style fish tacos and Brazilian paella with shrimp, clams and crawfish.

DOUBLE CROWN   British-Asian Fusion $$$
☎ 212-254-0350; 316 Bowery at Bleecker St; 🕒 lunch & dinner Mon-Fri, brunch & afternoon tea Sat & Sun; 🚇 B, D, F, M to Broadway-Lafayette St, 6 to Bleecker St

One of the tastiest – and most gorgeous – elements of the Bowery's ongoing up-scale makeover is this Asian-inspired, design-detailed den of sophisticated treats. Chef Dan Rafalin marries Britain, India and other spots in the East to create wow-factor foods: spicy-pork stuffed ly-chees, house-cured ham with figs, twice-cooked chicken with ginger-garlic relish, butternut squash curry with snake-bean salad (plus bangers and mash!).

MOMOFUKU NOODLE BAR
                          Japanese Ramen $$
☎ 212-777-7773; www.momofuku.com; 171 First Ave btwn 10th & 11th Sts; 🕒 lunch & dinner; 🚇 L to 1st Ave

With just 30 stools and a no-reservations policy, you will always have to wait to cram into this tiny phenomenon – part of a crazily popular restaurant group that now includes Momofuku Ko (139 First Ave btwn 10th & 11th Sts; ⊕ L to 1st Ave) for pricey tasting menus and a prohibitive, we-dare-you-to-try reservations scheme; Momofuku Ssäm Bar (207 Second Ave at 13th St; ⊕ L to 1st Ave) for large and small meat-heavy dishes; and Momofuku Milk Bar (207 Second Ave at 13th St; ⊕ L to 1st Ave) and its to-die-for desserts and snacks. Queue up for the namesake special: homemade ramen noodles in broth, served with poached eggs, shredded pork, braised oxtail, roasted rice cakes or some interesting combos (the only vegetarian option is a broth-free bowl with ginger and veggies).

ANGELICA KITCHEN   Vegan Cafe $$
☎ 212-228-2909; 300 E 12th St btwn First & Second Aves; ⓧ lunch & dinner; ⊕ L to 1st Ave
This enduring herbivore classic has a calming vibe – candles, tables both intimate and communal and a mellow, long-time staff – and enough creative options to make your head spin. Standards such as the Pantry Plate – which lets you choose from a list of a dozen or so veggie concoctions and special salads – or the Dragon Bowl, a Buddha's delight with seasonal greens, tubers, tofu, seaweed and brown rice piled high, will leave you feeling both virtuous and full.

IL BAGATTO   Italian $$
☎ 212-228-0977; 192 E 2nd St btwn Aves A & B; ⓧ lunch & dinner Tue-Sat; ⊕ F to Lower East Side-2nd Ave
A bustling yet romantic little nook, this spot has thoroughly delicious Italian creations at exceptionally reasonable prices – plus an excellent wine list and a dedicated sommelier who will pour you tastes before you decide (a wonderful oddity in such an affordable and casual dining room). Menu items tend toward the sinful side, with highlights that include cheese and spinach ravioli swimming in butter and sage sauce, homemade gnocchi in gorgonzola sauce, and paper-thin beef slices sautéed in olive oil and white wine.

DRINKING

DBA   Beer Nerds
☎ 212-475-5097; 41 First Ave btwn 2nd & 3rd Sts; ⊕ F to Lower East Side-2nd Ave, 6 to Bleecker St
Ever tried to pick up *Led Zeppelin IV* at an indie CD store? You'll get the same jeers if you try for a Sam Adams at this testosterone-fueled, dark-wood bar built for beer nerds disguised as the hip. (We mean that as a compliment.) There are more than 200 beers here, plus 130 single-malt scotches and a few dozen tequilas.

HEATHERS   Cocktail Bar
☎ 212-254-0979; 506 E 13th St; ⊕ L to 1st Ave
Heathers is a tiny and stylish unsigned drinking den with frosted windows, a painted tin ceiling and white-washed brick walls. A mishmash of regulars lingers over eye-catching artworks (courtesy of the artist owner and her friends), two-for-one drink specials and gluten-free beer options.

HOLIDAY COCKTAIL LOUNGE
                                     Dive Bar
☎ 212-777-9637; 75 St Mark's Pl btwn First & Second Aves; ⊕ 6 to Astor Pl
No $12 cocktails at this long-term classic bad-behavior HQ – just a mix of penny-pinching alcoholic guys, students on a budget and dive-hounds who find crotchety service, a mix of nostalgia and $4 rum-and-cokes the perfect night out.

EAST VILLAGE

DRINKING

AMSTERDAM BILLIARDS
Games & Booze

☎ 212-995-0333; 110 E 11th St at Fourth Ave;
Ⓜ L, N, Q, R, 4, 5, 6 to 14th St-Union Sq

The long-time Upper West Side icon of the cue ball moved its green-table HQ to the Village. It offers 26 tables, $24 private 'pool clinics,' tourneys and just plain ol' gaming with beer and cocktails – only some of the regulars are dorky NYU students.

11TH STREET BAR
Irish Pub

☎ 212-982-3929; www.11thstbar.com; 510 E 11th St btwn Aves A & B; Ⓜ L to 1st Ave

When a Liverpool game's on, the place may go nuts, but at other, non-football times it's about the homiest watering hole in the 'hood, with soft sofas, exposed-brick walls, pressed-tin ceiling and candle-lit tables.

KGB BAR
Lit Bar

☎ 212-505-3360; www.kgbbar.com; 85 E 4th St; Ⓜ F to Lower East Side-2nd Ave, 6 to Bleecker St

The propaganda posters and deepest commie-red walls of KGB long pre-date the retro tongue-in-cheek of 'CCCP' T-shirts you see on St Mark's Pl. Set up in a former 1930s HQ for the Ukrainian socialist party, it's a lit bar, with interesting readings for free – more new fiction than Marx – several nights a week.

LAKESIDE LOUNGE
Live Music

☎ 212-529-8463; www.lakesidelounge.com; 162 Ave B btwn 10th & 11th Sts; Ⓜ L to 1st Ave

This battered East Village stalwart is a great spot to start the night when you're looking for a welcoming watering hole with one of the city's best jukeboxes. Some folks come for the free bands – indie rock and rockabilly four or five nights a week – others for the photo booths ($4 for four pics) and happy-hour drink specials.

MCSORLEY'S OLD ALE HOUSE
Old-Time Bar

☎ 212-474-9148; 15 E 7th St btwn Second & Third Aves; Ⓜ 6 to Astor Pl

Around since 1854, McSorley's feels far removed from the East Village veneer of cool: you're more likely to drink with firemen, Wall St refugees and a few tourists. It's hard to beat the cobwebs and sawdust floors and flip waiters who slap down two mugs of the house's ale for every one ordered.

DECIBEL
Sake Bar

☎ 212-979-2733; 240 E 9th St btwn Second & Third Aves; Ⓜ 6 to Astor Pl

Barely signed, this dark basement sake bar is an East Village icon. Once you get past the line (on weekends: certain) you may wonder whether the chatty staff think they know you. Up front it feels like a 19th-century Japanese bar, with a few seats wrapped around the sake bottle-backed bar.

PDT
Secret Bar

☎ 212-614-0386; www.pdtnyc.com; 113 St Mark's Pl btwn First Ave & Ave A Ⓜ L to 1st Ave

The worst-kept secret in New York: PDT (or 'Please Don't Tell') is a basement bar reached via a telephone booth – Superman would like it – inside tiny Crif Hot Dogs. Call ahead for a reservation, or have a hot dog while waiting. It's no East Village dive – well-swirled cocktails go for $12.

NEVADA SMITH'S
Sports Bar

☎ 212-982-2591; www.nevadasmiths.net; 74 Third Ave btwn 11th & 12th Sts; Ⓜ L to 3rd Ave, N, Q, R, 4, 5, 6 to 14th St-Union Sq

New York's greatest soccer bar gets filled with European expats and other assorted fist-pumping adult males in sports jerseys. Some 100 matches get

ANGUS OBORN

Anthology Film Archives

played a week on the wall-to-wall flat-screen TVs (just past the signed jersey of Ronaldinho).

BOURGEOIS PIG
Wine Bar

☎ 212-475-2246; 111 E 7th St; Ⓔ 6 to Astor Pl

Amid a setting of royal-hued wallpaper, gilded mirrors and a glowing chandelier, you can sink into a velvety armchair, drink wine and nibble on tartines, cheese plates or fondue, and contemplate the nature of your bourgeois pig existence. On Mondays and Tuesdays, bottles of wine are half price.

ENTERTAINMENT & ACTIVITIES

RECYCLE-A-BICYCLE
Bike Rental

☎ 212-475-1655; 75 Ave C btwn 5th & 6th Sts; rentals 1hr/day $10/35; Ⓨ noon-7pm Mon-Sat; Ⓔ F to Lower East Side-2nd Ave

The Recycle folks offer several youth-related programs, sell good used bikes and rent a few single-speed cruisers, too.

SIDEWALK CAFÉ
Country, Folk & Blues

☎ 212-473-7373; www.sidewalkmusic.net; 94 Ave A at 6th St; Ⓔ 6 to Astor Pl, F to Lower East Side-2nd Ave

Never mind the Sidewalk's burger-bar appearance outside; inside is the home of New York's 'anti-folk' scene, where the Moldy Peaches carved out their legacy before Juno got knocked up.

ANTHOLOGY FILM ARCHIVES
Film & TV

☎ 212-505-5181; www.anthologyfilmarchives. org; 32 Second Ave at 2nd St; Ⓔ F to Lower East Side-2nd Ave

This theater, opened in 1970 by film buff Jonas Mekas and a supportive crew, is dedicated to the idea of film as an art form. It screens indie works by new film-makers and also revives classics and obscure oldies that are usually screened in programs organized around a specific theme or director, from Luis Buñuel to Ken Brown's psychedelia.

RUSSIAN & TURKISH BATHS
Health & Fitness

☎ 212-674-9250; www.russianturkishbaths. com; 268 E 10th St btwn First Ave & Ave A; day pass $30; ⏰ noon-10pm Mon, Tue, Thu & Fri, 10am-10pm Wed, 9am-10pm Sat, 8am-10pm Sun; Ⓜ L to 1st Ave, 6 to Astor Pl

In a constantly glossed-up neighborhood, these historic Russian and Turkish steam baths remain a beloved constant. Since 1892, this has been the spa for anyone who wants to get naked (or stay in their swimsuit) and romp in steam baths, an ice-cold plunge pool, a sauna and on the sundeck. All-day access includes the use of lockers, locks, robes, towels and slippers.

The baths are open to both men and women most hours (wearing shorts is required at these times), except between 10am and 2pm Wednesday (women only) and between noon and 5pm Thursday and 8am to 2pm Sunday (men only). These are widely considered the best times to visit, as the vibe is more open, relaxed and communal.

LA MAMA ETC
Off-Broadway & Off-Off-Broadway

☎ 212-475-7710; www.lamama.org; 74A E 4th St btwn Second & Third Aves; Ⓜ F to Lower East Side-2nd Ave

Led by founder Ellen Stewart and begun in a small East Village basement, this home for onstage experimentation (the 'ETC' stands for 'experimental theater club') has grown into a complex of three theaters, a cafe, an art gallery and a separate rehearsal studio building.

NEW YORK THEATER WORKSHOP
Off-Broadway & Off-Off-Broadway

☎ 212-460-5475; www.nytw.org; 79 E 4th St btwn Second & Third Aves, East Village; Ⓜ F to Lower East Side-2nd Ave

Recently celebrating its 25th year, this innovative production house is a treasure to those seeking cutting-edge, contemporary plays with purpose.

PERFORMANCE SPACE 122
Off-Broadway & Off-Off-Broadway

PS 122; ☎ 212-477-5288; www.ps122.org; 150 First Ave at 9th St; Ⓜ N, R to 8th St-NYU, 6 to Astor Pl

This former schoolhouse has been committed to fostering new artists and their far-out ideas since its inception in 1979. Its two stages have hosted such now-known performers as Meredith Monk, Eric Bogosian and the late Spalding Gray, and it's also home to dance shows, film screenings and various festivals for up-and-coming talents.

AMORE OPERA
Opera

www.amoreopera.org; Connelly Theater, 220 E 4th St btwn Aves A & B; Ⓜ F to Lower East Side-2nd Ave

This new company, formed by several members of the recently defunct Amato Opera, presents affordable ($35) works.

BOWERY POETRY CLUB
Readings

☎ 212-614-0505; www.bowerypoetry.com; 308 Bowery btwn Bleecker & Houston Sts; Ⓜ 6 to Bleecker St

Just across from the old CBGB site on the East Village/NoHo border, this funky cafe and performance space has eccentric readings of all genres, from plays to fiction, plus frequent themed poetry slams and literary-focused parties that celebrate new books and their authors.

SHOPPING

You'll have to pound the pavement to see it all; the old-school stuff is on St Mark's Pl between Third and First Aves, and much of the new stuff along its parallel strips, from 13th St to Houston St, and as far east as Ave C. The blocks of E 2nd through E 7th Sts, between Second Ave and Ave B especially, are good for finding vintage wear, curiosity shops and record stores.

ST MARK'S BOOKSHOP — Books
☎ 212-260-7853; 31 Third Ave; 🕙 10am-midnight Mon-Sat, 11am-midnight Sun; 🚇 6 to Astor Pl
Actually located around the corner from St Mark's Pl (it moved long ago), this indie bookshop specializes in political literature, poetry, new nonfiction and novels, and academic journals. There's also a superior collection of cookbooks, travel guides and magazines, both glossy and otherwise.

TOKIO 7 — Consignment Store
☎ 212-353-8443; 64 E 7th St; 🕙 noon-8:30pm Mon-Sat, noon-8pm Sun; 🚇 6 to Astor Pl
This revered and hip consignment shop, down a few steps on a shady stretch of E 7th St, has good-condition designer labels

(Issey Miyake, Gucci, D&G, Prada) for men and women at some 'come again?' prices.

PATRICIA FIELD — Designer Clothing
☎ 212-966-4066; 302 Bowery at 1st St; 🕙 11am-8pm Mon-Thu, 11am-9pm Fri & Sat, 11am-7pm Sun; 🚇 F to Lower East Side-2nd Ave
The fashion-forward stylist for *Sex and the City*, Patricia Field isn't afraid of flash, with feather boas, pink jackets, disco dresses, graphic and color-block T-shirts and leopard-print heels, plus colored frizzy wigs, silver spandex and some wacky gift ideas for good measure.

SUNRISE MART — Japanese Groceries
☎ 212-598-3040; 29 Third Ave at Stuyvesant St; 🕙 10am-11pm Sun-Thu, 10am-midnight Fri & Sat; 🚇 6 to Astor Pl
A bright, 2nd-floor supermarket dedicated to all foods Japanese, this is where you'll find clutches of homesick, well-dressed New York University kids stocking up on wasabi, plus plenty of locals who have discovered a new craving for Poki sweets.

Patricia Field

DAN HERRICK

OBSCURA ANTIQUES
Oddities

☎ 212-505-9251; 280 E 10th St; ⏲ 2-8:30pm;
Ⓢ L to 1st Ave

This small cabinet of curiosities pleases both lovers of the macabre and inveterate antique hunters. Here you'll find taxidermy specimens (such as a bear's head), butterfly displays in glass boxes, photos of dead people, a mounted deer-hoof, disturbing little (dental?) instruments, old poison bottles, glass eyes, frock coats, Victorian corsets, miscellaneous beakers and other items not currently available at the local department store.

ACADEMY RECORDS
Records

☎ 212-780-9166; 415 E 12th St at First Ave;
Ⓢ L to 1st Ave

The East Village outpost of this excellent music store is a vinyl-lovers Valhalla with a brilliant assortment of new and used LPs. The jazz and world-music collection is particularly strong, with decks to listen to used albums before buying.

DE LA VEGA
Street Art

☎ 212-876-8649; 102 St Mark's Pl; ⏲ 1-8pm Mon, Tue & Thu-Sat, 1-6pm Sun; Ⓢ 6 to Astor Pl

The 30-something artist De La Vega is sometimes described as a blend of Keith Haring and Francisco de Goya. If you don't have time to hunt for his street murals in Spanish Harlem, head to his small gallery space in the East Village.

TOY TOKYO
Toys

☎ 212-673-5424; 121 Second Ave; ⏲ 1-9pm;
Ⓢ 6 to Astor Pl

For a nostalgic journey into the past, head to this 2nd-floor toy emporium. The narrow warren of rooms hides all sorts of icons from previous decades. You'll find Superman watches, scowling Godzillas, shiny Transformers, painted toy soldiers and action figures from all genres.

GREENWICH VILLAGE, CHELSEA & THE MEATPACKING DISTRICT

GREENWICH VILLAGE & AROUND

GREENWICH VILLAGE, CHELSEA & THE MEATPACKING DISTRICT

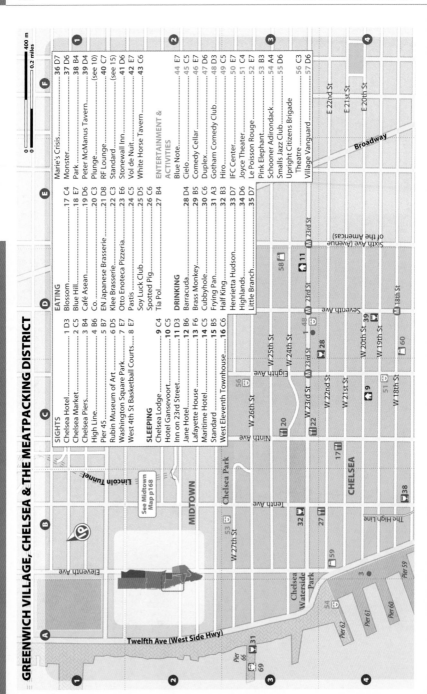

SIGHTS

Chelsea Hotel	1 D3
Chelsea Market	2 C5
Chelsea Piers	3 B4
High Line	4 B6
Pier 45	5 B7
Rubin Museum of Art	6 D5
Washington Square Park	7 E7
West 4th St Basketball Courts	8 E7

SLEEPING

Chelsea Lodge	9 C4
Hotel Gansevoort	10 C5
Inn on 23rd Street	11 D3
Jane Hotel	12 B6
Lafayette House	13 F6
Maritime Hotel	14 C5
Standard	15 B5
West Eleventh Townhouse	16 C6

EATING

Blossom	17 C4
Blue Hill	18 E7
Café Asean	19 D6
Co.	20 C3
EN Japanese Brasserie	21 D8
Klee Brasserie	22 C3
Otto Enoteca Pizzeria	23 E6
Pastis	24 C5
Soy Luck Club	25 D5
Spotted Pig	26 C6
Tia Pol	27 B4

DRINKING

Barracuda	28 D4
Brass Monkey	29 B5
Cubbyhole	30 C6
Frying Pan	31 A3
Half King	32 B3
Henrietta Hudson	33 D7
Highlands	34 D6
Little Branch	35 D7

Marie's Crisis	36 D7
Monster	37 D6
Park	38 B4
Peter McManus Tavern	39 D4
Plunge	(see 10)
RF Lounge	40 C7
Standard	(see 15)
Stonewall Inn	41 D6
Vol de Nuit	42 C7
White Horse Tavern	43 C6

ENTERTAINMENT & ACTIVITIES

Blue Note	44 E7
Cielo	45 C5
Comedy Cellar	46 E7
Duplex	47 D6
Gotham Comedy Club	48 D3
Hiro	49 C5
IFC Center	50 E7
Joyce Theater	51 C4
Le Poisson Rouge	52 E7
Pink Elephant	53 B3
Schooner Adirondack	54 A4
Smalls Jazz Club	55 D6
Upright Citizens Brigade Theatre	56 C3
Village Vanguard	57 D6

0   400 m
0   0.2 miles

Lincoln Tunnel

See Midtown Map p168

MIDTOWN

Chelsea Park

CHELSEA

Chelsea Waterside Park

The High Line

Twelfth Ave (West Side Hwy)

Eleventh Ave

Tenth Ave

Ninth Ave

Eighth Ave

Seventh Ave

Sixth Ave (Avenue of the Americas)

Broadway

W 27th St
W 26th St
W 25th St
W 24th St
W 23rd St
W 22nd St
W 21st St
W 20th St
W 19th St
W 18th St

E 22nd St
E 21st St
E 20th St

Pier 66
Pier 62
Pier 61
Pier 60
Pier 59
Pier 54

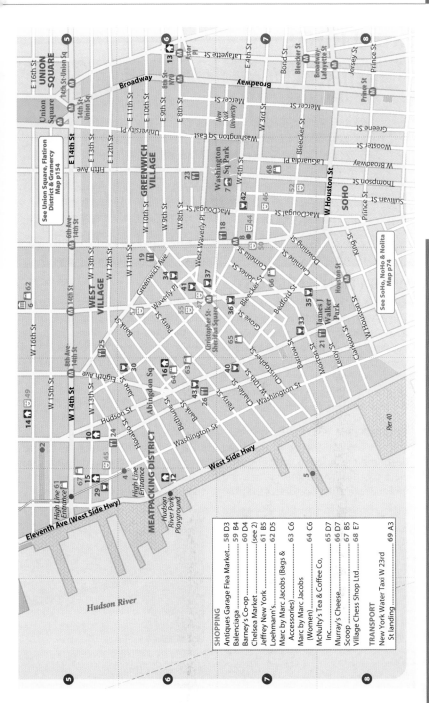

See Union Square, Flatiron District & Gramercy Map p154

See SoHo, NoHo & Nolita Map p74

SHOPPING

Antiques Garage Flea Market...	58 D3
Balenciaga	59 B4
Barney's Co-op	60 D4
Chelsea Market	(see 2)
Jeffrey New York	61 B5
Loehmann's	62 D5
Marc by Marc Jacobs (Bags & Accessories)	63 C6
Marc by Marc Jacobs (Women)	64 C6
McNulty's Tea & Coffee Co, Inc	65 D7
Murray's Cheese	66 D7
Scoop	67 B5
Village Chess Shop Ltd	68 E7

TRANSPORT

New York Water Taxi W 23rd St landing	69 A3

HIGHLIGHTS

1 HIGH LINE

With the opening of the High Line, a 30ft-high abandoned stretch of elevated railroad track that has been transformed into a long ribbon of parkland (from Gansevoort St to 34th St), there's finally some greenery amid the asphalt jungle. Only three stories above the streetscape, this thoughtfully designed mix of contemporary, industrial and natural elements is a refuge from the ordinary. The completed park will eventually extend to 30th Street and then loop around half of the West Side Rail Yards towards the Hudson River.

⬎ OUR DON'T MISS LIST

❶ AMPHITHEATER

This glass-front **amphitheater** sits just above 10th Avenue. Bleacherlike seating faces a huge pane of glass that allows you to view the traffic, buildings and pedestrians below as living works of urban art. Bring some food and join the local workers on their lunch break.

❷ WALKING THE LINE

Start at 20th St and work your way down the meandering concrete pathways past lushly planted grasses and flowers. Take a break on one of the fixed or movable seating along the rail tracks and enjoy the spectacular views of the city and the Hudson River. Entrances are at Gansevoort, 14th, 16th, 18th & 20th Sts; elevator access is at 14th & 16th Sts. It's open from 7am to 10pm.

❸ THE STANDARD

Rising on concrete stilts over the High Line, **The Standard** (p145) is one of the celebrated destinations of the moment, with two choice drinking spots and a grill (plus hotel rooms where high-paying guests sometimes expose

Clockwise from top: Views across the High Line; Exploring the nooks and crannies; Strolling on the High Line; Taking a break; Walkers on the High Line

themselves in front of their floor-to-ceiling windows in a towel – or less). Judging by the crowds who gather below, voyeurism is alive and well in New York.

❹ HISTORY

The tracks, constructed in 1930, were used by freight trains to service warehouses along Manhattan's west side (an area once home to more than 200 slaughterhouses and meat-packing plants). Before that, trains used to run along 10th Avenue, but ran over so many pedestrians that the street became known as Death Avenue. In 1980, the last train ran on the line and it fell into decay, with weeds growing thick among the tracks. When the city announced it was demolishing the line, a conservation group formed and fought to save it, eventually winning the city's support; work crews went into action in 2006 and the first section opened in 2009.

↘ THINGS YOU NEED TO KNOW

Feature tip Visit after dark, when the lighting system creates a beautiful nighttime landscape **Future Tip** One of the leading art institutions, the Whitney, is building a museum at the High Line's southern terminus **For more on the High Line, see p137.**

HIGHLIGHTS

⬂ GALLERY HOPPING

Among the showcases that create the most buzz in these parts are the so-called 'blue-chip' galleries: the **Andrea Rosen Gallery** (525 West 24 St); the **Mary Boone Gallery** (541 W 24th St); and the **Matthew Marks Gallery** (522 W 22nd St, 523 W 24th St, & 526 W 22nd St), a Chelsea pioneer with three galleries, known for exhibiting big names from Jasper Johns to Ellsworth Kelly.

⬂ WASHINGTON SQUARE PARK

Despite its recent makeover, **Washington Square Park** (p138) is still the Village's town square. The same odd characters still dance around the fountain, NYU undergrads still flip through used editions of Nietzche, and shifty amateur chess masters still hustle for games. Only now it's among immaculately landscaped gardens and grounds; for better or worse, it's less scruffy and more inviting to strangers.

▲ LIVE MUSIC

Several of the city's more prominent jazz clubs – **Blue Note** (p148), **Village Vanguard** (p149) and **Smalls Jazz Club** (p145) – are down in Greenwich Village. **Le Poisson Rouge** (p148), a relative newcomer, has been receiving praise for its eclectic line up of musicians, from avant-garde to traditional.

▲ SHOPPING

At the **Antiques Garage Flea Market** (112 W 25th St at Sixth Ave), more than 100 vendors sell their wares. The picturesque streets of the West Village are home to some lovely boutiques, bookstores, and curio shops. Foodies should head to **Chelsea Market** (p139), while the fashion conscious should visit Bleecker St between Bank and W 10th.

▲ CHELSEA PIERS

New York's biggest sporting center is at the historic **Chelsea Piers** (p140), a 30-acre sporting village where you can golf, work out, play soccer, baseball and basketball, get a massage, swim, box and bowl. There's even waterfront dining and drinking, where you can carb-load after a workout.

2 MICHELLE BENNETT; 3 BILL WASSMAN; 4 ANGUS OBORN; 5 DAN HERRICK; 6 DAN HERRICK

2 Photography gallery in Chelsea (p139); 3 Washington Square Park (p138); 4 Smalls Jazz Club (p145); 5 Chelsea Market (p139); 6 Chelsea Piers (p140)

VILLAGE RADICALS WALKING TOUR

This walk begins at Christopher St and ends at E 11th St near Sixth Ave. It covers 1.5 miles and should take around 1½ hours.

❶ CHRISTOPHER PARK

To begin, disembark the subway at Christopher St and head back to **Christopher Park**, where two life-sized statues of same-sex couples (*Gay Liberation,* 1992) stand guard. On its north side is the **Stonewall Inn** (p147), where a clutch of fed-up drag queens rioted for their civil rights in 1969, signaling the start of the gay revolution.

❷ LITTLE RED SQUARE

Head down Seventh Ave South and turn left onto Bleecker St, strolling until its intersection with Sixth Ave. To the south you'll see a plaque marking **Little Red Square**, named for the original site of the experimental Little Red Schoolhouse, founded in 1921 and still thriving.

❸ FAT BLACK PUSSYCAT SITE

Continue east on Minetta St, home to Panchito's Mexican Restaurant. Above its rear red facade is the faded sign for the former site of the **Fat Black Pussycat (103 MacDougal St)** – called the Commons in 1962 when a young Bob Dylan wrote and first performed 'Blowin' in the Wind' here.

❹ MINETTA TAVERN

Turn right on Minetta Lane and right on MacDougal St to the **Minetta Tavern (113 MacDougal St)**. It opened as a speakeasy in 1922 and was later frequented by a famous local eccentric, Joe Gould, who was immortalized through the writings of journalism great, Joseph Mitchell.

❺ FOLKLORE CENTER SITE

Also on this block is the former site of the **Folklore Center (110 MacDougal St)**, where Izzy Young established a hangout for folk artists, including Bob Dylan, who found his first audience at the music venue **Cafe Wha? (115 MacDougal St)**.

❻ CAFÉ REGGIO

Further along MacDougal is the cozy **Café Reggio (119 MacDougal St)**, whose original 1927 owners claimed to be the first to bring cappuccino from Italy to the US.

❼ WASHINGTON SQUARE PARK

Head further up MacDougal to the southwest entrance to **Washington Square Park** (p138), which has a long history for attracting radicals

VILLAGE RADICALS

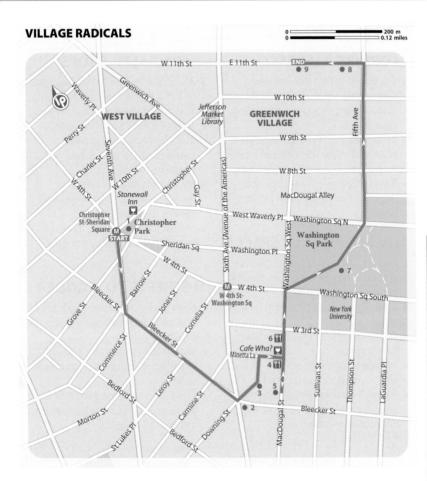

hosting antiwar, pro-marijuana or dyke pride demonstrations, among others. Leave the park through the iconic arch and head up Fifth Ave.

❽ WEATHERMAN HOUSE

Make a left on W 11th St, where you'll find two notable town houses. First is the infamous **Weatherman house** (18 W 11th St), used in 1970 as a hideout and bomb factory for the radical antigovernment group, Weatherman, until an accidental explosion killed three members and destroyed the house; it was rebuilt in its current angular form in 1978.

❾ OSCAR WILDE'S HOUSE

Just a bit further west, the tour comes to an end at the former, albeit brief, **home of Oscar Wilde** (48 W 11th St). The famed Irish wit lived here for a few weeks following a US lecture tour in 1882.

GREENWICH VILLAGE & AROUND

BEST...

BEST...

⬎ DRINKS ALFRESCO

- **Standard** (p141) The outdoor beer garden of the hotel of the same name; it rises over the High Line.
- **Frying Pan** (p147) Laze on a deck chair and enjoy the views of New Jersey.
- **Brass Monkey** (p144) The roof deck is a fine destination in warm weather.

⬎ PERFORMANCE SPACES

- **Le Poisson Rouge** (p148) Diverse and exciting line up across musical genres.
- **Blue Note** (p148) High-end jazz club.
- **Joyce Theater** (p149) Innovative dance venue.
- **Village Vanguard** (p149) Venerable institution for jazz stars.
- **Upright Citizens Brigade** (p149) Improv comedy with occasional big names dropping in.

⬎ SPECIALTY SHOPS

- **Murray's Cheese** (p151) Founded in 1914, this is probably New York's best cheese shop.
- **Village Chess Shop Ltd** (p151) Buy one of the spectacular thematic chess sets: Aztec, Crusades, Vegas etc.
- **Mc Nulty's Tea & Coffee, Inc** (p150) Selling gourmet teas and coffees here since 1895.
- **Flower District** (p151) Blocks of flower shops for every bouquet need.

⬎ STREETS TO WANDER

- **Christopher** Stores selling leather play gear and rainbow-colored T-shirts.
- **West Fourth** Southern end of Washington Square Park and heart of NYU.
- **West 20th to West 26th** Any of these streets in Chelsea has at least a dozen art galleries.

DAN HERRICK

Quirky shopfront, Meatpacking District

DISCOVER GREENWICH VILLAGE, MEATPACKING DISTRICT & CHELSEA

Locals generally don't use the term 'Greenwich Village'; instead they refer to anything west of Sixth Ave as 'the West Village,' and the central part between Sixth and Fourth Aves as simply 'the Village.' New York University (NYU) now dominates much of the central Village, but the vibe turns mellow just west of the park. Nestled in the few circuitous blocks just below 14th St is the Meatpacking District, now an official historic landmark area. Once known for its lascivious blend of working slaughterhouses, kink clubs and transgendered prostitutes, this nook is now the picture of hyper-gentrification.

Chelsea has great nightlife and a vibrant restaurant scene, streets both intimate and industrial, a slew of shopping opportunities and the most stellar collection of art galleries in the city. The area is known to many as a 'gayborhood,' as it's home to many beautiful men (as well as women and children, of course) who strut their stuff while running between the gym, work and various happy-hour gatherings.

SIGHTS
GREENWICH VILLAGE, WEST VILLAGE & MEATPACKING DISTRICT
HIGH LINE

☎ 212-500-6035; www.thehighline.org; Gansevoort St to 20th St btwn Ninth & Eleventh Aves, entrances at Gansevoort, 14th, 16th, 18th & 20th Sts; elevator access at 14th & 16th Sts; ⏱ 7am-10pm

For years now, the big buzz in Chelsea and Hell's Kitchen has been all about the coming of the first section of which finally and officially opened to the public in the summer of 2009. Now you can stroll, sit and picnic 30ft above the city below on what was, since the 1960s, an abandoned stretch of elevated railroad track. The perks thus far are numerous, and include stunning vistas of the Hudson River, public art installations, fat lounge chairs for soaking up some sun, willowy stretches of native-inspired landscaping (including a miniforest of trees), a cupcake vendor and a thoroughly unique perspective on the neighborhood streets below – especially at 10th Ave Square, where bleacherlike seating faces a huge pane of glass that allows you to view the traffic, buildings and pedestrians below as living works of urban art. There's also Andre Balazs' luxury hotel, the Standard (p141), which straddles the park, as well as a still-to-come branch of the Whitney Museum, which will reside at the southern end.

WEST 4TH STREET BASKETBALL COURTS

Sixth Ave btwn 3rd & 4th Sts; ⊕ A, C, E, B, D, F, M to W 4th St-Washington Sq

Also known as 'the Cage,' this small basketball court that stands enclosed within chain-link fencing is home to some of the best streetball in the country. Prime time is summer, when the W 4th St Summer Pro-Classic League, with daily high-energy games, hits the scene.

KIM GRANT

Washington Square Arch

↘ WASHINGTON SQUARE PARK

A park that began as a potter's field (and, conveniently, a public-execution ground), this is the town square of the Village, host to book-toting NYU students, fire-eating street performers, dog-run canines and their owners, and speed-chess champs alike. Mint-condition town houses and large modern structures, all belonging to NYU, surround the space on all sides. But its biggest claim to fame is that it's home to the iconic Stanford White Arch, colloquially known as the Washington Square Arch, which dominates the park with its 72ft of beaming white Dover marble. Originally designed in wood to celebrate the centennial of George Washington's inauguration in 1889, the arch proved so popular that it was replaced with stone six years later and adorned with statues of the general in war and peace (the latter work is by A Stirling Calder, father of artist Alexander Calder). In 1916 artist Marcel Duchamp famously climbed to the top of the arch by its internal stairway and declared the park the 'Free and Independent Republic of Washington Square.'

This little republic has just completed a controversial, $16-million renovation. And while plenty of change-phobic locals were wary about the plans, most reviews so far have been glowing – which is no wonder, since a new fountain, relocated dog run and lush lawn have added a clean, fresh feel to what had become a ramshackle (though charmingly so) spit of green.

Things you need to know: ⊖ A, C, E, B, D, F, M to W 4th St-Washington Sq, N, R to 8th St-NYU

PIER 45

Christopher St at Hudson River; ⊖ 1 to **Christopher St-Sheridan Sq**

Still known to many as the Christopher St Pier, this is an 850ft-long finger of concrete, spiffily renovated with a grass lawn, flowerbeds, a comfort station, an outdoor cafe, tented shade shelters and a stop for the New York Water Taxi as part of the ongoing Hudson River Park project.

And it's a magnet for downtowners of all stripes, from local families with toddlers in daylight to mobs of young gay kids who flock here at night from all over the city (and beyond) because of the pier's long-established history as a gay cruising hangout.

CHELSEA

CHELSEA GALLERIES

Chelsea is home to the highest concentration of art galleries in the entire city – and the number of them just keeps increasing. Most lie in the 20s, on the blocks between Tenth and Eleventh Aves, and wine-and-cheese openings for their new shows are typically held on Thursday evenings. For a complete guide and map, pick up Art Info's **Gallery Guide** (www.artinfo.com/gallery guide), available for free at most galleries, or visit www.westchelseaarts.com. Note that galleries are typically closed on Mondays.

CHELSEA HOTEL

☎ 212-243-3700; 222 W 23rd St btwn Seventh & Eighth Aves; ⊕ 1, C, E to 23rd St
It's probably not any great shakes as far as hotels go – and besides, it mainly houses long-term residents. But as a place of mythical proportions, the Chelsea Hotel is top of the line. The red-brick hotel, featuring ornate iron balconies and no fewer than seven plaques declaring its literary landmark status, has played some major roles in pop-culture history. It's where the likes of Mark Twain, Thomas Wolfe, Dylan Thomas and Arthur Miller hung out; Jack Kerouac allegedly crafted *On the Road* during one marathon session here; and it's where Arthur C Clarke wrote *2001: A Space Odyssey*. Dylan Thomas died of alcohol poisoning while staying here in 1953, and Nancy Spungeon died here after being stabbed by her Sex Pistols boyfriend Sid Vicious in 1978. The art-filled lobby is worth a look-see, and its basement-level **Star Lounge** is a sexy, low-lit spot for a martini.

CHELSEA MARKET

www.chelseamarket.com; 75 Ninth Ave at 15th St; ⊕ A, C, E to 14th St, L to 8th Ave
In a shining example of redevelopment and preservation, the Chelsea Market has taken a former factory of cookie giant Nabisco (creator of the Oreo) and turned it into an 800ft-long shopping concourse that caters to foodies. You can also sit down and indulge at lunch spots such as the Green Table organic-food cafe, and buy nonfood items at Imports from Marrakesh (specializing in Moroccan art and design) and the expert-staffed Chelsea Wine Vault.

MICHELLE BENNETT
Chelsea Hotel

Street basketball

DAN HERRICK

CHELSEA PIERS
☎ 212-336-6000; www.chelseapiers.com;
Twelfth Ave at 23rd St; ◉ C, E to 23rd St,
🚍 M23 westbound

This massive waterfront sports center caters to the athlete in everyone. You can set out to hit a bucket of golf balls at the four-level driving range, ice skate on the complex's indoor rink or rent in-line skates to cruise along the new Hudson River Park waterfront bike path – all the way down to Battery Park. There's a jazzy bowling alley, Hoop City for basketball, a sailing school for kids, batting cages, a huge gym facility with an indoor pool (day passes for nonmembers are $50), indoor rock-climbing walls – the works.

RUBIN MUSEUM OF ART
☎ 212-620-5000; www.rmanyc.org; 150 W 17th St at Seventh Ave; adult/under 12yr/senior & student $10/free/7, 7-10pm Fri free; 🕙 11am-5pm Mon & Thu, to 7pm Wed, to 10pm Fri, to 6pm Sat & Sun; ◉ 1 to 18th St

The Rubin Museum of Art is the first museum in the Western world to dedicate itself to art of the Himalayas and surrounding regions. Its impressive collections include embroidered textiles from China, metal sculptures from Tibet, Pakistani stone sculptures and intricate Bhutanese paintings, as well as ritual objects and dance masks from various Tibetan regions, spanning from the 2nd to the 19th centuries.

SLEEPING
GREENWICH VILLAGE, WEST VILLAGE & MEATPACKING DISTRICT
HOTEL GANSEVOORT
Boutique Hotel $$$
☎ 212-206-6700, 877-426-7386; www.hotel gansevoort.com; 18 Ninth Ave at 13th St; r from $355; ◉ A, C, E to 14th St, L to 8th Ave; 🅿 🖥 🛉

Coated in zinc-colored panels, and booming up top where rooftop bar Plunge attracts block-long lines (and guests swim in the skinny pool overlooking the Hudson River), the 14-floor Gansevoort has been a swank swashbuckler of the Meatpacking District since it opened in 2004. Rooms are luscious and airy, with fudge-colored suede headboards, plasma-screen TVs and illuminated bathroom doors.

STANDARD   Boutique Hotel $$$
☎ 212-645-4646, 877-550-4646; www.standard hotels.com; 848 Washington St at 13th St; r from $350; ⊕ A, C, E to 14th St, L to 8th Ave; ✗ 🖵 📺

Hipster hotelier André Balazs has built a wide, boxy, glass tower that straddles the High Line (p137), an old elevated train track recently turned into a public park. Every room has sweeping Meatpacking District views and fills with cascading sunlight that makes the Standard's glossy, wood-framed beds and marbled bathrooms glow in a particularly homey way.

LAFAYETTE HOUSE   Boutique Hotel $$$
☎ 212-505-8100; www.lafayettenyc.com; 38 E 4th Ave; r from $350; ⊕ B, D, F, M to Broadway-Lafayette St, 6 to Bleecker St; ✗ 🖵

A former town house that's been turned into homey, spacious suites (each with a working fireplace), Lafayette House feels very Victorian. Suites have big beds, desks, thick drapes and old-fashioned armoires. Bathrooms are large, with claw-footed tubs, and some rooms have kitchenettes.

WEST ELEVENTH TOWNHOUSE
B&B $$
☎ 212-675-7897; www.west-eleventh.com; 278 W 11th St, btwn W 4th & Bleecker Sts; r $235-350; ⊕ 1 to Christopher St, A, C, E, B, D, F, M to W 4th St-Washington Sq; ✗ 🖵

Ring bell 11 when you show up at this gracious West Village town house, which of-

fers five spacious suites – more like small apartments than hotel rooms – with tiny kitchenettes, cozy living areas with artfully decorated nooks and crannies, and handsome four-poster beds.

JANE HOTEL   Hotel $
☎ 212-924-6700; www.thejanenyc.com; 113 Jane St near Hudson River; r $99-250; ⊕ A, C, E to 14th St, L to 8th Ave; ✗ 🖵

The claustrophobic will want to avoid the Jane's tiny, 50ft rooms, but if you can stomach living like a luxury sailor, check into this recently renovated gem. Now it's outfitted for modern travelers, with air-con, wi-fi, iPod docks and a gorgeous communal lobby/lounge that looks like it belongs in a five-star hotel.

CHELSEA

MARITIME HOTEL   Boutique Hotel $$$
☎ 212-242-4300; www.themaritimehotel.com; 363 W 16th St btwn Eighth & Ninth Aves; r $229-725; ⊕ A, C, E to 14th St, L to 8th Ave; ✗ 🖵

Originally the site of the National Maritime Union headquarters (and more recently a shelter for homeless teens), this tower dotted with portholes has been transformed into a marine-themed luxury inn by a hip team of architects. It feels like a luxury *Love Boat* inside, as its 135 rooms, each with their own round window, are compact and teak-paneled, with extras in the form of flat-screen TVs and DVD players.

INN ON 23RD ST   B&B $$
☎ 212-463-0330; www.innon23rd.com; 131 W 23rd St btwn Sixth & Seventh Aves; r $210; ⊕ F, M, 1 to 23rd St; ✗ 🖵

Housed in a lone 19th-century, five-story town house on busy 23rd St, this 14-room B&B is a Chelsea gem. Bought in 1998 and extensively renovated by the Fisherman family (who wisely installed an elevator), the rooms are big and welcoming, with fanciful fabrics on big brass or poster beds and TVs held in huge armoires.

CHELSEA LODGE   B&B $

☎ 212-243-4499; www.chelsealodge.com; 318 W 20th St btwn Eighth & Ninth Aves; r $119; ◉ C, E to 23rd St; ▨

Housed in a landmark brownstone in Chelsea's lovely historic district, the European-style, 20-room Chelsea Lodge is a super deal, with homey, well-kept rooms. Space is tight, so you won't get more than a bed, with a TV (and cable) plopped on an old wooden cabinet. Six suite rooms have private bathrooms, and two come with private garden access.

EATING

GREENWICH VILLAGE, WEST VILLAGE & MEATPACKING DISTRICT

While the West Village is known for classy, cozy, intimate spots that cause quiet envy among the most casual of passersby, the adjacent Meatpacking District's dining scene is a bit more… ostentatious, complete with nightclub-like queues behind velvet ropes, eye-popping decor and crowds of trend-obsessed young folk. The most solidly pleasing option here is the original cool-kid spot, **Pastis** (☎ 212-929-4844; 9 Ninth Ave at Little W 12th St; ☽ breakfast, lunch, dinner, late night; ◉ A, C, E, L to 8th Ave-14th St), Keith McNally's perfect homage to the French brasserie. The central Village, meanwhile, falls somewhere in between the vibe of those two 'hoods, and includes the many student-geared budget options (falafel, pizza etc) of NYU-land.

BLUE HILL   American $$$

☎ 212-539-1776; 75 Washington Pl btwn Sixth Ave & Washington Sq W; ☽ dinner; ◉ A, C, E, B, D, F, M to W 4th St-Washington Sq

A place for Slow Food junkies with deep pockets, Blue Hill was an early crusader in the local-is-better movement. Expect barely seasoned, perfectly ripe vegetables, which serve to highlight centerpieces of cod in almond broth, Berkshire pork stewed with four types of beans, and grass-fed lamb with white beans and new

DAN HERRICK

Pier 45 (p138)

potatoes. The space itself, slightly below street level and housed in a landmark former speakeasy on a quaint Village block, is sophisticated and serene.

EN JAPANESE BRASSERIE
Modern Japanese $$$

☎ 212-647-9196; 5 Hudson St at Leroy St; ⊙ lunch & dinner; ⊚ 1 to Houston St
This high-ceilinged space is anchored by a wide sushi bar, and you'll know you've entered some place special by the amazing earthy yet modern decor – not to mention the exuberant welcome call you'll get from the chefs in the open kitchen. Menu options are sublime.

OTTO ENOTECA PIZZERIA
Pizza & Italian $$

☎ 212-995-9559; 1 Fifth Ave at 8th St; ⊙ lunch & dinner; ⊚ A, C, E, B, D, F, M to W 4th St-Washington Sq
An intimate trattoria in the heart of the Village, this is (a refreshingly affordable) part of Mario Batali's empire, a pizza palace, where thin pizzas are cooked on flat iron griddles till they crackle perfectly. They come topped with items far beyond your standard pizza joint – fennel, goat cheese, egg, fresh chilies, capers, the best fresh mozzarella – and sauce that has the perfect balance of smoky and sweet.

CAFÉ ASEAN
Pan-Asian $$

☎ 212-633-0348; 117 W 10th St at Greenwich Ave; ⊙ lunch & dinner; ⊚ A, C, E, B, D, F, M to W 4th St-Washington Sq
A tiny spot on a short stretch of street, this eclectic and homey crevice is easy to miss. It serves up refreshing takes on Malaysian, Thai and Vietnamese concoctions to a low-key, cool-cat crowd who know you don't need to plunk down wads of cash for authentic flavor.

SPOTTED PIG
Pub Fare $$

☎ 212-620-0393; 314 W 11th St at Greenwich St; ⊙ lunch & dinner till 2am, brunch weekends; ⊚ A, C, E to 14th St, L to 8th Ave
This diminutive hideaway in a romantic, residential West Village pocket has been quite celebrated, receiving the coveted Michelin star each of the three years it's been open. It packs in folks nightly with its hearty, upscale blend of Italian-English-Irish pub fare.

SOY LUCK CLUB
Soy-Themed Vegetarian Cafe $

☎ 212-229-9191; 115 Greenwich Ave at Jane St; ⊙ 7am-10pm Mon-Fri, 9am-10pm Sat & Sun; ⊚ A, C, E to 14th St, L to 8th Ave
Panini, salads and brunch items, some even containing meat, abound. Best of all, everything is fresh and tasty, especially the signature drinks, which consist of soymilk, either steamed or iced, mixed with additions from dark chocolate to honey and ginger.

CHELSEA

KLEE BRASSERIE
Eclectic $$$

☎ 212-633-8033; 200 Ninth Ave btwn 22nd & 23rd Sts; ⊙ dinner; ⊚ C, E to 23rd St
A fun and thoroughly unique neighborhood option, this joyously designed space – with wood-paneled walls, low banquettes and whimsically colored tile detailing – does an impressive job of creating a cool scene without throwing too much 'tude. It also creates magic in its open kitchen with some wholesome, fresh ingredients.

TÍA POL
Spanish Tapas $$

☎ 212-675-8805; 205 Tenth Ave btwn 22nd & 23rd Sts; ⊙ dinner Tue-Sun; ⊚ C, E to 23rd St
This closet-sized, authentic and romantic Spanish tapas bar is the real deal – and the hordes of locals who crowd into the

front-bar waiting area to get one of six teeny tables filled with massive doses of deliciousness know it. The red-wine options will have your tongue doing backflips, as will the array of tapas.

CO
Wood-Fired Pizza $$
☎ 212-243-1105; 230 Ninth Ave at 24th St; ☽ dinner Mon, lunch & dinner Tue-Sun; ⊕ C, E to 23rd St

For a prime example of the upper-crust, Neapolitan-inspired pizza wave that's overtaken the city, step into this soothing, blonde-wood-filled dining room, where the lovingly crafted pizzas of Jim Lahey are served. Salads of artichoke, beet or radicchio – as well as global wines and a sprinkling of sweets – round out the offerings.

Spotted Pig (p143)

DAN HERRICK

DRINKING
GREENWICH VILLAGE, WEST VILLAGE & MEATPACKING DISTRICT

The word in the West Village is 'west' – the further towards the Hudson you go, the more likely you are to sidestep the frat-boy scenes found around the NYU campus. (There are a handful of exceptions, of course, as well as a few worthy gay bars, listed on p147). Just to the north, the Meatpacking District is strictly contemporary in vibe, with sprawling, modern spaces boasting long cocktail lists, velvet-roped entrances and dins that'll rattle your brain.

VOL DE NUIT
Beer Nerds
☎ 212-982-3388; 148 W 4th St; ⊕ A, C, E, B, D, F, M to W 4th St-Washington Sq

Even all the NYU students can't ruin this – a cozy Belgian beer bar, with a few dozen zonkers such as Lindemans Framboise (strawberry beer!) and *frites* (fries) to share in the front patio seats, the lounge, the communal wood tables or under the dangling red lights at the bar.

BRASS MONKEY
Chill Bar
☎ 212-675-6686; 55 Little W 12th St at Washington St; ⊕ A, C, E to 14th St, L to 8th Ave

While most Meatpacking District bars tend toward the chic, the Brass Monkey is more for beer lovers than those worrying about what shoes to wear. At first step in, the multifloor Monkey is at ease and down-to-earth, with squeaking wood floors and a nice long list of beers and scotch.

LITTLE BRANCH
Cocktail Bar
☎ 212-929-4360; 22 Seventh Ave S at Leroy St; ⊕ 1 to Houston St

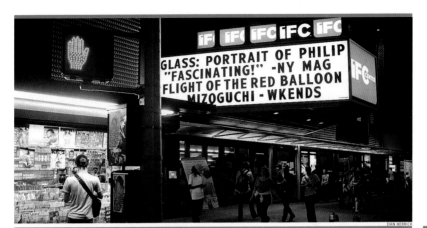

DAN HERRICK

IFC Center

⤵ IF YOU LIKE...

If you like the eclectic musical offerings at Le Poisson Rouge (p148), then we think you'll like:

- **Dance Theater Workshop** (☎ 212-924-0077; www.dancetheaterworkshop.org; 219 W 19th St btwn Seventh & Eighth Aves, Chelsea; ◉ 1 to 18th St) You'll find a program of more than 110 experimental, contemporary works annually at this sleek dance center; shows often include pre- or post-show discussions with choreographers or dancers.
- **Gotham Comedy Club** (☎ 212-367-9000; http://gothamcomedyclub.com; 208 W 23rd St btwn Seventh & Eighth Aves, Chelsea; ◉ F, M, N, R to 23rd St) Fancying itself as a NYC comedy hall of fame, and backing it up with regular big names and Gotham All-Stars shows.
- **IFC Center** (☎ 212-924-7771; www.ifccenter.com; 323 Sixth Ave at 3rd St, West Village; ◉ A, C, E, B, D, F, M to W 4th St-Washington Sq) This art house in NYU-land has a great cafe and a solidly curated lineup of new indies, cult classics and foreign films.
- **Smalls Jazz Club** (☎ 212-283-9728; www.smallsjazzclub.com; 183 W 10th St at Seventh Ave, West Village; ◉ 1 to Christopher St-Sheridan Sq) Living up to its name, this cramped but appealing basement jazz den offers a grab-bag collection of jazz acts who take the stage nightly.

Down from Seventh in an unassuming, gray, triangular building, this alluring, stylish speakeasy keeps the lights and jazz low, so the focus in two- and four-person booths is on the gin, rum and scotch cocktails, all stirred with precision.

STANDARD
Hotel Bar

☎ 212-645-4646; 848 Washington St; ◉ A, C, E to 14th St, L to 8th Ave

There's an outdoor beer garden with a classic German menu and frothy drafts, plus the Living Room bar, a swankier indoor affair with marvelous views over the Hudson and a Euro-loving crowd.

WHITE HORSE TAVERN — Old-Time Bar

☎ 212-243-9260; 567 Hudson St at 11th St; ◉ 1 to Christopher St-Sheridan Sq

It's a bit on the tourist trail, but that doesn't dampen the century-old, pubby, dark-wood, tin-ceilinged atmosphere.

PLUNGE — Rooftop Bar

☎ 212-206-6700; Hotel Gansevoort, 18 Ninth Ave at 13th St; ◉ A, C, E to 14th St, L to 8th Ave

Located in the 15th-floor penthouse of the hopelessly trendy Hotel Gansevoort, this Meatpacking District star affords great views of the Hudson River in a Miami Beach–type club with long lines.

HIGHLANDS — Scottish Bar

☎ 212-229-2670; 150 W 10th St; ◉ 1 to Christopher St-Sheridan Sq

This unpretentious Scottish gastropub is a fine place to while away an evening. Exposed brick, a fireplace and a mix of animal heads, oil paintings and tartans

on the walls bring in more than a touch of the old country.

CHELSEA

PARK — Dining, Drinking & Dancing

☎ 212-352-3313; 118 Tenth Ave btwn 17th & 18th Sts; ◉ A, C, E to 14th St, L to 8th Ave

The party may have moved elsewhere but the Park, with its multiple rooms and over-the-top design, has lost none of its appeal. The main dining room boasts a stand of 30-ft-tall bamboo and wide glass doors leading into the garden.

HALF KING — Lit Bar

☎ 212-462-4300; 505 W 23rd St at Tenth Ave; ◉ C, E to 23rd St

A unique marriage of cozy bar, bistro and casual writers' lair; you'll often experience top-notch literary readings in this wood-accented, candlelit watering hole.

PETER MCMANUS TAVERN — Old-Time Bar

☎ 212-929-9691; 152 Seventh Ave at 19th St; ◉ A, C, E to 14th St

Little Branch (p144)

DAN HERRICK

GAY & LESBIAN GREENWICH VILLAGE, MEATPACKING DISTRICT & CHELSEA
Drinking & Nightlife

- **Barracuda** (☎ 212-645-8613; 275 W 22nd St at Seventh Ave; ☺ C, E to 23rd St) This long-time gay favorite holds its own even as newer places come and go. That's because it's got a simple, winning formula: affordable cocktails, a cozy rec-room vibe and free entertainment from some of the city's top drag queens.

- **Cubbyhole** (☎ 212-243-9041; 281 W 12th St; ☺ A, C, E to 14th St, L to 8th Ave) A tiny hideaway festooned with brightly patterned bar stools and strings of color-ful lights, this no-attitude neighborhood watering hole has a mix of lesbians and gay men who are out to make friends rather than hit the road with the first trick they find.

- **Henrietta Hudson** (☎ 212-924-3347; 438 Hudson St; ☺ 1 to Houston St) All sorts of cute young dykes, many from neighboring New Jersey and Long Island, storm this sleek lounge, where varying theme nights bring in spirited DJs who stick to particular genres (hip-hop, house, rock).

- **Marie's Crisis** (☎ 212-243-9323; 59 Grove St btwn Seventh Ave S & Bleecker St; ☺ 1 to Christopher St-Sheridan Sq) Aging Broadway queens, wide-eyed, out-of-town gay boys, giggly tourist girls and various other fans of musical theater assemble around the piano here and take turns belting out campy numbers, often joined by the entire crowd.

- **Monster** (☎ 212-924-3558; 80 Grove St at Sheridan Sq; ☺ 1 to Christopher St-Sheridan Sq) It's old-school, gay-man heaven in here, with a small dance floor as well as a piano bar and cabaret space. Spirited theme nights range from Latino parties to drag-queen-hosted soirees.

- **RF lounge** (☎ 917-262-0836; 531 W Hudson St at Charles St; ☺ 1 to Christopher St-Sheridan Sq) The former site of longtime lesbian favorite Rubyfruit Bar & Grill, RF is a redesigned loungey sort of place, now drawing a new crowd of women who find they have fewer and fewer places to call their own over the years.

- **Stonewall Inn** (☎ 212-463-0950; 53 Christopher St; ☺ 1 to Christopher St-Sheridan Sq) Site of the Stonewall riots in 1969, this historic bar was losing its fan base to trendier spots until new owners came along, gave it a facelift and opened it to a new and welcoming crowd several years back. Since then, it's been pulling in varied crowds nightly for parties catering to everyone under the gay rainbow.

Pouring drafts since the 1930s, this family-run dive is something of a museum to the world of the McManuses: photos of yesteryear, an old telephone booth and Tiffany glass. There's also greasy bar food to eat at the cute green booths.

FRYING PAN Waterfront Bar
☎ 212-989-6363; Pier 66 at W 26th St; ☺ C, E to 23rd St

Salvaged from the bottom of the sea (or at least the Chesapeake Bay), the *Frying Pan* and the two-tiered dockside bar where it's parked is a fine spot for a sundowner.

ENTERTAINMENT & ACTIVITIES

GREENWICH VILLAGE, WEST VILLAGE & MEATPACKING DISTRICT

DUPLEX
Cabaret

☎ 212-255-5438; www.theduplex.com; 61 Christopher St at Seventh Ave S; ⊕ 1 to Christopher St-Sheridan Sq

It's way gay at this tiny spot, where you'll find a near-constant roster of drag queens and piano-bar shows from a range of up-and-comers.

CIELO
Clubbing

☎ 212-645-5700; www.cieloclub.com; 18 Little W 12th St btwn Ninth Ave & Washington St; admission $15-25; ⊕ A, C, E to 14th St, L to 8th Ave

Known for its intimate space and free or low-cost parties, this Meatpacking District staple packs in a fashionable, multiculti crowd nightly for its blend of deep house, tribal, Latin-spiced grooves and soul.

COMEDY CELLAR
Comedy

☎ 212-254-3480; www.comedycellar.com; 117 MacDougal St btwn 3rd & Bleecker Sts; ⊕ A, C, E, B, D, F, M to W 4th St- Washington Sq

This long-established basement club features mainstream material and a good list of regulars (eg Colin Quinn, SNL's Darrell Hammond), plus an occasional high-profile drop-in such as Dave Chappelle.

BLUE NOTE
Jazz & Experimental

☎ 212-475-8592; www.bluenote.net; 131 W 3rd St btwn Sixth Ave & MacDougal St; ⊕ A, C, E, B, D, F, M to W 4th St-Washington Sq

This is by far the most famous (and expensive) of the city's jazz clubs. Most shows are $20 at the bar, $35 at a table, but can rise for the biggest jazz stars, and a few outside the normal jazz act (um, Doobie Brothers' Michael McDonald, anyone?).

LE POISSON ROUGE
Jazz & Experimental

☎ 212-505-3474; www.lepoissonrouge.com; 158 Bleecker St; ⊕ A, C, E, B, D, F, M to W 4th St-Washington Sq

DAN HERRICK

Joyce Theater

This newish high-concept art space (complete with dangling fish aquarium) hosts a highly eclectic lineup, with the likes of Deerhunter, Marc Ribot, Lou Reed and Laurie Anderson performing in past years.

VILLAGE VANGUARD
Jazz & Experimental

☎ 212-255-4037; www.villagevanguard.com; 178 Seventh Ave at 11th St, West Village; ⊙ 1, 2, 3 to 14th St

More intimate and real than the bigger legends, the Vanguard's been around since 1935, still pushing a no-talking policy that keeps the focus on jazz. It's seen the best in its seven decades – Bill Evans, John Coltrane, Sonny Rollings and Wynton Marsalis have recorded live albums here.

CHELSEA

SCHOONER ADIRONDACK
Boating

☎ 646-336-5270; www.sail-nyc.com; Chelsea Piers, Pier 62 at W 22nd St, Chelsea; tours $40-50; ⊙ C, E to 23rd St

The two-masted 'Dack hits the New York Harbor with four two-hour sails daily from May to October. The 1920s-style, 80ft *Manhattan* yacht makes three-hour circumnavigation sunset tours at 6pm, night tours at 8:30pm and day tours at 1pm or 3:30pm.

HIRO
Clubbing

☎ 212-242-4300; www.themaritimehotel.com; 371 W 16th St, Chelsea; ⊙ Thu-Sun; ⊙ A, C, E to 14th St, L to 8th Ave

In the Maritime Hotel, this chic Japanese space looks like the place where Uma kicked a lot of ass at the end of *Kill Bill: Vol 1*. It's Japanese chic, with bamboo wall dividers and low-slung banquettes. It's most popular on Thursday and Sunday nights when a gay crowd hits the dance floor.

PINK ELEPHANT
Clubbing

☎ 212-463-0000 ext 1844; www.pinkelephant club.com; 527 W 27th St, Chelsea; admission $25; ⊙ Thu-Sun; ⊙ 1 to 28th St

The name is coy, but the place is all class – so much so that it can be tough getting in the door. DJ-blasted deep house resonates throughout the tight, low-ceilinged dance floor, so don't expect to hear your taxi driver's chatter at 4am.

UPRIGHT CITIZENS BRIGADE THEATRE
Comedy

☎ 212-366-9176; www.ucbtheatre.com; 307 W 26th St btwn Eighth & Ninth Aves, Chelsea; ⊙ C, E to 23rd St

Pros of comedy sketches and outrageous improvisations reign at this popular 74-seat venue, which gets drop-ins from casting directors. Getting in is cheap ($5 to $8) – so is the beer (from $2 a can) – and you may recognize pranksters on stage from late-night comedy shows; it's free on Wednesday after 11pm, when newbies take the reins.

JOYCE THEATER
Dance

☎ 212-242-0800; www.joyce.org; 175 Eighth Ave at 19th St, Chelsea; ⊙ A, C, E to 14th St, L to 8th Ave

A favorite among dance junkies because of its excellent sight lines and offbeat offerings, this is an intimate venue, seating 470 in a renovated cinema. Its focus is on traditional modern companies such as Pilobolus and Parsons Dance

SHOPPING
GREENWICH VILLAGE, WEST VILLAGE & MEATPACKING DISTRICT

High-end shoppers stick to top-label stores along Bleecker St between Bank and W 10th. There's much more color along Christopher St, with its stores selling leather play gear and rainbow-colored T-shirts. Tourist hordes, meanwhile, come to the more central poster and T-shirt shops along Bleecker between Seventh Ave and La Guardia Pl.

The Meatpacking District is all about that new, sleek, high-ceilinged industrial-chic vibe, with ultramodern designers reigning at expansive boutiques that are among the most fashionable haunts in town (some stores indeed look like sets for futuristic and beautifully stylized Kubrick films).

MCNULTY'S TEA & COFFEE CO, INC
Coffee & Tea
☎ 212-242-5351; 109 Christopher St; ⏰ 10am-9pm Mon-Sat, 1-7pm Sun; ⊕ 1 to Christopher St-Sheridan Sq
Just down from a few sex shops, sweet McNulty's, with worn wooden floorboards and fragrant sacks of coffee beans and large glass jars of tea, flaunts a different era of Greenwich Village. It's been

selling gourmet teas and coffees here since 1895.

JEFFREY NEW YORK   Designer Clothing
☎ 212-206-1272; 449 W 14th St; ⏰ 10am-8pm Mon-Sat, 12:30-6pm Sun; ⊕ A, C, E to 14th St, L to 8th Ave
One of the pioneers in the Meatpacking makeover, Jeffrey sells several high-end designer clothing lines – Versace, Pucci, Prada, Michael Kors and company – as well as accessories, shoes and a small selection of cosmetics.

MARC BY MARC JACOBS
Designer Clothing
☎ 212-924-0026; www.marcjacobs.com; 403-405 Bleecker St; ⏰ noon-8pm Mon-Sat, noon-7pm Sun; ⊕ A, C, E to 14th St, L to 8th Ave
With five small shops sprinkled around the West Village, Marc Jacobs has established a real presence in this well-heeled neighborhood. Large front windows allow easy peeking – assuming there's not a sale, during which you'll only see hordes of fawning shoppers.

DAN HERRICK

Village Vanguard (p149)

SCOOP   Designer Clothing

☎ 212-929-1244; 430 W 14th St; ⏰ 11am-7pm Mon-Sat, noon-6pm Sun; ⓔ A, C, E to 14th St, L to 8th Ave

Scoop is a great one-stop destination for unearthing top contemporary fashions by Theory, Stella McCartney, Marc Jacobs, James Perse and many others.

VILLAGE CHESS SHOP LTD   Games

☎ 212-475-9580; 230 Thompson St; ⏰ 11am-midnight; ⓔ A, C, E, B, D, F, M to W 4th St-Washington Sq

A crusty crew of chess-o-philes frequents this hole-in-the-wall chess shop for $1 games in a no-frills sitting area. Come to play, buy a book to study up, or buy one of the chess sets.

MURRAY'S CHEESE   Gourmet Cheese

☎ 212-243-3289; www.murrayscheese.com; 254 Bleecker St btwn Sixth & Seventh Aves; ⏰ 8am-8pm Mon-Sat, 10am-7pm Sun; ⓔ 1 to Christopher St-Sheridan Sq

You'll find (and be able to taste) all manner of *fromage*, be it stinky, sweet or nutty, from European nations and from small farms in Vermont and upstate New York. There's also prosciutto and smoked meats, freshly baked breads, olives, antipasto, chocolate and all manner of goodies for a gourmet picnic – plus a counter for freshly made sandwiches and melts.

CHELSEA

The neighborhood standout is the beloved **Chelsea Market** (p139), a huge concourse packed with minimarkets selling fresh baked goods, wines, veggies, imported cheeses and other temptations. Eighth Ave has the densest (but not the best) selections, with chain stores such as Gap and Banana Republic among the smaller stores.

RICHARD I'ANSON
Chess sets for sale, Thompson St

For a unique DIY adventure beginning at the northern edge of this 'hood, wander through the small but fascinating **Flower District** (around Sixth Ave btwn 26th & 29th Sts) on a weekday morning, when trucks unload massive amounts of fragrant, fresh flowers and plants.

LOEHMANN'S   Discount Department Store

☎ 212-352-0856; www.loehmanns.com; 101 Seventh Ave at 16th St; ⏰ 9am-9pm Mon-Sat, 11am-7pm Sun; ⓔ 1 to 18th St

A starting point for local hipsters looking for designer labels on the cheap (though some may not admit it), Loehmann's is a five-story department store that allegedly inspired a young Calvin Klein to make clothes.

BALENCIAGA — Designer Clothing

☎ 212-206-0872; 522 W 22nd St at Eleventh Ave; ⊗ noon-7pm Mon-Sat, noon-5pm Sun; ⊕ C, E to 23rd St

Come and graze at this cool, grey, Zen-like space, the gallery district's showcase, appropriately enough, for the artistic, post-apocalypse avant-garde styles of this French fashion house.

BARNEYS CO-OP — Designer Clothing

☎ 212-593-7800; 236 W 18th St; ⊗ 11am-8pm Mon-Fri, 11am-7pm Sat, noon-6pm Sun; ⊕ 1 to 18th St

The edgier, younger, more affordable version of Barneys has (relatively) affordable apparel at this expansive, loftlike space. You'll find a spare, well-edited inventory of clothing for men and women, as well as stocks of shoes, cosmetics and bags.

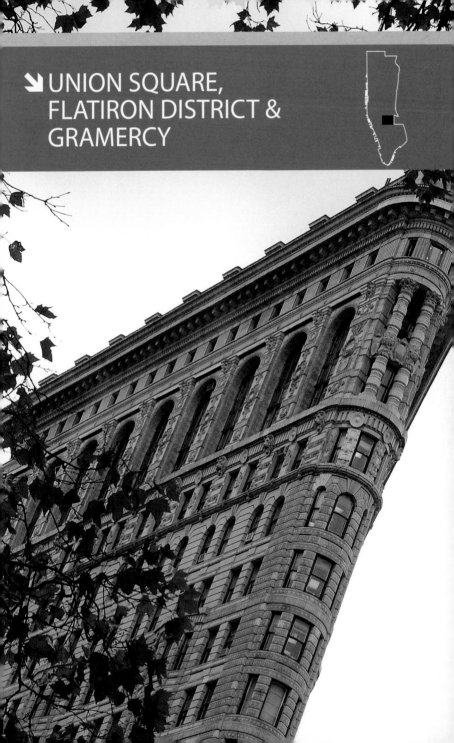

UNION SQUARE, FLATIRON DISTRICT & GRAMERCY

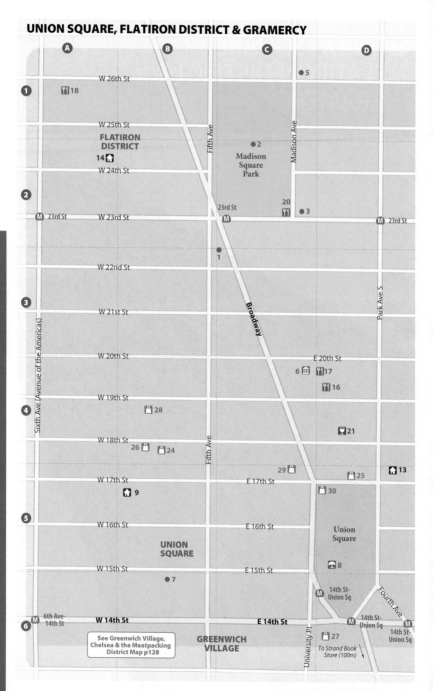

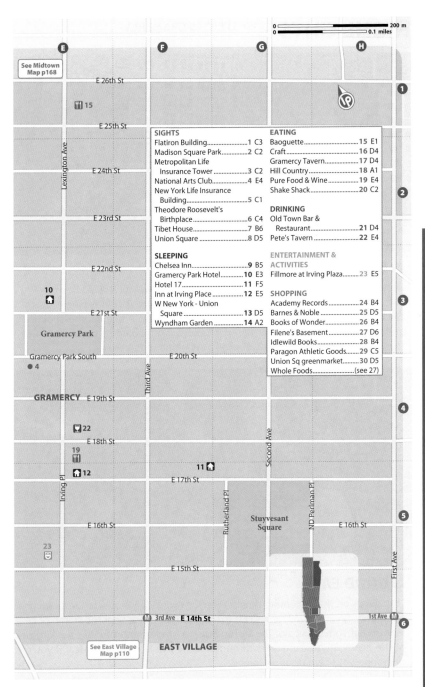

0 _____ 200 m
0 _____ 0.1 miles

See Midtown Map p168

SIGHTS
Flatiron Building............................1 C3
Madison Square Park....................2 C2
Metropolitan Life
    Insurance Tower 3 C2
National Arts Club.........................4 E4
New York Life Insurance
    Building.....................................5 C1
Theodore Roosevelt's
    Birthplace.................................6 C4
Tibet House....................................7 B6
Union Square.................................8 D5

SLEEPING
Chelsea Inn....................................9 B5
Gramercy Park Hotel..................10 E3
Hotel 17..11 F5
Inn at Irving Place 12 E5
W New York - Union
    Square 13 D5
Wyndham Garden 14 A2

EATING
Baoguette....................................15 E1
Craft..16 D4
Gramercy Tavern.........................17 D4
Hill Country..................................18 A1
Pure Food & Wine 19 E4
Shake Shack.................................20 C2

DRINKING
Old Town Bar &
    Restaurant...............................21 D4
Pete's Tavern................................22 E4

**ENTERTAINMENT &
ACTIVITIES**
Fillmore at Irving Plaza............23 E5

SHOPPING
Academy Records 24 B4
Barnes & Noble............................25 D5
Books of Wonder.........................26 B4
Filene's Basement........................27 D6
Idlewild Books.............................28 B4
Paragon Athletic Goods.........29 C5
Union Sq greenmarket..........30 D5
Whole Foods.........................(see 27)

See East Village Map p110

EAST VILLAGE

UNION SQUARE & AROUND

HIGHLIGHTS

HIGHLIGHTS

↘ UNION SQUARE

Despite its prosaic etymology – it was simply the 'union' of the old Bowery and Bloomingdale (now Broadway) roads – **Union Square** (p160) is where downtowners come together, if not always in agreement with one another. Political and social activists gather for demonstrations, skateboarders do tricks, office workers grab a quick break; it's the very definition of multi-use.

↘ GOOD EATS

This area is on the discerning diner's map for two widely respected restaurants, **Gramercy Tavern** (p163) and **Craft** (p163), both of which bear the stamp of celebrity chef Tom Colicchio. The **Union Square greenmarket** (p162), the largest of the nearly 50 greenmarkets throughout the five boroughs, is ideal if you're preparing your own gourmet picnic.

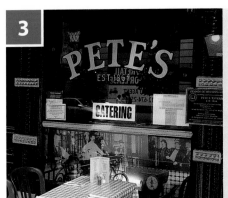

⊾ CLASSIC BARS

For memorable, turn-of-the-century vibe you can't do better than to pull up a stool or grab a hard bench at **Pete's Tavern** (p165) or the **Old Town Bar & Restaurant** (p164). These neighborhood watering holes, open since 1864 and 1892 respectively, will have you feeling wistful for a time gone by. Both also serve food, including good burgers.

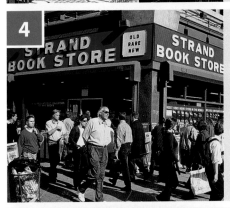

⊾ BOOK SHOPS

Bibliophiles beware of stimulation overload. The **Strand Book Store** (p165), a veritable warehouse of books, is one of the city's most famous for autodidacts, academics, students and everyone in between. Browse your way around the world at **Idlewild Books** (p165) and of course there's the flagship **Barnes & Noble** (p165) at the northern end of the park.

⊾ FLATIRON BUILDING

At the intersection of Broadway, Fifth Ave and 23rd St, the famous (and absolutely gorgeous) 1902 **Flatiron Building** (p159) has a distinctive triangular shape to match its site. It was New York's first iron-frame high-rise, and the world's tallest building until 1909. The surrounding district is a fashionable area of boutiques and loft apartments.

1 RICHARD CUMMINS; 2 DAN HERRICK; 3 DAN HERRICK; 4 ANGUS OBORN; 5 SUNE WENDELBOE

1 Union Square (p160); 2 Union Square greenmarket (p162); 3 Pete's Tavern (p165); 4 Strand Book Store (p165);
5 Flatiron Building (p159)

BEST...

⬎ BLOCKS TO WANDER

- **West Fourteenth Street** Store-upon-store – from bargain indies to chains – hawking discount electronics, cheap linens, a range of shoes and hit-or-miss clothing.
- **East Fourteenth Street** Immediately south of Union Sq Park there's a Whole Foods; further east there's a Trader Joe's for cheaper grocery fare.
- **Fifth Avenue** You'll find more upmarket chain stores heading up Fifth Ave, with Paul Smith, BCBG, Anthropologie, Zara and Intermix among the standouts.

⬎ OVERLOOKED NUGGETS

- **The Factory** (231 East 47th St) Andy Warhol's famous studio on Union Sq West now houses a Puma store.
- **Mohandas K Gandhi Statue** This beautiful likeness by Kantilal Patel stands in Union Sq Park.
- **NYC Manhole Covers** Lawrence Weiner's collection of 19 arty manhole covers south of Union Sq bears the phrase: 'In direct line with another and the next.'

⬎ FOOD ON THE GO

- **Burgers** Gourmet versions can be had at Shake Shack at the southern end of Madison Square Park.
- **Falafel** Three quick-serve restaurants and at least one food truck surround Union Sq Park.
- **Tacos** On any given day there are usually at least two trucks serving tacos and other Mexican fare.

⬎ DIVERSIONS

- **Yoga** Several well-known large studios are in the vicinity, and yoga is sometimes practiced in Union Sq Park.
- **See a movie** There's a behemoth of a cinema a block south of Union Sq Park and a smaller one on 19th and Broadway.
- **Street for shoes** Fourteenth St from Union Sq Park west is chock-a-block with stores.

RICHARD CUMMINS

Madison Square Park

DISCOVER UNION SQUARE, FLATIRON DISTRICT & GRAMERCY

This trio of east-side neighborhoods boasts lovely architecture, diverse public spaces and a smattering of offerings that are quite hip, but in a subtle, less frenzied way than, say, the Lower East Side or the Meatpacking District.

Union Sq was one of New York's first business districts, providing a convenient site for many workers' rallies and political protests throughout the mid-19th century. By the 1960s, junkies and gigolos took over, but were ushered out in the 1990s during a massive revival. Today, shops and eateries surround Union Sq Park, whose interior hops with activity.

To the northwest is the Flatiron District, loaded with loft buildings and boutiques, and doing a good imitation of SoHo without the pretensions, prices or crowds. The neighborhood takes its name from the Flatiron Building, a thin, gorgeous work of architecture that sits just south of Madison Square Park. The Gramercy area, loosely comprising the 20s blocks east of Park Ave South, is named after one of New York's loveliest parks.

SIGHTS

FLATIRON BUILDING

23rd St & Broadway; ⊕ F, M, N, R, 6 to 23rd St

Built in 1902, the 20-story Flatiron Building, designed by Daniel Burnham, has a uniquely narrow triangular footprint that resembles the prow of a massive ship, and a traditional Beaux Arts limestone facade, built over a steel frame, that gets more complex and beautiful the longer you stare at it. Best viewed from the traffic island north of 23rd St between Broadway and Fifth Ave, this unique structure dominated the plaza back in the skyscraper era of the early 1900s. Images of the Flatiron that were published before its official opening – many thanks to the fact that this was also the time of the first mass-produced picture postcards – aroused a buzz of curiosity around the globe. Publisher Frank Munsey was one of the building's first tenants, and from his 18th-floor offices his firm published *Munsey's Magazine,* which featured the writings of short-story writer O Henry ('The Gift of the Magi'). His musings, along with the paintings of John Sloan and photographs by Alfred Stieglitz, best immortalized the Flatiron back in the day – along with a famous comment by actress Katherine Hepburn, who said in a TV interview once that she'd like to be admired as much as the grand old building. Today it remains one of the most photographed architectural sites in New York.

MADISON SQUARE PARK

www.madisonsquarepark.org; 23rd to 26th Sts btwn Fifth & Madison Aves; ⊕ F, M, N, R, 6 to 23rd St

This park defined the northern reaches of Manhattan until its population exploded after the Civil War. It has enjoyed a rejuvenation in the past few years thanks to a renovation and re-dedication project.

Book and music stalls, Union Sq

ANGUS OBORN

⬎ UNION SQUARE

Town square for an eclectic crowd, this park hosts loungers and local workers catching some fresh air, throngs of young skateboarders doing tricks on the southeastern stairs and frequent antiwar or general antigovernment protestors. Opened in 1831, the park soon became the central gathering place for surrounding mansions and grand concert halls and eventually an explosion of high-end shops along Broadway, which became known as the Ladies' Mile. Then, from the start of the Civil War until well into the 20th century, this became the site for protests of all kinds – for everyone from union workers to political activists. By the time of WWI, the area had become neglected and depressed, but eventually was home to all sorts of working-class headquarters, including the American Civil Liberties Union, the Communist and Socialist Parties and the Ladies' Garment Workers Union. The 1960s ushered in an era of lounging hippiedom.

Its latest transformation has been that of a $20-million redesign that is going on in stages, bringing with it an expanded playground, additional landscaping with Japanese Pagoda trees, better lighting and new bathrooms. There will also be a new as-yet-to-be-named restaurant, to the chagrin of a local-resident organization, which filed suit to stop that project, claiming the space was better suited for community rather than for-profit use. It was dismissed, and now the development marches on.

It's all brought a lot of upheaval to the weekly greenmarket, which has been temporarily displaced to other corners of Union Sq, but which still remains one of the most popular farmers markets in the city.

Things you need to know: 14th to 17th Sts btwn Broadway & Park Ave S; Ⓜ L, N, Q, R, 4, 5, 6 to 14th St-Union Sq

Now locals unleash their dogs here in the popular dog-run area and workers enjoy lunches – which can be bought from the hip, on-site **Shake Shack** (☎ 212-889-6600; ⏰ 11am-11pm) – while perched on the shaded benches or sprawled on the wide lawn. These are perfect spots from which to gaze up at the landmarks that surround the park, including the **Flatiron Building** (p159) to the southwest, the art-deco **Metropolitan Life Insurance Tower** to the southeast and the **New York Life Insurance Building**, topped with a gilded spire, to the northeast. And, at the southeast corner of the park, you'll find one of the city's few self-cleaning, coin-operated toilets, which lets you do your business for only 25¢.

TIBET HOUSE
☎ 212-807-0563; www.tibethouse.org; 22 W 15th St btwn Fifth & Sixth Aves; $5 suggested donation; ⏰ noon-5pm Mon-Fri, by appointment Sat; ◉ F to 14th St, L to 6th Ave
With the Dalai Lama as the patron of its board, this nonprofit cultural space is dedicated to presenting Tibet's ancient traditions through art exhibits, a research library and various publications, while programs on offer include educational workshops, open meditations, retreat weekends and docent-led tours to Tibet, Nepal and Bhutan.

THEODORE ROOSEVELT'S BIRTHPLACE
☎ 212-260-1616; www.nps.gov/thrb; 28 E 20th St btwn Park Ave S & Broadway; adult/child $3/free; ⏰ 9am-5pm Tue-Sat; ◉ N, R, 6 to 23rd St
This National Historic Site is a bit of a cheat, since the physical house where the 26th president was actually born was demolished in his own lifetime. But this building is a worthy reconstruction by his

relatives, who joined it with another family residence next door. Included in the admission price are half-hour house tours, offered on the hour from 10am to 4pm.

NATIONAL ARTS CLUB
☎ 212-475-3424; www.nationalartsclub.org; 15 Gramercy Park South; ◉ 6 to 23rd St
This club, founded in 1898 to promote public interest in the arts, boasts a beautiful, vaulted, stained-glass ceiling above the wooden bar in its picture-lined front parlor. Calvert Vaux, who was one of the creators of Central Park, designed the building, and it was originally the private residence of Samuel J Tilden, governor of New York and failed presidential candidate in 1876. The club holds art exhibitions, ranging from sculpture to photography, that are sometimes open to the public from 1pm to 5pm (check the website for schedules). Other events include sketch classes, jazz lunches and French lessons.

SLEEPING

Even though Union Sq is a pretty bustling section of town, this often-overlooked region actually has an abundance of upscale, quiet and romantic hotel options. Full of inns and opulent boutique hotels, the leafy, residential streets in close proximity (walking distance) to both Midtown and East Village attractions will make you feel at home.

W NEW YORK – UNION SQUARE
Classy Chain Hotel $$$
☎ 212-253-9119, 888-625-5144; www.whotels.com; 201 Park Ave S at 17th St; r $389; ◉ L, N, Q, R, 4, 5, 6 to 14th St-Union Sq; 🖳 💻
The ultra-hip W demands a black wardrobe and credit card. The standard rooms aren't big but – set in a 1911 one-time insurance building – benefit from high

ceilings, and are decked out with all the modern bells and whistles (flat-screen TVs, iPod docks, wi-fi and so on). If rooms here are sold out, investigate W's other Manhattan hotels.

INN AT IRVING PLACE B&B $$$

☎ 212-533-4600, 800-685-1447; www.innat irving.com; 56 Irving Pl btwn 17th & 18th Sts; r $379; ◎ L, N, Q, R, 4, 5, 6 to 14th St-Union Sq; 🚣 💻

Richly Victorian, this intimate and exquisite 11-room red-brick town house dates from 1834 and is stuffed with period pieces and rosy patterns of days past. The spacious rooms have massive four-poster beds, plump easy chairs, cozy sofas and handsome armoires set atop dark-wood floors.

GRAMERCY PARK HOTEL
Indie Boutique Hotel $$$

☎ 212-475-4320; www.gramercyparkhotel.com; 2 Lexington Ave at 21st St; r from $350; ◎ 6 to 23rd St; 🚣 💻

Formerly a grand old dame, the Gramercy's had a major facelift and emerged looking young and sexy. Dark wood paneling and red suede rugs and chairs greet you in the lobby, while the rooms – overlooking nearby Gramercy Park – have customized oak furnishings, 400-count Italian linens and big, feather-stuffed mattresses on sprawling beds. Be sure to visit the celebrity-studded Rose and Jade bars, the guest-only rooftop terrace and Maialino, the on-site rustic Italian eatery run by Danny Meyer.

WYNDHAM GARDEN Hotel $$

☎ 212-243-0800; www.wyndham.com; 37 W 24th St btwn Fifth & Sixth Aves; r $159-269; ◎ 4, 5, 6, N, R to 14th St; 🚣 💻

Nearly equal distance between Chelsea and Union Square, the Wyndham's color-ful checked entrance fits in with the surrounding, unique neighborhoods. The whimsy disappears once you're inside – it's beige walls, taupe carpet and plain work stations, are what you'd expect from a chain hotel (but one that caters to business folk). Still, it's a fantastic location, and the rooms are as clean as a whistle.

CHELSEA INN B&B $

☎ 212-645-8989, 800-640-6469; www.chelsea inn.com; 46 W 17th St btwn Fifth & Sixth Aves; s $89-289; ◎ F, M, L to 6th Ave-14th St; 🚣

Made up of two adjoining 19th-century town houses, this funky hide-away (a four-story walk-up) has small but comfortable rooms that look like they were furnished entirely from flea markets or grandma's attic. It's character on a budget, just a bit east of the most desirable part of its namesake 'hood. Most of the rooms have private bathrooms; the two rooms that go for the lowest prices share facilities.

HOTEL 17 Budget Hotel $

☎ 212-475-2845; www.hotel17ny.com; 225 E 17th St btwn Second & Third Aves; r $89-150; ◎ L to 3rd Ave, N, Q, R, 4, 5, 6 to 14th St-Union Sq; 🚣

Right off Stuyvesant Sq on a leafy residential block, this popular eight-floor town house has old New York charm with cheap prices. Only four of the 120 rooms have private bathrooms (all are free of the film's dead bodies). Rooms are small with basic furnishings (gray carpet, striped wallpaper, chintzy bedspreads, burgundy blinds) and lack natural light.

EATING

One precious perk is the **Union Square greenmarket** (a sprawling sensory delight held Monday, Wednesday, Friday and Saturday), when discerning chefs

Chelsea Inn

both pro and amateur scour the wares of upstate farmers and get inspired for their next meals. Madison Square Park is host to the mega-popular, alfresco **Shake Shack** (p161), with foodie-focused burgers and the like. Lexington Ave in the high 20s is known as Curry Hill, thanks to its preponderance of spots serving South Indian fare.

GRAMERCY TAVERN
American Creative $$$

☎ 212-477-0777; 42 E 20th St btwn Broadway & Park Ave S; 🕑 lunch & dinner; ◉ 6 to 23rd St

Though superstar chef Tom Colicchio (who put this legendary spot on the foodie map) recently passed the torch, Michael Anthony was the capable guy who grabbed it. And so the country-chic restaurant, aglow with copper sconces, bright murals and dramatic floral arrangements, is still in the spotlight – perhaps more than ever. That's thanks to the lighter fish-and-vegetable menu that has replaced what was meat-heavy and hearty.

PURE FOOD & WINE
Raw-Food Vegetarian $$$

☎ 212-477-1010; 54 Irving Pl btwn 17th & 18th Sts; 🕑 dinner; ◉ L, N, Q, R, 4, 5, 6 to 14th St-Union Sq

The 'chef' (there's no oven in the kitchen) at this gem achieves the impossible, churning out not just edible but extremely delicious and artful concoctions, made completely from raw organics that are put through blenders, dehydrators and the capable hands of Pure's staff. The dining room is sleek and festive, but in warmer months don't miss a chance to settle into a table in the shady oasis of the backyard.

CRAFT
American Creative $$$

☎ 212-780-0880; 43 E 19th at Park Ave S; 🕑 dinner; ◉ L, N, Q, R, 4, 5, 6 to 14th St-Union Sq

When superchef Tom Colicchio opened this fine-food palace in a sweeping architectural space several years ago, the concept was completely new: create your own meal with à la carte items, and enjoy the feeling that not a plate on your table

Pure Food & Wine (p163)

DAN HERRICK

was cookie-cutter. Copycats sprang up around town, but this spot still reigns as items change seasonally and are always finely prepared. If you can't decide, you can always go for the tasting menu: a seven-course feast paired with wines.

BAOGUETTE   Eclectic Bánh Mì $
☎ 212-518-4089; 61 Lexington Ave at 25th St; ⊗ 8am-8pm Mon-Sat; ◉ 6 to 23rd St
Part of the current *bánh mì* (Vietnamese sandwich) obsession is this little joint, which puts its own spin on what is traditionally a stack of smoked, sliced pork piled high with fresh cucumbers, pickled carrots and hot sauce on a baguette. You can get that here – along with catfish, barbecued chicken and the odd option of spicy red curried corned beef with hot peppers.

HILL COUNTRY   Texan BBQ $$
☎ 212-255-4544; 30 W 26th btwn Broadway & Sixth Ave; ⊗ lunch & dinner; ◉ N, R to 28th St
City slickers have been going gaga for good ol'-fashioned BBQ for a while now,

finally able to tell the difference between smoked meats of the Carolinas, Mississippi and various other Southern states. Here it's all about the sausage, fatty brisket, beef shoulder and pork ribs cooked in the Texas style (the Hill Country is a country area between Austin and San Antonio), plus an array of imaginative side dishes including smoky deviled eggs, baked beans braised with beer and penne with three cheeses.

DRINKING

OLD TOWN BAR & RESTAURANT
Old-Time Bar
☎ 212-529-6732; 45 E 18th St; ◉ L, N, Q, R, 4, 5, 6 to 14th St-Union Sq
It still looks like 1892 in here, with the original tile floors and tin ceilings – the Old Town is an 'old world' drinking-man's classic (and woman's: Madonna lit up at the bar here, when lighting up was still legal, in her *Bad Girl* video). There are cocktails around, but most people come

for an afternoon beer and burger ($10.25), both very good.

PETE'S TAVERN
Old-Time Bar

☎ 212-473-7676; 129 E 18th St at Irving Pl; ⊕ L, N, Q, R, 4, 5, 6 to 14th St-Union Sq

Around since 1864, this dark and atmospheric watering hole is a New York classic – all pressed tin and carved wood and an air of literary history. You can get a respectable burger here, plus choose from more than 15 draft beers. The crowd draws a mix of post-theater couples, Irish expats and no-nonsense NYU students.

ENTERTAINMENT & ACTIVITIES

FILLMORE AT IRVING PLAZA
Rock & Indie

☎ 212-777-6800; www.livenation.com; 17 Irving Pl at 15th St; ⊕ L, N, Q, R, 4, 5, 6 to 14th St-Union Sq

A great in-between stage for quirky mainstream acts – from Cat Power to a reunited Animals – the Fillmore is nominally linked with San Francisco's famed Fill. There's a cozy floor around the stage, and good views from the mezzanine.

SHOPPING

There's plenty of shopping to be had in this big block of neighborhoods. First and foremost is Union Sq, home to a delightful **greenmarket**, which hits the park several times a week all year round. Meanwhile, huge chain stores flank the park to the north and south, offering books, discount fashion and music.

STRAND BOOK STORE
Books

☎ 212-473-1452; 828 Broadway at 12th St; ⊕ 9:30am-10:30pm Mon-Sat, 11am-10:30pm Sun; ⊕ L, N, Q, R, 4, 5, 6 to 14th St-Union Sq

Book fiends (or even those who have casually skimmed a few) shouldn't miss this bookstore, selling new, used and rare titles. Operating since

MICHELLE BENNETT

Books galore in NYC

⤷ IF YOU LIKE...

If you like stocking up on reading material at the **Strand Book Store**, we think you'll enjoy these other book stores:

- **Barnes & Noble** (☎ 212-253-0810; www.bn.com; 33 E 17th St; ⊕ 10am-10pm; ⊕ L, N, Q, R, 4, 5, 6 to 14th St-Union Sq) With a dozen locations in NYC (visit the website for more), this heavy-hitter superstore is a massive space, with four floors of books and magazines.
- **Books of Wonder** (☎ 212-989-3270; 18 W 18th St; ⊕ 10am-7pm Mon-Sat, 11am-6pm Sun; ⊕ F, M, L to 6th Ave-14th St) Small, fun-loving bookstore devoted to children's and young-adult titles.
- **Idlewild Books** (☎ 212-414-8888; www.idlewildbooks.com; 12 W 19th St; ⊕ 11:30am-8pm Mon-Fri, noon-7pm Sat & Sun; ⊕ L, N, Q, R, 4, 5, 6 to 14th St-Union Sq) Divided into regions of the world; includes guidebooks, fiction, travelogues, history, cookbooks and other stimulating fare.

1927, the Strand is New York's most famous bookstore, with an incredible 18 miles of books (more than 2.5 million of them), spread over three floors.

FILENE'S BASEMENT
Discount Department Store

☎ 212-358-0169; 4 Union Sq S; ⊙ 9am-10pm Mon-Sat, 11am-8pm Sun; ⊕ L, N, Q, R, 4, 5, 6 to 14th St-Union Sq

This outpost of the Boston-based chain is not actually in a basement but three flights up, with a tremendous view of Union Sq. The best stuff to see is inside, though, where you will find labels for up to 70% less than the price at regular retail outlets. Like similar discount department stores, it's got clothing, shoes, jewelry, accessories, cosmetics and some housewares (such as bedding).

WHOLE FOODS
Gourmet Supermarket

☎ 212-673-5388; 4 Union Sq S; ⊙ 8am-11pm; ⊕ L, N, Q, R, 4, 5, 6 to 14th St-Union Sq

One of several locations of the healthy food chain that is sweeping the city, this is an overwhelming spot to shop for a picnic. Find endless rows of gorgeous produce, both organic and conventional, plus a butcher, a bakery, a health and beauty section, and aisles packed with natural packaged goods.

ACADEMY RECORDS
Music

☎ 212-242-3000; 12 W 18th St; ⊙ 11am-7pm; ⊕ F, M, L to 6th Ave-14th St

This tiny music shop brings in the crowds for its excellent selection of new and used CDs. There's an astounding classical selection on vinyl, while LP collectors of other genres should visit the East Village store (p126).

PARAGON ATHLETIC GOODS
Sporting Goods

☎ 212-255-8889; 867 Broadway; ⊙ 10am-8pm Mon-Sat, 11am-7pm Sun; ⊕ L, N, Q, R, 4, 5, 6 to 14th St-Union Sq

A mazelike, windowless behemoth, Paragon offers a comprehensive collection of sports merchandise featuring basketballs, tennis rackets, hiking gear, swim goggles, ski poles, baseball bats, all sorts of sneakers and apparel – you name it.

MIDTOWN

MIDTOWN

INFORMATION	
Australian Consulate	**1** G4
Circle Line Boat Tours	**2** B4
German Consulate	**3** H3
New York General Post Office	**4** D5
SATH	**5** F5
UK Consulate	**6** G2

SIGHTS	
Chrysler Building	**7** G4
Empire State Building	**8** F5
Grand Central Terminal	**9** G4
Herald Square	**10** E5
Intrepid Sea, Air & Space Museum	**11** B3
Japan Society	**12** H3
Little Korea	**13** F5
Museum of Arts & Design	**14** D1
Museum of Sex	**15** F6
St Patrick's Cathedral	**16** F2
United Nations Visitors' Entrance	**17** H3

SLEEPING	
414 Hotel	**18** C3
6 Columbus	**19** D1
70 Park Avenue Hotel	**20** G4
Dream	**21** E2
Four Seasons	**22** F1
Hotel Metro	**23** F5
Kitano	**24** G4
Murray Hill Inn	**25** G6
Pierre	**26** F1
Ritz-Carlton - New York, Central Park	**27** E1
Strand	**28** F5
Waldorf-Astoria	**29** G3

EATING	
Blue Smoke	**30** G6
Brasserie	**31** G2
Chennai Garden	**32** G6
Convivio	**33** H4
Hangawi	**34** F5
Russian Tea Room	**35** E1
Sparks	**36** G3

DRINKING	
Bar-Tini Ultra Lounge	**37** C3
Campbell Apartment	**38** G4
Club 57	**39** D1
Ginger Man	**40** F5
King Cole Bar	**41** F2
MOBAR	**42** D1
Tillman's	**43** E6
Top of the Tower	**44** H3

ENTERTAINMENT & ACTVITIES	
Carnegie Hall	**45** E1
Central Park Bicycle Tours & Rentals	**46** E1
Clearview's Ziegfeld Theater	**47** E2
Hammerstein Ballroom	**48** D5
Jazz Standard	(see 30)
Madison Square Garden	**49** D5
New York City Center	**50** E2
Pacha	**51** B3
Playwrights Horizons	**52** C4
Rodeo Bar & Grill	**53** G6
Scandinavia House	**54** G5

SHOPPING	
B&H Photo-Video	**55** D5
Barneys	**56** F1
Bergdorf Goodman	**57** F1
Bloomingdale's	**58** G1
Clothingline/SSS Sample Sales	**59** D5
Complete Traveller Antiquarian Bookstore	**60** F5
Dylan's Candy Bar	**61** G1
FAO Schwartz	**62** F1
H&M	**63** E5
Henri Bendel	**64** F2
Lord & Taylor	**65** F4
Macy's	**66** E5
Rizzoli	**67** F1
Saks Fifth Avenue	**68** F3
Shops at Columbus Circle	(see 42)
Takashimaya	**69** F2
Tiffany & Co	**70** F1

TRANSPORT	
New York Water Taxi W 44th St Landing	**71** B4
Penn Station	**72** E5
Transportation Alternatives	**73** E6

See Greenwich Village, Chelsea & the Meatpacking District Map p128

MIDTOWN

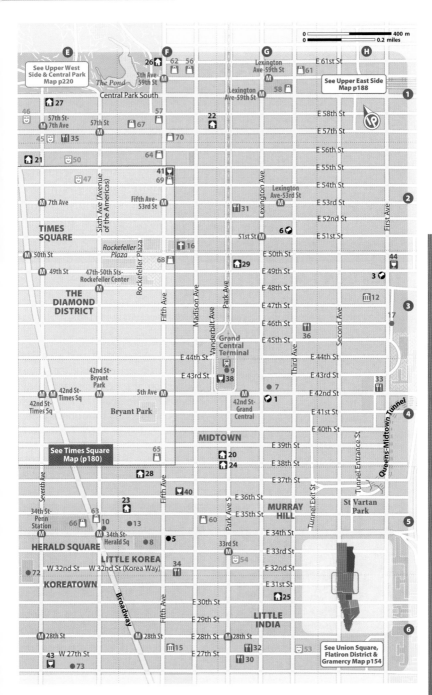

MIDTOWN

HIGHLIGHTS

1 | TIMES SQUARE

Smack in the middle of Midtown Manhattan, this area around the intersection of Broadway and Seventh Ave has become so intertwined with NYC in the minds of non–New Yorkers (think gaudy billboards and glittery marquees) that regardless of how Disneyfied it has become, it's still considered quintessential New York. Better-known in the 1970s for its seedy strip clubs, hookers and pick pockets, the square today is once again the 'Crossroads of the World,' and draws 27 million visitors annually.

HIGHLIGHTS

⇖ OUR DON'T MISS LIST

❶ BROADWAY THEATER
Times Sq is home to New York's Theater District, with dozens of Broadway and off-Broadway theaters located in an area that stretches from 41st to 54th Sts between Sixth and Ninth Aves. As well as the money-making revivals, musicals such as *In the Heights* and *Spring Awakening,* and dramas including *August: Osage County* and *Race,* attract large mobs: walking through the area just before showtime can be a challenge. Evening performances begin at 8pm; Wednesday and weekend matinees start at 2pm.

❷ MUSIC HISTORY
This is where post–Civil War vaudeville exploded, spurred on by 'Tin Pan Alley,' a collection of songwriters and music publishers who changed music with their contributions to ragtime blues, show tunes, folk and jazz. The historic Colony (Map p180), located in the Brill Building, once sold sheet music to the likes of Charlie Parker and Miles Davis.

Clockwise from top: Times Sq neon; Rudy's Music Stop; New York Marriott Marquis; Times Sq at night; Signs at Times Sq

CLOCKWISE FROM TOP: RICHARD CUMMINS; ADAM SLINGER/ALAMY; MICHELLE BENNETT; JEAN-PIERRE LESCOURRET; EPI/IMAGE BROKER

Its collection remains the city's largest. The stretch of 48th St just off Times Sq used to be known as Music Row and it's where Benny Goodman, the Beatles, Jimi Hendrix, the Stones, the Who, Bob Dylan and countless other musical legends paid a visit for the latest acoustic essentials. Today **Rudy's Music Stop** (Map p180) is one of the last vestiges of this venerable block.

❸ RETAIL THERAPY
Most of the stores around Times Sq are megasized and themed (M&Ms and MTV), and massive chains, including Sephora, Skechers and Cold Stone Creamery, take up much of the real estate. But you can still find kitschy souvenir shops, pretzel vendors and caricature artists out on the streets.

❹ REVOLVING ROOFTOP
Hop in one of the express elevators to the 48th floor of the **New York Marriott Marquis** for 360-degree views of the city and New Jersey across the Hudson. And you don't even have to turn your head.

⭲ THINGS YOU NEED TO KNOW

New development Broadway from 47th to 42nd St is a vehicle-free zone. Grab one of the public chairs for a rest. **Back-up plan** If you can't score theater tickets, head to the Stardust Diner, where talented hopefuls belt out show tunes while serving food **For more on Times Square, see p179.**

HIGHLIGHTS

MIDTOWN

HIGHLIGHTS

The Museum of Modern Art

◥ MUSEUM OF MODERN ART

The **Museum of Modern Art** (MoMA, p182) is a gleaming gem. It's easy to spend a day here, starting at the top and strolling downward from floor to floor, and chronologically through the major art movements of the 20th century. Floors four and five are MoMA's intro to modern art, with Picassos, Matisses, Dalis, Mondrians, Pollocks, de Koonings and a few Marcel Duchamp originals.

◥ ROCKEFELLER CENTER

A ritzy enclave full of media companies and wine bars, **Rockefeller Center** (p180) also doubles as a public art plaza. Prometheus overlooks the famous skating rink; there's an Atlas Carrying the World on Fifth Ave; and the aptly named News, an installation by Isamu Noguchi, sits not far from NBC studios. Inside, you can zip up to its observation deck, **Top of the Rock** (p181), for views into Central Park.

⌞ SKYLINE

No matter where you are in the city, the **Empire State Building's** (p177) jutting silhouette is the perfect landmark. Its legendary observation decks, although encased in safety wire, are not for the faint of heart. Just east of Grand Central Terminal, the **Chrysler Building** (p175), an art deco masterpiece, is magnificent when viewed from a distance.

⌞ CULINARY TOUR

While Midtown isn't generally considered a foodie destination, the area has its fair share of quality eating options. **Little Korea** (p177) has loads of restaurants, while **Little India** (on Lexington between 27th and 30th) features South Indian fare. **Hell's Kitchen** (along Ninth Ave) has a huge range of restaurants with cuisines from all over the world.

⌞ WORLD'S GREATEST SPORTS ARENA

Typical of New York braggadocio and despite the local teams recent travails, **Madison Square Garden** is still known by this moniker. Most famously home to the NBA's New York Knicks (p194), as well as the New York Rangers hockey team, catching a game here is a chance to immerse yourself in the city's passionate sports culture.

MIDTOWN

HIGHLIGHTS

2 RICHARD CUMMINS; 3 MARK DAFFEY; 4 GAVIN GOUGH; 5 DAN HERRICK; 6 COREY WISE

2 Museum of Modern Art (p182); 3 Rockefeller Center (p180); 4 Empire State Building (p177); 5 Restaurants in Hell's Kitchen; 6 Madison Square Garden

MIDTOWN

BEST...

BEST...

⬃ LONG-RUNNING BROADWAY MUSICALS

- **Hair** Revival of the rock-driven 1968 musical.
- **Lion King** Disney musical with magical story about kings, with an African-beat score.
- **Chicago** Classic musical about a showgirl and the sordid goings-on of the Chicago underworld.
- **Mamma Mia!** Musical revue based on hits of the 1970s supergroup Abba.

⬃ TV TAPINGS

- **Saturday Night Live** Most popular, longest-running NYC-based sketch comedy show.
- **The Daily Show with John Stewart** Influential, satiric look at the day's headlines.
- **Late Show With David Letterman** Talk show with celebrity guests.

⬃ DRINKS WITH VIEWS

- **Ava** (p188) Rooftop hangout in the Dream Hotel.
- **Top of the Tower** (p192) Date turf in Midtown Beekman Tower's rooftop bar.
- **Mobar** (p172) The Mandarin Hotel's upper-floor perch with similarly elevated drink prices.
- **Dizzy's Club Coca Cola** High-quality music and Central Park vistas are an unbeatable combination.

⬃ SPOTS FOR CROWD WATCHING

- **Broadway between 42nd & 47th Streets** Closed-off pedestrian areas allow you to gawk without danger.
- **Grand Central Terminal** (p176) Focus on the clock at the center of the terminal as commuters race for their train.

RICHARD CUMMINS

DISCOVER MIDTOWN

This is, in some ways, the heart of Manhattan – the New York most outsiders thrill over in films or daydream about before they ever set foot in the city. It's classic NYC, home to Broadway and larger-than-life billboards, seas of taxis and crushing crowds, skyscraping icons and an inimitable, frenzied energy.

Midtown West is a general term that refers to any part of Midtown (between 34th and 59th Sts) that lies west of Fifth Ave (the east–west dividing line). Its collection of neighborhoods includes the trendy far-west reaches of Hell's Kitchen, the office-worker crush of harried suit-wearers along Sixth Ave, the bustle of Times Sq, and Columbus Circle, located at the southwest corner of Central Park.

From the sophisticated shops of storied Fifth Ave to a handful of iconic sights, Midtown East is the quieter side of Manhattan's full belly. It's where you'll find the Chrysler Building, the UN Building, St Patrick's Cathedral and the Beaux Arts–style Grand Central train station – plus iconic stores such as Tiffany & Co and Saks Fifth Avenue.

SIGHTS

CHRYSLER BUILDING Map p168
Lexington Ave at 42nd St; ⊚ S, 4, 5, 6, 7 to Grand Central-42nd St

An art deco masterpiece designed by William Van Alen in 1930, this 1048ft-high skyscraper, just across the avenue from Grand Central Terminal, has been widely named since its opening as a favorite work of architecture by laypeople and aficionados alike. The building, constructed to be the headquarters for Walter P Chrysler and his automobile empire, reigned briefly as the tallest structure in the world until superseded by the Empire State Building a few months later. Fittingly, the facade's design celebrates car culture, with gargoyles that resemble hood ornaments, radiator caps and thatched-steel designs, all best viewed with binoculars.

The Chrysler Building has no restaurant or observation deck, but is filled with unexciting offices for lawyers and accountants. Still, it's worth wandering into the lobby to admire the elaborately veneered elevators and the profusion of marble, plus the ceiling mural (purportedly the world's largest at 97ft by 100ft) depicting the promise of industry. But even at a distance, there are few more poignant symbols of New York than the Chrysler Building lit up at night.

FIFTH AVENUE & MIDTOWN EAST

UNITED NATIONS Map p168
☎ 212-963-8687; www.un.org/tours; First Ave btwn 42nd & 48th Sts; adult/child/student & senior $16/9/11; ◷ 9:45am-4:45pm Mon-Fri; ⊚ S, 4, 5, 6, 7 to Grand Central-42nd St

Welcome to the headquarters of the UN, a worldwide organization that oversees international law, international security and human rights. The building is located on a patch of technically international territory, overlooking the East River. Take a guided tour of the facility and you'll get

MIDTOWN

LOU JONES

Grand Central Terminal

SIGHTS

GRAND CENTRAL TERMINAL

Completed in 1913, Grand Central Terminal – more commonly, if technically incorrectly, called Grand Central Station – is another of New York's stunning Beaux Arts buildings, boasting 75ft-high, glass-encased catwalks and a vaulted ceiling bearing a mural of the constellations streaming across it – backwards (the designer must've been dyslexic). The balconies overlooking the main concourse afford an expansive view; perch yourself on one of these at around 5pm on a weekday to get a glimpse of the grace that this terminal commands under pressure.

There are no teary good-byes for people traveling across the country from here today, though, as Grand Central's underground electric tracks serve only commuter trains en route to northern suburbs and Connecticut. But whether you're traveling somewhere or not, the station merits a special trip for the architecture alone – not to mention for the fine-dining restaurants and gourmet food court, cool bars, funky shops, holiday craft fairs and occasional music performances.

The Grand Central Partnership leads free tours of both the terminal and the surrounding neighborhood on Fridays at 12:30pm.

Things you need to know: Grand Central Partnership (www.grandcentralpartnership.com); Grand Central Terminal (Map p168; www.grandcentralterminal.com; 42nd St at Park Ave; ⊕ S, 4, 5, 6, 7 to Grand Central-42nd St)

to see the General Assembly, where the annual convocation of member nations takes place every fall; the Security Council Chamber, where crisis management continues year-round; and the Economic & Social Council Chamber. There is a serene park to the north of the complex, which is home to Henry Moore's *Reclining Figure* as well as several other sculptures with a peace theme.

English-language tours of the UN complex depart every 30 minutes; limited tours in several other languages are also available. (The visitors' entrance is at 46th St.)

LITTLE KOREA Map p168

btwn 31st & 36th Sts & Broadway & Fifth Ave;
Ⓔ B, D, F, M, N, Q, R to 34th St-Herald Sq

You'll be spoiled for choice when it comes to eateries serving Korean fare, with authentic BBQ available around the clock at many of the all-night spots on 32nd St, some with the added treat of karaoke.

EMPIRE STATE BUILDING Map p168

☎ 212-736-3100; www.esbnyc.com; 350 Fifth Ave at 34th St; adult/child/senior & student $19/13/17; ⏱ 8:30am-2am, last elevator up at 1:15am; Ⓔ B, D, F, M, N, Q, R to 34th St-Herald Sq, 6 to 33rd St

Featured prominently in almost a hundred Hollywood films over the years, the Empire State Building – actually a very glorified office building – is the most famous member of the New York skyline. It's a limestone classic built in just 410 days (using seven million hours of labor) during the Great Depression, at the astounding cost of $41 million. Located on the site of the original Waldorf-Astoria Hotel, the 102-story, 1472ft-high (to the top of the antenna) building opened in 1931 after the laying of 10 million bricks, the installation of 6400 windows and the setting of 328,000 sq ft of marble. The famous antenna was originally meant to be a mooring mast for zeppelins, but the *Hindenberg* disaster slammed the brakes on that plan. Later an aircraft did (accidentally) meet up with the building: a B-25 bomber crashed into the 79th floor on a foggy day in 1945, killing 14 people.

The view of the vast city from the Empire State Building is just exquisite, but be prepared – the lines to get to the observation decks, found on the 86th and 102nd floors, are notorious. And the basement area where you must buy tickets and queue up for the elevator ride is a shabby, poorly ventilated waiting pen, especially in summer. Getting here very

United Nations headquarters (p175)

GREG GAWLOWSKI

MIDTOWN

SIGHTS

MIDTOWN

SIGHTS

New York Public Library

RICHARD CUMMINS

early or very late will help you avoid delays – as will buying your tickets ahead of time, online, where an extra $2 purchase charge is well worth the hassle it will save you. Sunset is one of the most magical times to be up here because you can see the city don its nighttime cloak in dusk's afterglow.

NEW YORK PUBLIC LIBRARY
Map p180

☎ 212-930-0830; www.nypl.org; Fifth Ave at 42nd St; ⏰ 11am-6pm Mon, to 7:30pm Tue & Wed, 10am-6pm Thu-Sat, 1-5pm Sun; ⊕ B, D, F, M to 42nd St-Bryant Park, 7 to Fifth Ave
When it was dedicated in 1911, New York's flagship library ranked as the largest marble structure ever built in the US, with a vast, 3rd-floor reading room designed to hold 500 patrons – not to mention the famous marble lions ('Patience' and 'Fortitude') at the entrance, profligate use of gold leaf throughout, chandeliers, carved porticoes and ceiling murals. On a rainy day, hide away with a book in the airy Reading Room and admire the

original Carre-and-Hastings lamps, or stroll through the Exhibition Hall, which contains precious manuscripts by just about every author of note in the English language, including an original copy of the Declaration of Independence and a Gutenberg Bible. The free **guided tour** (⏰ 11am & 2pm Mon-Sat, 2pm Sun) is a bonanza of interesting tidbits; it leaves from the information desk in Astor Hall.

PALEY CENTER FOR MEDIA Map p180

☎ 212-621-6800; www.paleycenter.org; 25 W 52nd St btwn Fifth & Sixth Aves; adult/child/ senior & student $10/5/8; ⏰ noon-6pm Wed & Fri-Sun, to 8pm Thu; ⊕ E, M to Fifth Ave-53rd St
Formerly called the Museum of Television and Radio, the institution changed its name both to honor its founder, William S Paley, and to reflect both its changing mission and collection in this day of shifting media forms. But it's still a couch potato's smorgasbord, with more than 150,000 TV and radio programs from around the world available from the museum's computer catalog with the click of a mouse.

ST PATRICK'S CATHEDRAL Map p168

☎ 212-753-2261; www.saintpatrickscathedral.
org; Fifth Ave btwn 50th & 51st Sts; ⊙ 6am-
9pm; ⊚ B, D, F, M to 47th-50th Sts–Rockefeller
Center

The largest Gothic-style Catholic cathedral in the country, this is the seat of the Archbishop of New York, the staunchly conservative Timothy Dolan, and the place that's been largely recognized as the center of Catholic life in the United States – drawing a steady stream of both revelers and protesters alike. Although it seats a modest 2400 worshippers, most of New York's 2.2 million faithful will have been inside at one time or another.

Know that St Patrick's is not a place for truly restful, spiritual contemplation because of the constant buzz from loud, videorecording and generally disrespectful visitors. Also, while frequent masses take place on the weekend, with New York's archbishop presiding over the Sunday service at 10:15am (which also includes music from the church choir), casual visitors are allowed in only between services (which are also held at 7am, 8am, 9am, noon, 1pm, 5:30pm and, in Spanish, at 4pm) – so dress up and plan on staying for the long haul if you're interested.

MIDTOWN WEST & TIMES SQUARE

TIMES SQUARE Map p180

☎ 212-869-5667; www.timessquarenyc.org; 1560 Broadway btwn 46th & 47th Sts; ⊙ 8am-8pm; ⊚ N, Q, R, S, 1, 2, 3, 7 to Times Sq-42nd St),

Spiffed up Times Sq, whose name once evoked images of drug peddlers, porn theaters and various other dregs of society, has for a while been an utterly safe and clean tourist area, bursting at the seams with massive chain stores, famed Broadway theaters and the gaudy billboards and marquees that this area

has long been synonymous with. With more than 60 mega-billboards and 40 miles of neon, it's startling how it always looks like daytime here. Once called Longacre Sq, Times Sq took its present name from the famous *New York Times* newspaper, whose headquarters are still located nearby, albeit now in a sparkly new tower just across Eighth Ave from the Port Authority bus terminal.

Unless there's a specific show you're after, the best – and most affordable – way to score tickets is at the **TKTS Booth** (Map p168; ☎ 212-768-1818; www.tdf.org/tkts; ⊙ 3-8pm Mon-Sat, 11am-8pm Sun), where you can line up and get same-day half-price tickets for top Broadway and off-Broadway shows at the recently renovated location in **Duffy Square** (Broadway at 47th St).

St Patrick's Cathedral

LOU JONES

MIDTOWN

SIGHTS

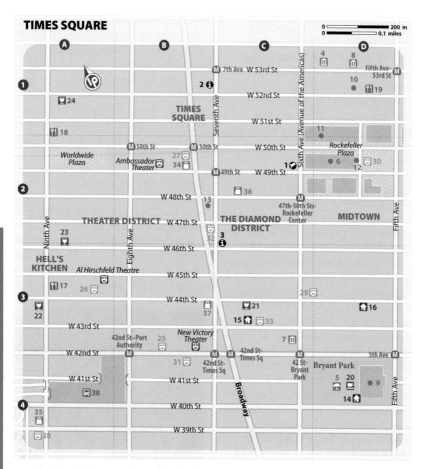

TIMES SQUARE

ROCKEFELLER CENTER Map p180
☎ 212-632-3975; www.rockefellercenter.com;
from Fifth to Seventh Aves & 48th to 51st Sts;
ⓢ B, D, F, M to 47th-50th Sts–Rockefeller Center
Built during the height of the Great
Depression in the 1930s, the 22-acre
Rockefeller Center, named after developer
John D Rockefeller, Jr, was the first project
to combine retail, entertainment and office space in what is often referred to as a
'city within a city.' Built over nine years by
70,000 workers, this complex features several outdoor plazas and 19 buildings (14 of
which are the original art deco structures),

and spans from 48th to 51st Sts and Fifth
to Seventh Aves. Most popular highlights
include **Radio City Music Hall** (p183), the
GE Building (Map p180; 30 Rockefeller Plaza at
49th St), the **ice-skating plaza** and the **Top
of the Rock** (p181) observation deck.

Perhaps most impressive, though, is the
slew of public artwork – commissioned
around the theme 'Man at the Crossroads
Looks Uncertainly but Hopefully at the
Future' – created by 30 great artists of
the day.

Possibly the best-known feature of
Rockefeller Center is its gigantic Christmas

MIDTOWN

SIGHTS

tree, which overlooks the skating rink during the holidays. Today the annual lighting of the tree, held after Thanksgiving, attracts thousands of visitors to the area to cram around the felled spruce, selected each year with fanfare from an unlucky upstate forest.

NBC STUDIOS Map p180

☎ 212-664-3700; www.nbcuniversalstore.com; 30 Rockefeller Plaza at 49th St; tours adult/ senior & 6-16 yr $19.25/16.25 (under 6yr not admitted); ⏰ tours 8:30am-5:30pm Mon-Sat, to 4:30pm Sun; ◉ B, D, F, M to 47th-50th Sts–Rockefeller Center, E, M to Fifth Ave-53rd St

The NBC TV network has its headquarters in the 70-story GE Building that looms over the Rockefeller Center ice-skating rink (which is transformed into a cafe in the summer months). The *Today* show broadcasts live, 7am to 10am daily, from a glass-enclosed, street-level studio near the fountain, drawing plenty of admirers below who thrill over waving to and hamming it up for the camera. You're free to join them – or instead opt for a tour of the NBC studios, which leaves from inside the NBC Experience Store every half- hour (every 15 minutes on weekends); the walkabout lasts for about one hour and 10 minutes, but be

advised that there is a strict policy of 'no bathrooms,' so be sure to empty your bladder beforehand! Call ☎ 212-664-6298 to make a reservation.

TOP OF THE ROCK Map p180

☎ 212-698-2000; www.topoftherocknyc.com; 30 Rockefeller Plaza at 49th St; adult/child/ senior $21/14/19; ⏰ 8:30am-midnight; ◉ B, D, F, M to 47th-50th Sts–Rockefeller Center, E, M to Fifth Ave-53rd St

This open-air observation deck at the top of Rockefeller Center first wowed New Yorkers back in 1933. Designed in homage to ocean liners popular in the day, it was an incredible place – 70 stories above Midtown – from which to view the city. But it became off-limits for almost two decades starting in 1986, when renovation of the stunning Rainbow Room restaurant five floors below cut off access to the roof. The observation deck was reopened with much fanfare in 2005, and since then it's been proving to be an even better bet than the Empire State Building: it's much less crowded and has wider observation decks that span several levels – some are indoors, some are outside with Plexiglass walls and those at the very top are completely alfresco.

MIDTOWN

COREY WISE

Museum of Modern Art

SIGHTS

⬎ MUSEUM OF MODERN ART

Founded in 1929, the **Museum of Modern Art** (MoMA) is one of NYC's most popular museums, home to more than 100,000 pieces of modern artwork, most by heavy hitters – Matisse, Picasso, Cezanne, Rothko, Pollock and many others. It's dedicated to showcasing artwork based on the emerging creative ideas of the late 19th century through to those that dominate today. Also, the museum's cinema hosts a rich film program, with rotating screenings from its collection of more than 19,000 films, including the works of the Maysles Brothers and every Pixar animation film ever produced.

Since its grand reopening in 2004, following the most extensive renovation project in its 75-year history, the Museum of Modern Art has been widely hailed for its physical design, with a central, five-story atrium housing peaceful, airy galleries with works in areas such as painting, sculpture, architecture and design, and including drawings, prints, illustrated books, and film and media. The reconstruction, by architect Yoshio Taniguchi, doubled the museum's capacity and restored its tranquil sculpture garden to the original, larger vision of Philip Johnson's 1950s design. You can look over this area as you dine in high style at the **Modern**, a much-lauded foodie paradise of French-American cuisine courtesy of head chef Gabriel Kreuther (though you'll find more affordable cafes on-site, too).

Things you need to know: Map p180; ☎ 212-708-9400; www.moma.org; 11 W 53rd St btwn Fifth & Sixth Aves; adult/child/student/senior $20/free/12/16, Fri 4-8pm free; ☽ 10:30am-5:30pm Sat-Mon, Wed & Thu, to 8pm Fri; ◉ E, M to Fifth Ave-53rd St

Though the Chrysler Building is partially obscured, you do get an excellent view of the Empire State Building, as well as Central Park's perfect patch of green.

BRYANT PARK Map p180
☎ 212-768-4242; www.bryantpark.org; 42nd St btwn Fifth & Sixth Aves; ◉ B, D, F, M to 42nd St-Bryant Park, 7 to Fifth Ave

Nestled behind the grand New York Public Library building is this lovely square of green – once a patch of squalor, referred to as 'Needle Park' throughout the 1980s – where local Midtown workers gather for lunchtime picnics on warm afternoons. Among its offerings are impressive skyscraper views, European-style coffee kiosks, the Brooklyn-constructed, French-inspired **Le Carrousel** offering rides for $2, and frequent special events, from readings to concerts. This is where the famed Fashion Week tent goes up every winter, and is also the site of the wonderful outdoor **Bryant Park Summer Film Festival**, which packs the lawn with post-work crowds lugging cheese-and-wine picnics. The **Bryant Park Grill & Café** (p193), a lovely restaurant and bar situated at the eastern end of the park, is the site of many a New York wedding come springtime. And if you've got your laptop and it's a nice day, grab a seat and surf the web in the park, which is a free wi-fi hot spot.

MUSEUM OF ARTS & DESIGN
Map p168

☎ 212-956-3535; www.madmuseum.org; 2 Columbus Circle btwn Eighth Ave & Broadway; adult/under 13yr/senior $15/free/12; ⊗ 11am-6pm Tue-Sun, to 9pm Thu; ⊕ A, C, B, D, 1 to 59th St-Columbus Circle

This is an impressive palace of design and handicrafts, from blown glass and carved wood to elaborate metal jewelry. It also hosts innovative shows like the recent 'Read my Pins: the Madeleine Albright Collection,' including baubles that Albright wore during her diplomatic tenure, and 'Slash: Paper Under the Knife,' exploring the art world's renewed interest in paper as a creative medium.

RADIO CITY MUSIC HALL Map p180

☎ 212-247-4777; www.radiocity.com; 51st St at Sixth Ave; tours adult/child/senior $17/10/14; ⊕ B, D, F, M to 47th-50th Sts–Rockefeller Center

The interior of this 6000-seat, art deco movie palace is a protected landmark, and one peek inside tells you why: the sea of restored velvet seats and furnishings, the lush curtains, the famous pipe organ

Top of the Rock (p181), Rockefeller Center

RICHARD I'ANSON

and the decorative detailing are just as gorgeous as when the building opened in 1932. For a real treat, take a **guided tour** of the interior. You can join one every half-hour between 11am and 3pm, Monday to Sunday. As far as shows here go, though, be warned: the vibe does not quite match the theater's splendor now that it's managed by the folks from Madison Square Garden. Still, there are often some fabulous talents in the lineup – Rufus Wainwright, Aretha Franklin, Dolly Parton – but the annual Christmas Spectacular, starring the Rockettes, is best avoided.

HERALD SQUARE Map p168
⊕ B, D, F, M, N, Q, R to 34th St-Herald Sq

This crowded convergence of Broadway, Sixth Ave and 34th St is best known as the home of famous **Macy's** (p200) department store, where you can still ride some of the remaining original wooden elevators to floors ranging from women's casualwear and home furnishings to lingerie and linens. The busy square gets

its name from a long-defunct newspaper, the *New York Herald* (1835–1924), and the small, leafy park here bustles during business hours.

INTREPID SEA, AIR & SPACE MUSEUM Map p168
☎ 212-245-0072; www.intrepidmuseum.org; Pier 86, Twelfth Ave at 46th St; adult/youth/under 3yr/seniors/veterans $22/17/free/18/17; ⏱ 10am-5pm Tue-Sun; ⊕ A, C, E to 42nd St, 🚌 M42 bus westbound

This military museum, housed in a hulking aircraft carrier that survived both a WWII bomb and kamikaze attacks, is back in its slip after being gone for two years to undergo a $115-million renovation. That entailed a refurbishment of half of the 30 aircrafts onboard, a paint job for the entire carrier, a rebuilding of its Pier 86 and the installation of various new high-tech exhibits – including the G Force Encounter, which allows you to experience the virtual thrill of flying a supersonic jet plane, and the Transporter FX, a flight simulator that promises six full minutes of a

Radio City Music Hall

ANGUS OBORN

MIDTOWN

DAN HERRICK

International Center of Photography

SIGHTS

⤴ IF YOU LIKE...

If you like exploring the Museum of Modern Art (MoMA; p182), we think you'll enjoy the following museums:

- American Folk Art Museum (Map p180; ☎ 212-265-1040; www.folkart museum.org; 45 W 53rd St btwn Fifth & Sixth Aves; adult/child/senior & student $9/free/7; ☾ 10:30am-5:30pm Tue-Thu, Sat, Sun, 11am-7:30pm Fri; ⊕ E, M to Fifth Ave-53rd St) The main museum, housed in a beautiful eight-story building, focuses on traditional arts tied to moments in history or personal milestones. The expansive collection features objects such as flags, liberty figures, textiles, weather vanes and decorative arts.

- International Center of Photography (Map p180; ☎ 212-857-0000; www.icp.org; 1133 Sixth Ave at 43rd St; adult/senior & student $12/8, by donation Fri 5-8pm; ☾ 10am-6pm Tue-Thu, Sat & Sun) The city's most important showcase for major photographers, especially photojournalists. It's also a photography school, offering coursework (for credit) and a public lecture series.

- Japan Society (Map p168; ☎ 212-832-1155; www.japansociety.org; 333 E 47th St btwn First & Second Aves; admission free; ☾ 11am-6pm Tue-Thu, to 9pm Fri, to 5pm Sat & Sun; ⊕ S, 4, 5, 6, 7 to Grand Central-42nd St) Founded in 1907, this nonprofit society has played a large role in strengthening American–Japanese relations. Today its main draw can be found in its galleries and in its theater, which hosts a range of films and dance, music and theatrical performances.

- Museum of Sex (Map p168; ☎ 212-689-6337; www.museumofsex.org; 233 Fifth Ave at 27th St; adult/senior & student $14.50/13.50; ☾ 11am-6:30pm Sun-Fri, to 8pm Sat; ⊕ N, R to 23rd St) An intriguing house of culture, the Museum of Sex ('Mosex' for short) traces the interwoven history of NYC and sex, from tittie bars and porn to street hustling and burlesque shows. There's a $3 discount coupon available online.

THE
WORLD'S
LARGEST
STORE

★macy's

RICHARD CUMMINS

Macy's (p200)

'complete sensory overload.' The flight deck of the USS *Intrepid,* which served in WWII and Vietnam, features fighter planes and military helicopters, while the pier area contains the guided-missile submarine *Growler,* an *Apollo* space capsule, Vietnam-era tanks, the 900ft destroyer *Edson* and a decommissioned Concorde. The *Intrepid* is also the nexus for the **Fleet Week** (p47) celebrations each May, when thousands of the world's sailors descend on Manhattan for shore leave.

SLEEPING
MIDTOWN EAST & FIFTH AVENUE
FOUR SEASONS
Map p168   International Chain Hotel $$$
☎ 212-758-5700, 800-819-5053; www.four seasons.com/newyorkfs; 57 E 57th St btwn Madison & Park Aves; r $650; N, Q, R to 5th Ave-59th St;
Rising like a pyramid up 52 floors, the Four Seasons has a massive lobby (designed by IM Pei) that hits you like a Gothic cathedral gone mod, with limestone arches leading to the glass-tile skylight – plus there's an adjoining bar and restaurant. Even the smallest of the 368 rooms are giant things, with latte-colored carpets and 10in plasma TVs in the full-marble bathrooms.

PIERRE HOTEL
Map p168   International Chain Hotel $$$
☎ 212-838-8000; www.tajhotels.com; 2 E 61st St at Fifth Ave; r from $525; N, Q, R to Fifth Ave-59th St;
The lobby looks like a Gilded Age–period piece, the restaurant (La Caprice) imported from London has spawned some A-list celebrity sightings, and the rooms (in muted tones with delicate accent colors) beckon with wide beds, sweeping views of Central Park (at the hotel's front door) and private, full-sized bathrooms.

KITANO Map p168   Deluxe Indie Inn $$$
☎ 212-885-7000, 800-548-2666; www.kitano. com; 66 Park Ave at 38th St; r $350; S, 4, 5, 6, 7 to Grand Central-42nd St;
This sleek, 18-floor business hotel indeed has a hushed Eastern vibe (double-paned

windows guarantee quiet). Carpeted rooms are simple, with fluffy duvets, wi-fi access, flat-screen TVs and work desks.

WALDORF-ASTORIA

Map p168   Legendary Chain $$
☎ 212-355-3000, 800-925-3673; www.waldorf astoria.com; 301 Park Ave btwn 49th & 50th Sts; r $289-514; ◉ 6 to 51st St, E, F to Lexington Ave-53rd St; ⌗ ▢
An attraction in itself, the 416-room, 42-floor legendary hotel is an art deco landmark. It's massive, occupying a full city block – with 13 conference rooms, and shops and eateries keeping the ground floor buzzing with life. Elegant rooms conjure some old-world fussiness, with rose-petal rugs and embossed floral wallpaper.

70 PARK AVENUE HOTEL

Map p168   Business Boutique Hotel $$
☎ 212-973-2400; 877-707-2753; www.70parkave. com; 70 Park Ave at 38th St; r $280; ◉ S, 4, 5, 6, 7 to Grand Central-42nd St; ⌗ ▢
The earth-conscious aesthetic at 70 Park extends beyond the gorgeous limestone fireplace and long communal concierge/check-in table that greet you at the lobby. The rooms are packed with state-of-the-art technology (including great sound systems) and, while small, have comfy, plush beds, cute sofas tucked into corner nooks and soothing gold-and-brown palettes.

ROYALTON Map p180   Boutique Hotel $$

☎ 212-869-4400, 800-635-9013; www.royalton. com; 44 W 44th St btwn Fifth & Sixth Aves; d $279-620; ◉ B, D, F, M to 42nd St; ⌗ ▢ ▢
A funky mix of modern and classic, this Ian Schrager and Philippe Starck creation had a wee facelift recently but remains a chic choice in a primetime Midtown spot. A rich, mahogany-filled lobby greets you inside the Greek-pillar flanked outer door,

with African art. Up the dark hallways are midsized rooms with short, wide beds, leather headboards, light lavender drapes and baby-blue sofas.

STRAND Map p168   Boutique Hotel $$

☎ 212-991-6231; www.thestrandnyc.com; 33 W 37th St btwn Fifth & Sixth Aves; r $249; ◉ B, D, F, M, N, Q, R to 34th St-Herald Sq; ⌗ ▢
The eye-catching lobby has neon lights, a curving staircase, a two-story cascading waterfall, and a tinkling piano bar. Even the standard rooms are large enough for a settee and a plush chair, giving them a suite-like feel, and the superior rooms are even larger. Free breakfast buffet is offered.

MURRAY HILL INN

Map p168   Budget Hotel $
☎ 212-683-6900, 888-996-6376; www.murray hillinn.com; 143 E 30th St btwn Lexington & Third Aves; r $99-149; ◉ 6 to 33rd St; ⌗ ▢
Named for its pleasant, leafy residential nook of Midtown, this basic, friendly 47-room budget option is better than most in the price range. Rooms have small refrigerators, tiny closets, wi-fi and flat-screen TVs. All but two have private bathrooms. There's no elevator, so guests have to haul their bags up the stairs.

MIDTOWN WEST & TIMES SQUARE

RITZ-CARLTON – NEW YORK, CENTRAL PARK

Map p168   International Chain Hotel $$$
☎ 212-308-9100, 800-241-3333; www.ritz carlton.com; 50 Central Park S btwn Sixth & Seventh Aves; r $650; ◉ N, Q, R to 57th St-7th Ave, F to 57th St; ⌗ ▢
It's about as luxe as Manhattan gets: a landmark building with views of Central Park so giant you almost can't see New York. All 261 rooms are faintly French

MIDTOWN

SLEEPING

colonial, with tasseled armchairs, lovely inlaid-tile bathrooms and loads of space.

BRYANT PARK HOTEL

Map p180   Boutique Hotel $$$

☎ 212-869-0100; www.bryantparkhotel.com; 40 W 40th St btwn Fifth & Sixth Aves; r$365-665; ⊕ B, D, F, M to 42nd St, 7 to 5th Ave; 🍴 💻

Originally the American Standard Building (1934), this 130-room hotel is chic central, with bare-bone minimalist rooms, most with huge views. The lift up is padded in red leather; rooms come with flat-screen TVs, cashmere robes, full-sized soaking tubs and Pipino lotions.

DREAM Map p168   Boutique Hotel $$

☎ 212-247-2000, 866-437-3266; www.dreamny. com; 210 W 55th St btwn Broadway & Seventh Ave; r $299-509; ⊕ N, Q, R to 57th St-7th Ave; 🍴 💻

Museum of Arts & Design (p183)

DAN HERRICK

Some might find it a nightmare, but for those who like minimal all-white rooms with blue lights shining from under beds and inside glass-top desks, Dream is really a dream. The high-tech floating TV screens, iPod docks and wi-fi add to the futuristic feel. The rooftop hangout, Ava, is a hidden gem.

6 COLUMBUS Map p168   Boutique Hotel $$

☎ 212-204-3000; www.sixcolumbuscircle.com; 6 Columbus Circle at 59th St; r $250-600; ⊕ A, C, B, D, 1 to 59th St-Columbus Circle; 🍴 💻

Flashback to the 1960s at this ultramod boutique hotel. Rooms are as fun and whimsical as the decade that inspired the decor, but with all the high-tech hookups and glamorous touches of today. The location, steps from Central Park, next to Time Warner and backed by a major subway hub, can't be beat.

CASABLANCA HOTEL

Map p180   Boutique Hotel $$

☎ 212-869-1212, 888-922-7225; www. casablancahotel.com; 147 W 43rd St btwn Sixth Ave & Broadway; r $249-400; ⊕ N, Q, R, S, 1, 2, 3, 7 to 42nd St-Times Sq; 🍴 💻

Low-key and tourist-oriented, the popular 48-room Casablanca flexes the North African motif throughout (eg tiger statues, Moroccan murals, framed tapestries and a 2nd-floor lounge named Rick's Cafe, after the movie). Rooms are pleasant and comfortable, with sisal-like carpets and a window-side seating area, but not very big. You'll also find free internet, all-day espresso, wine at 5pm and roll-away beds.

HOTEL METRO

Map p168   International Hotel $$

☎ 212-947-2500; www.hotelmetronyc.com; 45 W 35th St btwn Fifth & Sixth Aves; r $189-365; ⊕ B, D, F, M, N, Q, R to 34th St-Herald Sq; 🍴 💻

Bryant Park Hotel

DAN HERRICK

Imbued with a faint whiff of 1930s art deco, the 179-room, 13-floor Metro has a rooftop deck with full-frontal looks at the nearby Empire State Building. Up from the black-and-gold lobby, rooms are rather plain but certainly comfortable, with caramel color schemes and more thinking space than most hotels in this price range.

414 HOTEL Map p168   Budget Hotel $$
☎ 212-399-0006; www.414hotel.com; 414 W 46th St btwn Ninth & Tenth Aves; r $159-249; Ⓑ B, D, F, M to 42nd St; ⌘ ▯
Set up like a guesthouse, this great budget deal offers 22 tidy rooms a couple of blocks west of Times Sq. All rooms are simple deals with desks, dressers, closets with minisafe, cable TV and sinks outside tiled bathrooms. There's a small courtyard between the town house's two buildings; breakfast is included in the rate and served up front, where there is a computer and a small kitchen for guests to use.

EATING
MIDTOWN EAST & FIFTH AVENUE

CONVIVIO Map p168   Southern Italian $$$
☎ 212-599-5045; 45 Tudor City Pl at 42nd St; ⊙ lunch & dinner Mon-Fri, dinner Sat & Sun; Ⓑ S, 4, 5, 6, 7 to Grand Central-42nd St
This bright and airy dining room – pimped out with lavish touches including cushiony red banquettes, shiny walls and silvery chairs at its roomy tables – is host to a veritable parade of incredible eats. Over-the-top mains include cleverly authentic takes on lobster, strip steak, duck breast and grilled tuna, with a slew of antipasto options, from sweetbreads to grilled zucchini.

SPARKS Map p168   Steakhouse $$$
☎ 212-687-4855; 210 E 46th St btwn Second & Third Aves; ⊙ lunch & dinner Mon-Fri, dinner Sat; Ⓑ S, 4, 5, 6, 7 to Grand Central-42nd St
Get an honest-to-goodness New York steakhouse experience at this classic joint,

MIDTOWN

EATING

DAN HERRICK

Russian Tea Room

a former mob hangout that's been around for nearly 50 years, and still packs 'em in.

BRASSERIE Map p168 French $$$
☎ 212-751-4840; 100 E 53rd St at Park Ave; ☘ breakfast, lunch, dinner daily, brunch Sat & Sun; ⊕ E, M to 5th Ave-53rd St

This sleek temple of classics – including onion soup, wine-laden mussels, duck confit and chocolate beignets – is actually most impressive because of its ultramodern design. To get just a taste of the high-class action, perch thyself at the elegant backlit bar, where you can enjoy a plate of miniburger or lobster-salad sliders with a bracing cucumber gimlet.

BLUE SMOKE Map p168 Southern BBQ $$$
☎ 212-447-7733; 116 E 27th St; ☘ lunch & dinner; ⊕ 6 to 28th St

Another contender in the city's ongoing BBQ cook-off, this soulful spot presents a potpourri of various Southern 'cue style: St Louis, Texas, Kansas and Memphis ribs are all representin', as is pulled pork, smoked chicken, peel-and-eat shrimp and

the classic 'salad' consisting of an iceberg-lettuce wedge.

SOBA NIPPON Map p180 Japanese $$
☎ 212-489-2525; 19 W 52nd St btwn Fifth & Sixth Aves; ☘ lunch & dinner; ⊕ B, D, F, M to 47th-50th Sts-Rockefeller Center

The chewy buckwheat soba noodle is the star of the menu here, in this quiet and intimate nook smack dab in the middle of high-bustle Midtown. Try this melt-in-your-mouth highlight in a chilled salad or soothing broth, flavored with sesame, soy and other subtle stabs, including tofu, duck and chicken.

HANGAWI Map p168 Vegetarian Korean $$
☎ 212-213-0077; 12 E 32nd St btwn Fifth & Madison Aves; ☘ lunch Mon-Sat, dinner daily; ⊕ B, D, F, M, N, Q, R to 34th St-Herald Sq

An oasis in Little Korea, this Zen-like dining room is strictly no meat and no shoes (cubbies and bathroom slippers are provided). Slip down into the cushiony, low seating and feast on unique dishes that include crispy mushrooms in sweet-and-sour sauce, tofu stone bowl rice with sesame leaves and organic vegetable stir-fries.

CHENNAI GARDEN
Map p168   Kosher South Indian $
☎ 212-689-1999; 129 E 27th St btwn Park Ave S & Lexington Ave; lunch & dinner; 6 to 28th St
Come to this low-key Curry Row standout for favorite Southern treats and a range of more expected northern favorites, including curries. The interior is bright and bustling – especially for the popular lunchtime buffet, which, for less than $10, lets you reload your plate again and again.

MIDTOWN WEST & TIMES SQUARE
Wandering up and down Ninth Ave will yield all sorts of ethnic-food-market surprises, from Middle Eastern spices sold in bulk to Amish country cheeses proffered by the pound.

RUSSIAN TEA ROOM
Map p168   Russian $$$
☎ 212-581-7100; 150 W 57th St btwn Sixth & Seventh Aves; lunch & dinner; F to 57th St, N, Q, R to 57th St-7th Ave
Bright-red banquettes, crystal bears, chandeliers and a colorful stained-glass ceiling make the various dining rooms here pop; borscht, lamb chops, and chicken Kiev, meanwhile, sing with flavor.

FIVE NAPKIN BURGER
Map p180   Eclectic Bistro $$
☎ 212-757-2277; 630 Ninth Ave at 44th St; lunch & dinner; A, C, E to 42nd St-Port Authority
The cavernous, atmospheric art deco dining room here is a lovely pre- or post-theater hangout, featuring fine wide-ranging bistro fare – sushi rolls, matzo-ball soup, big salads and barbecued ribs. Its

original, acclaimed burger comes topped with carmelized onions, gooey Comte cheese and herb aioli.

RICE 'N' BEANS Map p180   Brazilian $$
☎ 212-265-4444; 744 Ninth Ave btwn 50th & 51st Sts; lunch & dinner daily, brunch Sat & Sun; C, E, 1 to 50th St
The decor in this teensy storefront is nothing to speak of – but the high-flavor, low-priced Brazilian favorites that grace the small yellow tables certainly are. Even vegetarians are well cared for, with sautéed veggies, rice and beans, and fried plantains.

DRINKING
MIDTOWN EAST & FIFTH AVENUE
CAMPBELL APARTMENT
Map p168   1920s Lounge
☎ 212-953-0409; 15 Vanderbilt Ave at 43rd St; S, 4, 5, 6, 7 to 42nd St-Grand Central

This hidden-away spot in Grand Central was once the home of a 1920s railroad magnate fond of fussy European details: velvet, mahogany and Florentine-style carpets. Reach it from the lift beside the Oyster Bar or the stairs to the West Balcony.

KING COLE BAR Map p168   Cocktail Bar
☎ 212-753-4500; 2 E 55th St at Fifth Ave; E, M to 5th Ave-53rd St
Pretend life's posh at the St Regis Hotel's ultralux bar, named for the devilish 1906 mural behind the bar (you may have seen it in *The Devil Wears Prada*).

GINGER MAN Map p168   Snack Pub
☎ 212-532-3740; www.gingerman-ny.com; 11 E 36th St btwn Fifth & Madison Aves; 6 to 33rd St
A great Murray Hill beer post, this high-ceilinged, handsome pub is all about

MIDTOWN

DRINKING

⬐ GAY & LESBIAN MIDTOWN

DRINKING & NIGHTLIFE

Bar-Tini Ultra Lounge (Map p168; ☎ 917-388-2897; 642 Tenth Ave btwn 45th & 46th Sts; ⓔ A, C, E to 42nd St-Port Authority) The newest Hell's Kitchen watering hole is this sleek, all-white lounge, popular for happy hour and hosting nightly special events, with guest singers, drag-queen hosted game shows and a rotating lineup of local, favorite DJs.

Club 57 (Map p168; ☎ 917-388-2897; Providence, 311 W 57th St btwn Eighth & Ninth Aves; ⓔ A, C, E, 1, 9 to 59th St-Columbus Circle) This Saturday-night dance party is run by a couple of promoters who really know how to pack in the hotties. You'll find three distinct spaces – a cozy lounge, a pop-music dance scene and a main dance floor ruled by some of the biggest names in DJing, plus live performances from pop singers and drag queens.

HK Lounge (Map p180; ☎ 212-947-4208; 523 Ninth Ave at 39th St; ⓔ A, C, E to 42nd St-Port Authority) Enter on the 39th St side of this popular eatery and you'll find one of the sleekest, best-designed lounge spaces around. Handsome men gather to hear mellow DJs and rub elbows with local glitterati, from drag queens to porn stars.

Ritz (Map p180; ☎ 212-333-2554; 369 W 46th St btwn Eighth & Ninth Aves; ⓔ A, C, E to 42nd St-Port Authority) Gracing the western end of the city's Restaurant Row, in the Theater District, the Ritz has a front bar that's loud and abuzz, with a postwork, all-male crowd spilling onto the street in warm months. The upstairs space is a mellow retreat, while the downstairs back lounge, lined with banquettes, is often host to DJs or live vocal performers.

Therapy (Map p180; ☎ 212-397-1700; 348 W 52nd St btwn Eighth & Ninth Aves; ⓔ C, E, 1 to 50th St) This multileveled, airy and contemporary space was the first gay-man's hot spot to draw throngs to Hell's Kitchen. It presents nightly shows, from music to comedy, while the romantic 2nd-floor lounge has great fare (burgers, hummus, salads) served in front of a roaring fireplace.

good beer, good snacks and the suits who come to take part.

TOP OF THE TOWER
Map p168   Rooftop Bar
☎ 212-980-4796; 3 Mitchell Pl at First Ave, Beekman Tower; ⓔ 6 to 51st St
Hosting anniversary dates for half a century (and plenty of old-timers are still coming), the classy Beekman Tower's rooftop bar and restaurant puts its tables by the big windows that look over Queens' retro Pepsi-Cola sign and Midtown's twinkling soul.

MIDTOWN WEST & TIMES SQUARE

MOBAR Map p168   Cocktail Bar
☎ 212-805-8876; www.mandarinoriental.com; 35th fl, Mandarin Oriental New York, 80 Columbus Circle at 60th St; ⓔ A, B, C, D, 1 to 59th St-Columbus Circle
The Mandarin hotel is super-swank, and its lobby bar feels like you're in…well, in a hotel lobby, but the comfortable lounge seats look out from the 35th floor over the twinkling lights of buildings along the south end of Central Park – it's truly amazing.

JIMMY'S CORNER Map p180 Dive Bar
☎ 212-221-9510; 140 W 44th St;  N, Q, R, S, 1, 2, 3, 7 to 42nd St-Times Sq, B, D, F, M to 42nd St-Bryant Park

This skinny, welcoming, completely unpretentious dive off Times Sq is run by an old boxing trainer, as if you wouldn't guess by all the framed photos of boxing greats (and lesser-known fighters, too).

KEMIA BAR Map p180 DJ Bar
☎ 212-582-3200; www.kemiabarny.com; 630 Ninth Ave at 44th St;  A, C, E to 42nd St-Port Authority

Perfect for a pre- or post theater cocktail, the laid-back Moroccan-themed Kemia displays plenty of drama with its rose-petal-strewn staircase whisking you down to the underground hideaway decked in ottomans and billowing tapestries.

TILLMAN'S Map p168 Jazz Lounge
☎ 212-627-8320; 165 W 26th St btwn Sixth & Seventh Aves;  F, M, 1 to 23rd St

Jazzy and cool, with cubby booths, candles and vintage sepia prints reviving the jazz heyday, Tillman's is a bit dressed up – staff will take your jacket up front, and often help you put it on – but this Harlem import has a 'mingle o'er early-evening martini' ($12) vibe that sucks you in.

BRYANT PARK GRILL & CAFÉ
Map p180 Outside Bar
☎ 212-840-6500; 25 W 40th St btwn Fifth & Sixth Aves;  B, D, F, M to 42nd St-Bryant Park

If the weather's behaving (and it's between April and November), head to Bryant Park, where the outdoor cafe sets out its wicker chairs overlooking the lovely patch of green.

ENTERTAINMENT & ACTIVITIES
MIDTOWN EAST & FIFTH AVENUE

RODEO BAR & GRILL
Map p168 Country, Folk & Blues
☎ 212-683-6500; www.rodeobar.com; 375 Third Ave at 27th St;  6 to 28th St

Good shows of country, bluegrass and rockabilly are staged nightly for a

MAGNOLIA

RICHARD CUMMINS

Bryant Park (p182)

MIDTOWN

ENTERTAINMENT & ACTIVITIES

Carnegie Hall

DAN HERRICK

foot-tappin' Manhattan crowd. There are creative margaritas and plenty of steaks, fajitas, burgers and delicious veggie dishes, too.

JAZZ STANDARD

Map p168   Jazz & Experimental
☎ 212-576-2232; www.jazzstandard.net; 116 E 27th St btwn Lexington & Park Ave; ☻ 6 to 28th St
The lineup at this sleek and spacious music hall ranges from classic jazz to funk, blues, R&B and world. And adding real appeal to the music are the sizzling barbecue platters, courtesy of Danny Meyer's award-winning restaurant Blue Smoke.

MIDTOWN WEST & TIMES SQUARE

NEW YORK KNICKS   Basketball
Madison Square Garden; Map p168; ☎ 212-465-6073, tickets 866-858-0008; www.nyknicks.com; Seventh Ave btwn 31st & 33rd Stst; tickets $13-330; ☻ A, C, E, 1, 2, 3 to 34th St-Penn Station

Despite big crowds, including Spike Lee and 18,999 others, the Knicks haven't won a championship since 1973.

CENTRAL PARK BICYCLE TOURS & RENTALS Map p168   Bicycle Rental
☎ 212-541-8759; www.centralparkbiketours.com; 203 W 58th St at Seventh Ave; rentals 2hr/day $30/65, tours adult/child $49/40; ☻ A, C, B, D, 1 to 59th St-Columbus Circle
This place rents mountain bikes and leads various two-hour tours of the park, three to five times daily.

OAK ROOM Map p180   Cabaret
☎ 212-840-6800; Algonquin Hotel, 59 W 44th St btwn Fifth & Sixth Aves; ☻ B, D, F, M to 42nd St-Bryant Park
Dress up, order a martini and get the Dorothy Parker vibe at this famous piano lounge, which is known for launching the careers of Harry Connick Jr and Diana Krall.

CARNEGIE HALL Map p168   Classical Music
☎ 212-247-7800; www.carnegiehall.org; 154 W 57th St at Seventh Ave; ☻ N, Q, R to 57th St-7th Ave

Since 1891, this mostly classical and world-music historic performance hall has hosted Tchaikovsky, Mahler and Prokofiev, among others.

PACHA Map p168 Clubbing
☎ 212-209-7500; www.pachanyc.com; 618 W 46th St btwn Eleventh Ave & West Side Hwy; admission $20-40; Ⓔ A, C, E to 42nd St-Port Authority

A relative newcomer that's hyped for big-name visiting DJs, Pacha is definitely a massive and spectacular place: 30,000 sq ft and four levels of glowing, sleek spaces and cozy seating nooks that rise up to sur-round the main dance-floor atrium.

CAROLINE'S ON BROADWAY
Map p180 Comedy
☎ 212-757-4100; www.carolines.com; 1626 Broadway at 50th St; Ⓔ N, Q, R to 49th St, 1 to 50th St

You may recognize this big, bright, main-stream classic from comedy specials filmed here on location. Big names (Jerry Seinfeld, Jon Stewart) come here.

BB KING BLUES CLUB & GRILL
Map p180 Country, Folk & Blues
☎ 212-997-4144; www.bbkingblues.com; 237 W 42nd St btwn Seventh & Eighth Aves; Ⓔ N, Q, R, S, 1, 2, 3, 7 to 42nd St-Times Sq

Catch old-school blues performers – along with rock, folk and reggae acts and theme nights (eg Johnny Cash's birthday) at this two-tiered, horseshoe-shaped room in the heart of the new Times Sq.

NEW YORK CITY CENTER
Map p168 Dance
☎ 212-581-1212; www.citycenter.org; 131 W 55th St btwn Sixth & Seventh Aves; Ⓔ N, Q, R to 57th St-7th Ave

The New York City Center hosts the Alvin Ailey American Dance Theater and the American Ballet Theater in December, as well as the Paul Taylor Dance Company in spring.

CLEARVIEW'S ZIEGFELD THEATER
Map p168 Film & TV
☎ 212-307-1862; 141 W 54th St; Ⓔ 1 to 50th St

The last true movie palace in New York City, this stunner, built in 1969, seats a whopping 1131 moviegoers and is often used for glitzy celeb-studded premieres because of its opulence.

BIRDLAND Map p180 Jazz & Experimental
☎ 212-581-3080; www.birdlandjazz.com; 315 W 44th St btwn Eighth & Ninth Aves; Ⓔ A, C, E to 42nd St-Port Authority

Off Times Sq, it's got a slick look, not to mention the legend – its name dates from

---

HALF-PRICE BROADWAY TICKETS

Thanks to the Theatre Development Fund, an arts advocacy group that sells 2.5 million theater seats annu-ally, you can snag tickets to some of the most coveted seats at up to half the full price. Just head to the Times Sq **TKTS booth** (Map p180; ☎ 212-768-1818; Broadway at W 47th St), which sells cut-rate, same-day tick-ets to Broadway and off-Broadway shows. For evening shows, queue up from 3pm to 8pm Monday to Saturday; for matinees, line up from 10am to 2pm Wednesday to Saturday and from 11am to 3pm Sunday. Check the electric mar-quee to see what shows are avail-able, or visit the website (www.tdf.org/tkts) to see what has been available recently, to get an idea of what you might find.

BRENT WINEBRENNER

Bergdorf Goodman

A nonprofit entertainment organization founded in 1921 and housed in an elegant National Landmark building, Town Hall's 2000-plus seats get filled regularly with folks seeking eclectic musical performances.

PLAYWRIGHTS HORIZONS
Map p168   Off-Broadway & Off-Off-Broadway
☎ 212-564-1235; www.playwrightshorizons.org; 416 W 42nd St btwn Ninth & Tenth Aves; Ⓔ A, C, E to Port Authority-42nd St
Sitting on a quiet and windswept stretch of 42nd St, this is an excellent place to catch a new show that could very possibly be a rising hit. It's nearly 40 years old and known as a 'writers' theater,' and is dedicated to fostering contemporary American works.

ROUNDABOUT THEATRE COMPANY
Map p180   Off-Broadway & Off-Off-Broadway
☎ 212-719-1300; www.roundabouttheatre.org; 227 W 42nd St btwn Seventh & Eighth Aves; Ⓔ N, Q, R, S, 1, 2, 3, 7 to Times Sq-42nd St
The main stage for the Roundabout, unfortunately called the American Airlines Theatre, has been going strong for more than four decades.

bebop legend Charlie Parker (aka 'Bird'), who headlined at the previous location on 52nd St, along with Miles, Monk and just about everyone else.

RADIO CITY MUSIC HALL
Map p180   Live Music
☎ 212-247-4777; www.radiocity.com; 51st St at Sixth Ave; Ⓔ B, D, F, M to 47th-50th Sts–Rockefeller Center
This art deco masterpiece is a great place to see a show. Many throwback acts (eg Dolly Parton, Santana) take the stage, but newer names like Arcade Fire play, too.

TOWN HALL Map p180   Live Music
☎ 212-840-2824; www.the-townhall-nyc.org; 123 W 43rd St btwn Sixth & Seventh Aves; Ⓔ B, D, F, M to 42nd St-Bryant Park

HAMMERSTEIN BALLROOM
Map p168   Rock & Indie
☎ 212-279-7740; www.mcstudios.com; Manhattan Center, 311 W 34th St btwn Eighth & Ninth Aves; Ⓔ A, C, E to 34th St-Penn Station
It is not the most fun place to see a show – mobs being herded through security checks, pricey drinks, oft-rowdy crowds – but the faded grandeur inside makes it a tempting place to see some good bands, including the Flaming Lips and Coldplay.

SHOPPING
MIDTOWN EAST & FIFTH AVENUE

DYLAN'S CANDY BAR Map p168 Candy
☎ 646-735-0078; 1011 Third Ave at 60th St; 🕙 10am-9pm Mon-Thu, 10am-11pm Fri & Sat, 11am-9pm Sun; 🚇 N, Q, R to Lexington Ave-59th St

A candy junkie's worst nightmare, sweet Dylan's has giant swirly lollipops, crunchy candy bars, glowing jars of jelly beans, brightly colored Pez dispensers, soft-ball-sized cupcakes and a luminescent staircase embedded with scrumptious, unattainable candy. There's a cafe for hot chocolate, espresso, ice cream and other pick-me-ups on the 2nd floor.

BARNEYS Map p168 Department Store
☎ 212-826-8900; 660 Madison Ave; 🕙 10am-8pm Mon-Fri, 10am-7pm Sat, 11am-6pm Sun; 🚇 N, Q, R to 5th Ave-59th St

Perhaps offering Manhattan's best designer clothing selection, Barneys justifies its occasionally raised-nose staff with its spot-on collections of the best designer brands of the moment (Marc Jacobs, Prada, Helmut Lang, Paul Smith and Miu Miu shoes).

BERGDORF GOODMAN
Map p168 Department Store
☎ 212-753-7300; 754 Fifth Ave; 🕙 10am-8pm Mon-Fri, to 7pm Sat, noon-6pm Sun; 🚇 N, Q, R to Fifth Ave-59th St, F to 57th St

This classy, legendary, high-end department store is all about labels and fabulousness – the serious, not pretentious kind.

BLOOMINGDALE'S
Map p168 Department Store
☎ 212-705-2000; 1000 Third Ave at 59th St; 🕙 10am-8:30pm Mon-Thu, 9am-10pm Fri & Sat, 11am-7pm Sun; 🚇 4, 5, 6 to 59th St, N, Q, R to Lexington Ave-59th St

Massive 'Bloomie's' is something like the Metropolitan Museum of Art to the shopping world: historic, sprawling, over-whelming and packed with bodies, but you'd be sorry to miss it.

DAN HERRICK

Barneys

MIDTOWN

SHOPPING

FAO Schwarz

COREY WISE

HENRI BENDEL
Map p168   Department Store
☎ 212-247-1100; 712 Fifth Ave; ⊗ 10am-8pm
Mon-Sat, noon-7pm Sun; ⊖ E, M to 5th Ave-
53rd St, N, Q, R to 5th Ave-59th St
As boutique-cozy as a big-name, high-class department store can be, Bendel's makes for an easy pop-in-and-out. Its European collections include curious, stylish clothing by established and up-and-coming designers, as well as cosmetics and accessories.

LORD & TAYLOR
Map p168   Department Store
☎ 212-391-3344; www.lordandtaylor.com; 424
Fifth Ave; ⊗ 10am-8:30pm Mon-Fri, 10am-7pm
Sat, 11am-7pm Sun; ⊖ 7 to 5th Ave, S, 4, 5, 6, 7
to Grand Central-42nd St
Staying true to its traditional roots (Ralph Lauren, Donna Karen, Calvin Klein etc), this 10-floor classic tends to let shoppers browse pressure-free (even in the cosmetics department), and has a great selection of swimwear.

SAKS FIFTH AVE
Map p168   Department Store
☎ 212-753-4000; 611 Fifth Ave at 50th St;
⊗ 10am-8pm Mon-Sat, noon-7pm Sun; ⊖ B, D,
F, M to 47th-50th Sts–Rockefeller Center
This lovely flagship offers its updated collection of high-end women's and men's clothing, plus other lines including Gucci, Prada, Juicy Couture, Theory, Eli Tahari and Burberry.

TAKASHIMAYA
Map p168   Department Store
☎ 212-350-0100; 693 Fifth Ave; ⊗ 10am-7pm
Mon-Sat, noon-5pm Sun; ⊖ E, M to 5th Ave-
53rd St
The Japanese owners upped the ante on Fifth Ave's elegant, minimalist style with this stunning six-floor store, which sells high-end furniture, clothing and homewares from all over the world.

TIFFANY & CO Map p168   Jewelry & Home
☎ 212-755-8000; 727 Fifth Ave; ⊗ 10am-7pm
Mon-Fri, 10am-6pm Sat, noon-5pm Sun; ⊖ F
to 57th St

This famous jeweler, with the trademark clock-hoisting Atlas over the door, has won countless hearts with its fine diamond rings, watches, silver Elsa Peretti heart necklaces, and fine crystal vases and glassware.

FAO SCHWARZ Map p168 Toys
☎ 212-644-9400; 767 Fifth Ave; ☺ 10am-7pm Mon-Thu, 10am-8pm Fri & Sat, 11am-6pm Sun; ⊕ 4, 5, 6 to 59th St, N, Q, R to 5th Ave-59th St
The toy store giant, where Tom Hanks played footsy piano in the movie *Big*, is number one on the NYC wish list of most visiting kids.

COMPLETE TRAVELLER ANTIQUARIAN BOOKSTORE
Map p168 Used & Rare Travel Books
☎ 212-685-9007; 199 Madison Ave at E 35th St; ☺ 10am-6:30pm Mon-Fri, 10am-6pm Sat, noon-5pm Sun; ⊕ 6 to 33rd St
Stocking two rooms full with travel guides and maps from days past, the Complete Traveller Antiquarian arranges its stock by destination.

MIDTOWN WEST & TIMES SQUARE
Way west, in Hell's Kitchen, are a handful of boutiques along with the excellent but only-on-weekends **Hell's Kitchen Flea Market** (Map p180; ☎ 212-243-5343; 39th St btwn Ninth & Tenth Aves; ☺ 7am-4pm Sat & Sun; ⊕ A, C, E to 42nd St).

Gem hunters should not miss the wonderful Diamond District, a wild and wacky only-in-NYC experience, while self-made style mavens should hit the Garment District, around Seventh Ave in the 30s, home to massive, wonderfully stocked shops selling fabric, buttons, thread, zippers, sequins and such.

RIZZOLI Map p168 Books
☎ 212-759-2424; 31 W 57th St; ☺ 10am-7:30pm Mon-Fri, 10:30am-7pm Sat, 11am-7pm Sun; ⊕ F to 57th St
Set in a charming town house on W 57th, the US flagship store of the Italian publisher sells great art, architecture and design books (as well as general-interest titles).

H&M Map p168 Budget Fashions
☎ 646-473-1164; www.hm.com; 1328 Broadway at 34th St; ☺ 9am-10pm Mon-Sat, 10am-9pm Sun; ⊕ B, D, F, M, N, Q, R to 34th St-Herald Sq
The flagship H&M at Herald Sq is one of a dozen branches of the Swedish clothing giant (check online for other locations).

DAN HERRICK

Rizzoli

Both it and the store at 51st St and Fifth Ave have large selections of discount clothes.

B&H PHOTO-VIDEO
Map p168   Cameras & Electronics
☎ 212-444-6615; www.bhphotovideo.com; 420 Ninth Ave; ⏲ 9am-7pm Mon-Thu, 9am-1pm Fri, 10am-5pm Sun, closed Sat; Ⓜ A, C, E to 34th St-Penn Station

Visiting the city's most popular camera shop can be an experience in itself – it's massive and crowded, and bustling with black-clad, knowledgeable Hasidic Jewish salesmen bused in from communities in distant Brooklyn neighborhoods.

CLOTHINGLINE/SSS SAMPLE SALES Map p168   Clothing
☎ 212-947-8748; www.clothingline.com; 2nd fl, 261 W 36th St; ⏲ 10am-6pm Mon & Wed, 10am-7pm Tue & Thu; Ⓜ 1, 2, 3 to 34th St-Penn Station

Each week this Garment District space sells pieces from a different batch of designers – both small and well-known labels, with markdowns of up to 75%.

MACY'S Map p168   Department Store
☎ 212-695-4400; 151 W 34th St at Broadway; ⏲ 10am-8:30pm Mon-Sat, 11am-7pm Sun; Ⓜ B, D, F, M, N, Q, R to 34th St-Herald Sq

The world's largest department store has a bit of everything – clothing, furnishings, kitchenware, sheets, cafes, hair salons.

TOYS 'R' US Map p180   Toys
☎ 800-869-7787; 1514 Broadway; ⏲ 10am-10pm Mon-Thu, 10am-11pm Fri & Sat, 11am-9pm Sun; Ⓜ N, Q, R, S, 1, 2, 3, 7 to 42nd St-Times Sq

Sure, you have one of these at home, but this supersized Toys 'R' Us is its greatest bastion, with three thematic floors including a huge video-game area downstairs, an alley of stuffed animals and a 60ft-tall indoor Ferris wheel.

UPPER EAST SIDE

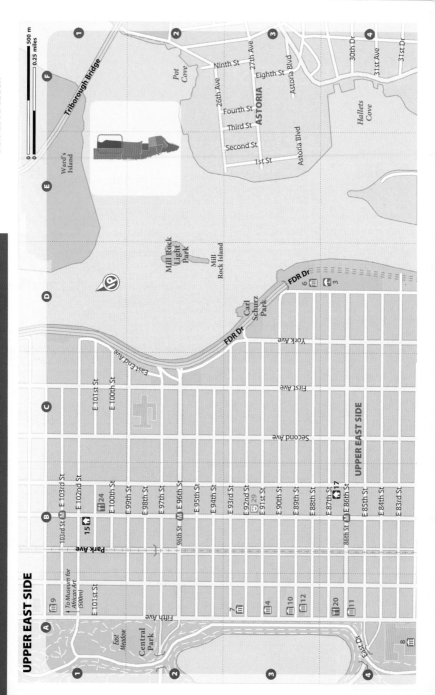

UPPER EAST SIDE

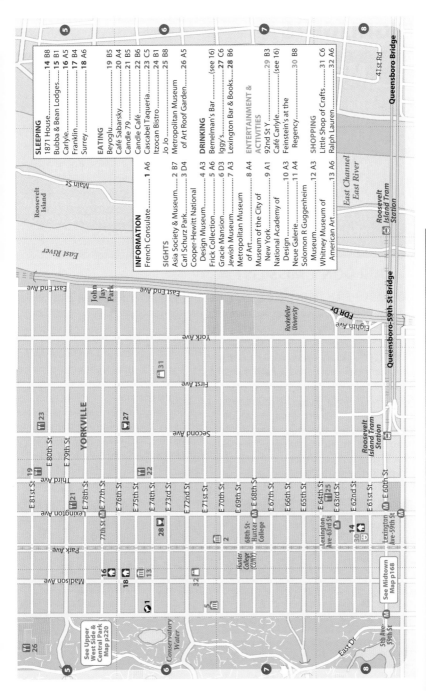

SLEEPING
1871 House............14 B8
Bubba & Bean Lodges......15 B1
Carlyle............16 A5
Franklin............17 B4
Surrey............18 A6

EATING
Beyoglu............19 B5
Café Sabarsky............20 A4
Candle 79............21 B5
Candle Café............22 B6
Cascabel Taqueria............23 C5
Itzocan Bistro............24 B1
Jo Jo............25 B8
Metropolitan Museum
of Art Roof Garden............26 A5

DRINKING
Bemelman's Bar............(see 16)
Iggy's............27 C6
Lexington Bar & Books......28 B6

**ENTERTAINMENT &
ACTIVITIES**
92nd St Y............29 B3
Café Carlyle............(see 16)
Feinstein's at the
Regency............30 B8

SHOPPING
Little Shop of Crafts............31 C6
Ralph Lauren............32 A6

INFORMATION
French Consulate............1 A6

SIGHTS
Asia Society & Museum........2 B7
Carl Schurz Park............3 D4
Cooper-Hewitt National
Design Museum............4 A3
Frick Collection............5 A6
Gracie Mansion............6 D3
Jewish Museum............7 A3
Metropolitan Museum
of Art............8 A4
Museum of the City of
New York............9 A1
National Academy of
Design............10 A3
Neue Galerie............11 A4
Solomon R Guggenheim
Museum............12 A3
Whitney Museum of
American Art............13 A6

UPPER EAST SIDE

HIGHLIGHTS

HIGHLIGHTS

1 | METROPOLITAN MUSEUM OF ART

The Metropolitan Museum of Art (Met) is a self-contained, cultural city–state of 17 acres, with two million individual objects in its collection. Its massive list of curatorial departments – from American Decorative Arts and Ancient Near Eastern Art to Greek and Roman Art, Medieval Art, Modern Art, Photography, Musical Instruments and the Costume Institute – can thrill, confound, inspire and exhaust. A stroll through the galleries provides an impressive record of the achievements of the human imagination.

↘ OUR DON'T MISS LIST

❶ EUROPEAN PAINTINGS
On the 2nd floor, in some of the oldest galleries, is the Met's famous collection of European paintings. The exhibition features works by every artist of note, including self-portraits by Rembrandt and Vincent van Gogh, and *Portrait of Juan de Pareja* by Diego Velázquez. An entire suite of rooms focuses on impressionist and postimpressionist art, and some of the canvases fill entire walls. The religious-themed triptychs, highlighted with dazzling gold leaf and exquisite detail, are particularly mesmerizing.

❷ AMERICAN WING
The newly renovated American Wing of furniture and architecture has a quiet, enclosed garden space that's a perennial favorite as a respite from the visiting hordes. Several stained-glass works by Louis Comfort Tiffany frame the garden, as does an entire two-story facade of the Branch Bank of the US, preserved when the downtown build-

Clockwise from top: Ocean Galleries; European Sculpture Court; Ancient Egyptian Wing; Roman & Greek Galleries; Metropolitan Museum of Art exterior

CLOCKWISE FROM TOP: RICK GERHARTER; MICHELLE BENNETT; GREG GAWLOWSKI; RICK GERHARTER; DAN HERRICK

ing was demolished in the early 20th century. Several Frederic Church and Thomas Cole landscapes offer romantic depictions of a pre-Edenic America.

❸ ROBERT LEHMAN COLLECTION

The Robert Lehman Collection of impressionist and modern art is housed in a pyramid-like addition. It features several works by Pierre-Auguste Renoir, Georges Seurat and Pablo Picasso (including *Portrait of Gertrude Stein*). An unexpected bonus in this gallery is the rear terra-cotta facade of the original 1880 museum building, completely encased by later additions and standing mutely on view – now an architectural artifact itself.

❹ ROOF GARDEN

It's nothing fancy, just a self-service area with sandwiches and drinks, but on flawless, balmy days, the roof garden – with constantly rotating installations and gorgeous views of the city below – is a true gem, especially in the summer, when a wine bar opens on weekend evenings.

↘ THINGS YOU NEED TO KNOW

Did you know? The suggested donation (truly, a suggestion) includes same-day admission to the Cloisters (p232) **Top tip** Audio tours (typically $6) of special exhibitions are highly recommended **When not to visit** Rainy days and Sundays are mobbed **For more on the Met, see p209.**

HIGHLIGHTS

⇲ SOLOMON R GUGGENHEIM MUSEUM

The **Guggenheim** (p212) sparked controversy during its construction in the '50s, but today has achieved landmark status. Most recently, the Frank Lloyd Wright–designed exterior has been restored. Head inside to view some of the museum's 5000 permanent works (plus changing exhibitions) on a path that coincides with the unique coiled design; take the elevator to the top and wind your way down.

⇲ FRICK COLLECTION

The wily and wealthy Henry Clay Frick, a Pittsburgh steel magnate, established a trust to open his private art collection as a **museum** (p211). On display are paintings by Titian and Johannes Vermeer, and portraits by Gilbert Stuart, El Greco, Goya and John Constable. Perhaps the best asset here is that it is never crowded, providing a welcome break from the swarms of gawkers at larger museums.

4

⇘ WINDOW SHOPPING

This well-scrubbed neighborhood boasts Gucci, Prada and Cartier, as well as stores such as the Gap. The main **shopping** (p218) is on, and just off, Madison Ave, from Midtown up to about E 75th St. You'll also find one-of-a-kind boutiques, mainly on Lexington and Third Aves in the 70s and 80s, as well as gourmet food shops.

5

⇘ 92ND ST Y

92nd St Y (p218) is a cultural hub offering classes, performances, readings and talks by folks ranging from writer Mario Vargas Llosa to TV business personality Jim Cramer. Almost all the big-name readings sell out, so if there's a particular person you want to hear, be sure to reserve well in advance. The venue also presents music and dance.

6

⇘ ROOSEVELT ISLAND

Not exactly part of the Upper East Side, **Roosevelt Island** (p213), in the middle of the East River, is really nothing more than a planned residential community that looks like an Olympic village from the 1960s. However, zipping across the river via the four-minute aerial tram is worth it for the stunning views. Bring along a picnic or a bike.

2 GAVIN GOUGH; 3 DAN HERRICK; 4 DAN HERRICK; 5 JEMAL COUNTESS/GETTY IMAGES; 6 DAN HERRICK

2 Centripetal walkway, Solomon R Guggenheim Museum (p212); 3 Frick Collection garden (p211); 4 Wine store; 5 92nd St Y (p218); 6 Queensboro Bridge, Roosevelt Island (p213)

UPPER EAST SIDE

BEST...

BEST...

⬐ AVENUES

- **Fifth** There are few more desirable addresses overlooking Central Park.
- **Madison** High-end boutiques and restaurants for ladies-who-lunch.
- **Park** Lined on either side with imposing apartment buildings, some of the most expensive real estate in the world.
- **Lexington** More modest and utilitarian than the others, Lex is the place for diners, delis and groceries.

⬐ FORMER MANSIONS

- **Frick Collection** (p211) Henry Clay Frick's flamboyantly opulent home-cum-musuem.
- **Cooper-Hewitt National Design Museum** (p211) Billionaire Andrew Carnegie's 64-room home.
- **Jewish Museum** (p212) This is how bankers used to live.
- **Neue Galerie** (p210) Once a Rockefeller abode; located near the Met.

⬐ DELUXE DRINKS

- **Café Sabarsky** (p210) At the Neue Galerie – high-minded, old world and luxurious.
- **Surrey** (p214) The Surrey hotel's downstairs bar, which carries Café Boulud dishes.
- **Bemelmen's Bar** (p217) Classic watering hole of the Hotel Carlyle.
- **Lexington Bar & Books** (p217) Mahogany, cigars, leather chairs... need we say more?

⬐ WAYS TO WEST SIDE

- **Walk** Once inside Central Park, you can scramble and wander whichever way you choose.
- **Horse-drawn carriage** Take the long, scenic way around; find one at 59th St (Central Park South).
- **Cross-town bus** Four options – 66th St, 79th St, 86th St, 97th St.
- **Taxi** If you don't hit any red lights, you can be on the other side in less than two minutes.

LEE FOSTER

Park Ave

DISCOVER UPPER EAST SIDE

The Upper East Side (often abbreviated UES) is home to New York's greatest concentration of cultural centers, including the grand dame that is the Metropolitan Museum of Art. A long section of Fifth Ave north of 79th St has even been officially designated 'Museum Mile.'

But beyond museums, you'll find plenty of less high-minded attractions in the form of seriously high-end shops. The neighborhood – whose residents, by the way, are in a never-ending contest with those of the Upper West Side just across the park – also includes many of the city's most exclusive hotels and residences (not to mention many of the city's most moneyed celebrities, from Woody Allen to Shirley MacLaine). The side streets from Fifth Ave to Third Ave between 57th and 86th Sts feature some stunning town houses and brownstones – walking through this area at night offers opportunities to see how the other half lives.

SIGHTS

METROPOLITAN MUSEUM OF ART

☎ 212-535-7710; www.metmuseum.org; Fifth Ave at 82nd St; suggested donation adult/child/senior & student $20/free/15; ☼ 9:30am-5:30pm Tue-Thu & Sun, to 9pm Fri & Sat; ◎ 4, 5, 6 to 86th St

With more than five million visitors per year, the Met is New York's most popular single-site tourist attraction, with one of the richest coffers in the arts world. Since the completion a multimillion-dollar remodeling project that brought works out of storage, renovated the halls of 19th- and early 20th-century paintings and sculptures, expanded the Ancient Hellenistic and Roman areas and sparklingly remade the American Wing, the place is looking more divine than ever – despite operating in the midst of a financial crisis that has led to major payroll cuts, a shrinking endowment and a donations slump.

To get organized once you arrive inside the **Great Hall**, pick up a floor plan and head to the ticket booths, where you'll find a list of any exhibitions closed that day, along with a lineup of special museum talks. The Met presents more than 30 special exhibitions and installations each year and it's best to target exactly what you want to see on the floor plan and head there first, before museum fatigue sets in. Then you can put the plan away and get lost trying to get back to the main entrance. To the right of the Great Hall, an information desk offers guidance in several languages (which change depending on the volunteers) and **audio tours** ($6) of the special exhibitions. The Met also offers free **guided tours** of museum highlights and specific galleries.

WHITNEY MUSEUM OF AMERICAN ART

☎ 212-570-3600, 800-944-8639; www.whitney.org; 945 Madison Ave at 75th St; adult/child/senior $18/free/12; ☼ 11am-6pm Wed, Thu, Sat & Sun, 1-9pm Fri; ◎ 6 to 77th St

Established in the 1930s by Gertrude Vanderbilt Whitney, who began a Greenwich Village salon for prominent artists, the stellar art collection here features works by famous folk such as Edward Hopper, Jasper Johns, Georgia O'Keeffe, Jackson Pollock and Mark

UPPER EAST SIDE

SIGHTS

DAN HERRICK

Neue Galerie

⤵ IF YOU LIKE...

If you like the wandering the galleries at the **Metropolitan Museum of Art** (p209), we think you'll enjoy these other museums:

- **Asia Society & Museum** (☎ 212-288-6400; www.asiasociety.org; 725 Park Ave at 70th St; adult/student/senior $10/5/7; ☯ museum 11am) Founded in 1956 by John D Rockefeller, this cultural center's museum features rare treasures from all across Asia, such as Jain sculptures from India, Buddhist paintings from Nepal and jade, and lacquer items from China.

- **Museum for African Art** (www.africanart.org; Fifth Ave at E 110th St; ☯ 2, 3, 6 to 110th St) This museum, dedicated to African artists, will open its doors at a grand new location in early 2011. In addition to wide-ranging exhibits, the programming will include lectures, film series and workshops.

- **National Academy of Design** (☎ 212-369-4880; www.nationalacademy.org; 1083 Fifth Ave at 89th St; adult/child under 16/senior & student $10/free/5; ☯ noon-5pm Wed & Thu, 11am-6pm Fri-Sun; ☯ 4, 5, 6 to 86th St) This complex includes a permanent collection of paintings and sculptures housed in yet another stunning Beaux Arts mansion.

- **Neue Galerie** (☎ 212-628-6200; www.neuegalerie. org; 1048 Fifth Ave at 86th St; adult/ senior $15/10, first Friday of the month 6-8pm free; ☯ 11am-6pm Thu-Mon, to 8pm first Friday of the month; ☯ 4, 5, 6 to 86th St) This showcase for German and Austrian art is a small gem among the Fifth Ave biggies. It also boasts the lovely Café Sabarsky, which serves Viennese meals, drinks and to-die-for pastries. Children under 12 years of age are not admitted.

Rothko. Known for its blockbuster shows, recent exhibits have included 'Georgia O'Keeffe: Abstraction,' and 'Modern Life: Edward Hopper and His Time.'

The Whitney makes no secret of its mission to provoke, which starts with the most brutal of structures housing the collection. Designed by Bauhaus architect Marcel Breuer, the rocklike edifice is a fitting setting for the Whitney's style of cutting-edge American art. The collection is highlighted every two years in the much ballyhooed Whitney Biennial, an ambitious survey of contemporary art that rarely fails to generate controversy – even if it's over the mediocrity of the works. It last hit town in 2010.

FRICK COLLECTION
☎ 212-288-0700; www.frick.org; 1 E 70th St at Fifth Ave; adult/student/senior $15/5/10; ⏰ 10am-6pm Tue-Sat, 11am-5pm Sun; ⊕ 6 to 68th St-Hunter College
This spectacular art collection sits in a mansion built by businessman Henry Clay Frick in 1914, one of the many such residences that made up 'Millionaires' Row.' The 2nd floor of the residence is not open for viewing, though the 12 rooms on the ground floor are grand enough and the garden beckons visitors on nice days. An audio tour (available in several languages) is included in the price of admission and helps visitors appreciate the displayed art

more fully; you can also dial up information on paintings and sculptures of your choosing on the ArtPhone. Classical music fans will no doubt be drawn here for the frequent piano and violin concerts that take place on Sunday. Children under 10 years of age are not admitted.

COOPER-HEWITT NATIONAL DESIGN MUSEUM
☎ 212-849-8400; www.si.edu/ndm; 2 E 91st St at Fifth Ave; adult/child/senior & student $15/free/10; ⏰ 10am-5pm Mon-Fri, to 6pm Sat, noon-6pm Sun; ⊕ 4, 5, 6 to 86th St
Part of the Smithsonian Institution in Washington, this house of culture is the only museum in the country that's dedicated to both historic and contemporary design. It's a must for anyone interested in architecture, engineering, jewelry or textiles. Exhibitions have examined everything from advertising campaigns to Viennese blown glass. Even if none of this grabs you, the mansion is stunning and the museum's garden and terrace are well worth a visit.

Cooper-Hewitt National Design Museum

KIM GRANT

UPPER EAST SIDE

SIGHTS

Solomon R Guggenheim Museum
ROB BLAKERS

⬇ SOLOMON R GUGGENHEIM MUSEUM

A sculpture in its own right, Frank Lloyd Wright's sweeping spiral building almost overshadows the collection of 20th-century art housed in this museum. The **Guggenheim** collection includes works by Picasso, Chagall, Pollock and Kandinsky. In 1976 Justin Thannhauser's major donation of impressionist and modern works added paintings by Monet, Van Gogh and Degas.

In 1992 the Robert Mapplethorpe Foundation gave 200 photographs to the museum, spurring curators to devote the 4th floor to photography exhibitions. Note that you can purchase tickets online in advance via the museum's website, which lets you avoid the sometimes brutal lines to get in.

Things you need to know: ☎ 212-423-3500; www.guggenheim.org; 1071 Fifth Ave at 89th St; adult/child under 12yr/senior & student $18/free/15; ☽ 10am-5:45pm Fri, Sun-Wed, to 7:45pm Sat; ⊕ 4, 5, 6 to 86th St

JEWISH MUSEUM

☎ 212-423-3200; www.jewishmuseum.org; 1109 Fifth Ave at 92nd St; adult/child/student/ senior $12/free/7.50/10, free; ☽ 11am-5:45pm Sat-Tue, to 8pm Thu, to 4pm Fri; ⊕ 6 to 96th St
This homage to Judaism primarily features artwork examining 4000 years of Jewish ceremony and culture; it also has a wide array of children's activities, including storytelling hour, arts and crafts workshops and more. The building, a gorgeous banker's mansion from 1908, houses more than 30,000 items of Judaica, as well as works of sculpture, paintings, numismatics, antiquities, prints, decorative arts and photography.

MUSEUM OF THE CITY OF NEW YORK

☎ 212-534-1672; www.mcny.org; 1220 Fifth Ave btwn 103rd & 104th Sts; suggested donation adult/senior & student/family $10/6/20; ☽ 10am-5pm Tue-Sun; ⊕ 6 to 103rd St
Housed in a 1932 Georgian-Colonial mansion, the Museum of the City of New York offers plenty of stimulation, both old-school and technology-based. You'll find internet-based historical resources and a decent scale model of New Amsterdam shortly after the Dutch arrival; the notable 2nd-floor gallery includes entire rooms from demolished homes of New York grandees, an exhibition dedicated to Broadway musicals and a collection of antique dollhouses, teddy bears and toys. Rotating exhibitions cast a clever eye on the city, with past subjects ranging from photographs of New York's waterfront to Catholics in NYC.

CARL SCHURZ PARK

☎ 212-459-4455; www.carlschurzparknyc.org; East End Ave btwn 84th & 89th Sts; ⊕ 4, 5, 6 to 86th St
The placid Carl Schurz Park has long been a favorite spot for a stroll along the East River, or to glimpse the blooming garden grounds of **Gracie Mansion**, the

1799 country residence of wealthy local merchant Archibald Gracie that was appropriated by the city in 1896. Since 1942, when Fiorello La Guardia moved in, this is where New York's mayors have lived – with the exception of the extremely wealthy Mayor Bloomberg, who already has his own plush city digs, thank you very much.

ROOSEVELT ISLAND

 F to Roosevelt Island

Floating in the East River between Manhattan's eastern edge and Queens, New York's anomalous, planned neighborhood sits on a tiny island no wider than a football field. It was once known as Blackwell's Island after the farming family who lived there; the city bought the island in 1828 and constructed several public hospitals and a psychiatric hospital on it. In the 1970s New York State built housing for 10,000 people along Roosevelt Island's Main St (the only street on the island).

Trams leave from the **Roosevelt Island tramway station** (☎ 212-832-4543; www.rioc. com; 60th St at Second Ave) every 15 minutes on the quarter-hour from 6am to 2am Sunday to Thursday, and until 3:30am Friday and Saturday; the one-way fare is $2. Roosevelt Island also has a subway station.

YORKVILLE

6 to 77th St

This area, east of Lexington Ave between 70th and 96th Sts, is known today as the one pocket of the Upper East Side with (relatively) affordable rental apartments. It was once the settling point for new Hungarian and German immigrants – the only trace left of that heritage today are places like **Schaller & Weber** (www.schaller weber.com), an old-world German grocery specializing in sausages, **Heidelberg** (www.heidelbergrestaurant.com), a homey restaurant and German beer garden serving sauerbraten and other traditional goodies (both are on Second Ave between

Museum of the City of New York

KIM GRANT

UPPER EAST SIDE

SLEEPING

Yorkville (p213)

DAN HERRICK

85th and 86th Sts), and the **Yorkville Meat Emporium** (www.hungarianmeatmarket.com; Second Ave at 81st St), which is stocked with fresh meats and prepared Hungarian dishes.

SLEEPING

SURREY   Deluxe Boutique Hotel $$$
☎ 212-288-3700; www.thesurrey.com; 20 E 76th St near Madison Ave; r from $629-7500; ◎ 6 to 77th St; ⊠ ▣

Part of the Affinia chain, the Surrey's been given a grand makeover and is now a sparkling Upper East Side gem. Guests are treated like rare treasures by attentive staff, who gently usher them into huge 'salons' with massive beds custom-made by Duxiana and with luxurious Egyptian cotton linens.

Lucky Surrey visitors can order room service from Café Boulud, the latest UES restaurant of Daniel Boulud. A nightcap on the private rooftop terrace is also in order.

CARLYLE   Indie Inn $$$
☎ 212-744-1600; www.thecarlyle.com; 35 E 76th St btwn Madison & Park Aves; r $595-800; ◎ 6 to 77th St; ⊠ ▣

A classic since its 1930 opening, the 179-room Carlyle is where Woody Allen played clarinet on Monday nights (and sometimes still does), where JFK and Jackie O stayed, and where Louis XIV might feel at home. The lobby's black-marble floors look like a pool of oil, the **Bemelman's Bar** (p217) is slick art deco, and rooms are as big as suites elsewhere, with old-fashioned luxury (such as 430-thread-count linens and jacuzzi bathtubs).

1871 HOUSE   Historic B&B $$$
☎ 212-756-8823; www.1871house.com; 130 E 62nd St btwn Park & Lexington Aves; r $425-800; ◎ N, Q, R to Lexington Ave-59th St; ▣

Named for the year it was built, this historic home has been turned into a classic B&B. Every room is like a mini apartment, with a kitchenette, private bathroom, huge bed, working fireplace and antique or period furnishings. The great location on Lexington and 62nd St means there's a subway nearby, Central Park around the corner and restaurants on all sides (plus a great cheese and salami shop).

FRANKLIN
Boutique Hotel $$

☎ 212-369-1000, 800-607-4009; www.franklin hotel.com; 164 E 87th St btwn Lexington & Third Aves; r $279-360; ❷ 4, 5, 6 to 86th St; ✂ ▢

Except for the small scale, the Franklin could pass for one of New York's grander hotels. Its gold-and-red facade, with uniformed doorman, is a gateway into an intimate lobby, full of fresh flowers and an old-fashioned, 1930s-style elevator. Bulgari amenities and Frette robes adorn the 50 lush rooms (some smaller than others), and a 24-hour espresso and wine bar adorns the lobby.

BUBBA & BEAN LODGES
B&B $

☎ 917-345-7914; www.bblodges.com; 1598 Lexington Ave btwn 101st & 102nd Sts; r/ste $120/220; ❷ 6 to 103rd; ✂ ▢

Owners Jonathan and Clement have turned their double-wide town house into a very nifty B&B that won't empty your pockets. The rooms are really more like full apartments (some fit up to six people). They come with private bathrooms and kitchens, except for the standard room, which uses a public kitchen off the foyer.

EATING

JO JO
French $$$

☎ 212-223-5656; 160 E 64th St at Lexington Ave; ☽ lunch & dinner; ❷ 6 to 68th St-Hunter College

French standards get the Midas touch with the addition of a little something special. And it's all turned out into a dining room that, following a recent renovation, feels so hushed, lush and intimate,

you feel as if you've been invited into an old-school, squeaky-clean bordello.

ITZOCAN BISTRO
French-Mexican Fusion $$

☎ 212-423-0255; 1575 Lexington Ave at 101st St; ☽ dinner Mon-Fri, brunch Sat & Sun; ❷ 6 to 103rd St

This small and lovely cafe, located at the edge of East Harlem, presents an intriguing array of items that combine the best of French and South of the Border cuisine. There's a huitlacoche (corn fungus) soufflé cake, and mussels steamed in tequila to start things off, and then a bevy of amazing mains: adobo-marinated duck breast, pistachio-crusted salmon with chipotle ragout and a batch of seafood tamales.

160

DAN HERRICK

Jo Jo

CAFÉ SABARSKY
Viennese $$

☎ 212-288-0665; Neue Gallerie, 1045 Fifth Ave at 86th St; ☼ 9am-6pm Mon & Wed, to 9pm Thu-Sun; ⊕ 6 to 86th St

You'll find a fresh and authentic array of cafe items here – a shimmering plate of *spaetzle* with corn, peas and wild mushrooms, smoked trout crepes, Viennese sausage with goulash sauce, and salads of red cabbage, pears and blue cheese – plus wines and perfect coffee drinks. But the most compelling reason to stop in lies in the dessert case, where a dizzying array of sweets awaits.

BEYOGLU
Turkish Meze $$

☎ 212-650-0850; 1431 Lexington Ave at 81st St; ☼ lunch & dinner; ⊕ 6 to 77th St

A charismatic, loungey space that's just a short stroll away from the Met, this is where to prolong your cultural imbibing with traditional small plates, such as yogurt soup, doner kebabs, eggplant puree and feta-flecked salads, even daily seafood specials, that are elegant and excellent.

CANDLE CAFÉ
Vegan Cafe $$

☎ 212-472-0970; 1307 Third Ave btwn 74th & 75th Sts; ☼ lunch & dinner; ⊕ 6 to 77th St

Offerings range from the most simple, such as 'good food plates,' a custom-made spread of greens, roots, grains and soy-based protein, to the more complex concoctions, such as the beloved 'paradise casserole,' a feast of layered sweet potatoes, black beans and millet topped with mushroom gravy. An outpost with a slightly more upscale take on the subject is **Candle 79** (☎ 212-537-7179; 154 E 79th St at Lexington Ave; ⊕ 6 to 77th St).

CASCABEL TAQUERIA
Modern Mexican $$

☎ 212-717-7800; 1542 Second Ave btwn 80th & 81st Sts; ☼ lunch & dinner Mon-Fri, brunch Sat & Sun; ⊕ 6 to 86th St

This recent addition to the 'hood has brought with it the bright and cheerful colors of a true taqueria. Head to the friendly counter to place your order for chicken-avocado or veal-tongue tacos, a plate of quinoa with fresh cheese and

Visitors on the steps of the Metropolitan Museum of Art (p209)

RICHARD CUMMINS

black beans, or hearty mains such as blue crab with corn and fresh salsa or grilled hangar steak.

DRINKING

LEXINGTON BAR & BOOKS   Cigar Bar
☎ 212-717-3902; 1020 Lexington Ave at 73rd St; ⊖ 6 to 77th St

Ashtrays and elbows – sometimes stars' elbows – line the elegant bar top in an ultrastylish space that allows the sipping of whiskies, $16 cocktails and cigar smoking. The shelves are lined with books (more for looks than reading), and jazzy lounge music eases the well-dressed night-outers into polite intoxication.

IGGY'S   Karaoke
☎ 212-327-3043; 1452 Second Ave; ⊖ 6 to 77th St

How much you love this skinny Irish-lite pub depends on how badly you need to misbehave in the Upper East Side. The karaoke mic certainly helps the raucous regulars, who bring on a bit of a frat atmosphere some nights.

BEMELMAN'S BAR   Lounge
☎ 212-744-1600; The Carlyle, 35 E 76th St at Madison Ave; ⊖ 6 to 77th St

Waiters wear white jackets, a baby grand piano is always being played and Ludwig Bemelman's *Madeline* murals surround you. It's a classic spot for a serious cocktail – the kind of place that could easily turn up in a Woody Allen film.

ENTERTAINMENT & ACTIVITIES

CAFÉ CARLYLE   Cabaret
☎ 212-744-1600; The Carlyle 35 E 76th St at Madison Ave; ⊖ 6 to 77th St

Jewish Museum (p212)

KIM GRANT

This swanky spot at the Carlyle hotel draws top-shelf talent, from Eartha Kitt to Woody Allen, who plays his clarinet here with his New Orleans jazz band on Mondays (September through May). Bring bucks: it's $75 to $150 per person, not including food or drinks.

FEINSTEIN'S AT THE REGENCY
Cabaret
☎ 212-339-4095; 540 Park Ave at 61st St; ⊖ F to Lexington Ave-63rd St, N, Q, R to Lexington Ave-59th St

You'll be puttin' on the ritz at this high-class joint from cabaret queen Michael Feinstein. You need reservations to get in to see Broadway greats on the small stage (including Betty Buckley, Jackie Mason, Donny Osmond and Tony Danza).

UPPER EAST SIDE

DRINKING

UPPER EAST SIDE

92ND ST Y   Lectures
☎ 212-415-5500; www.92y.org; 1395 Lexington Ave at 92nd St; ⊕ 6 to 96th St

In addition to its spectrum of wonderful readings, the Y hosts an excellent Lectures & Conversations series, which has recently featured thinkers from celeb doc Atul Gawande and actor William Hurt to writer Gail Collins and MSNBC anchor Mika Brzezinski.

SHOPPING

LITTLE SHOP OF CRAFTS   Crafts
☎ 212-717-6636; www.littleshopny.com; 431 E 73rd St; ⊙ 11am-6:30pm Mon & Tue, 11am-10pm Wed-Fri, 10am-7pm Sat, 10am-6:30pm Sun; ⊕ 6 to 68th St-Hunter College

Head to New York's largest craft house when you're in the mood for something crafty, and want to make it yourself. You can opt to paint ceramics (which they provide and then fire for you), create beaded jewelry, assemble a mosaic (picture frame, mirror etc), or even build your own stuffed animal.

RALPH LAUREN   Designer Clothing
☎ 212-606-2100; 867 Madison Ave; ⊙ 10am-7pm Mon-Wed, to 8pm Thu, to 6pm Fri & Sat, noon-6pm Sun; ⊕ 6 to 68th St-Hunter College

Housed in a beautiful 1890s mansion (one of Manhattan's few remaining residences of that era), Ralph's flagship store rewards the long stroll up Madison Ave, even if you've already stocked up on Polo gear elsewhere.

SHOPPING

UPPER WEST SIDE & CENTRAL PARK

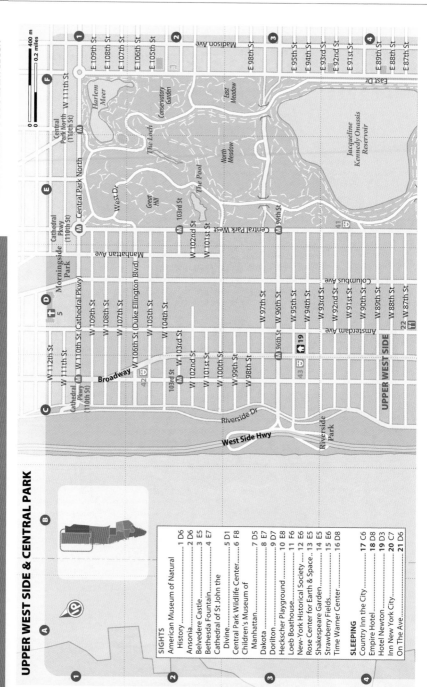

SIGHTS

American Museum of Natural History	1 D6
Ansonia	2 D6
Belvedere Castle	3 E5
Bethesda Fountain	4 E7
Cathedral of St John the Divine	5 D1
Central Park Wildlife Center	6 F8
Children's Museum of Manhattan	7 D5
Dakota	8 E7
Dorilton	9 D7
Heckscher Playground	10 E8
Loeb Boathouse	11 F6
New-York Historical Society	12 E6
Rose Center for Earth & Space	13 E5
Shakespeare Garden	14 E5
Strawberry Fields	15 E6
Time Warner Center	16 D8

SLEEPING

Country Inn the City	17 C6
Empire Hotel	18 D8
Hotel Newton	19 D3
Inn New York City	20 C7
On The Ave	21 D6

UPPER WEST SIDE & CENTRAL PARK

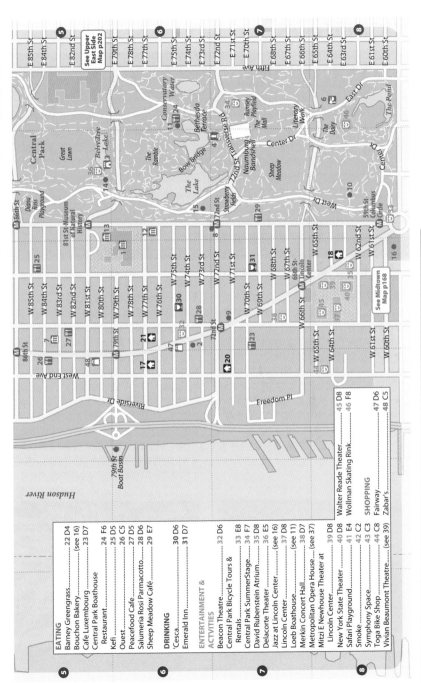

See Upper East Side Map p202

See Midtown Map p168

EATING

Barney Greengrass	22 D4
Bouchon Bakery	(see 16)
Cafe Luxembourg	23 D7
Central Park Boathouse Restaurant	24 F6
Kefi	25 D5
Ouest	26 C5
Peacefood Cafe	27 D5
Salumeria Rosi Parmacotto	28 D6
Sheep Meadow Café	29 E7

DRINKING

'Cesca	30 D6
Emerald Inn	31 D7

ENTERTAINMENT & ACTIVITIES

Beacon Theatre	32 D6
Central Park Bicycle Tours & Rentals	33 E8
Central Park SummerStage	34 F7
David Rubenstein Atrium	35 D8
Delacorte Theater	36 E5
Jazz at Lincoln Center	(see 16)
Lincoln Center	37 D8
Loeb Boathouse	(see 11)
Merkin Concert Hall	38 D7
Metropolitan Opera House	(see 37)
Mitzi E Newhouse Theater at Lincoln Center	39 D8
New York State Theater	40 D8
Safari Playground	41 E4
Smoke	42 C2
Symphony Space	43 C3
Toga Bike Shop	44 C8
Vivian Beaumont Theatre	(see 39)
Walter Reade Theater	45 D8
Wollman Skating Rink	46 F8

SHOPPING

Fairway	47 D6
Zabar's	48 C5

HIGHLIGHTS

1 | CENTRAL PARK

It's hard to imagine what New York City would be like without this refuge from the teeming sidewalks and clogged roadways. This enormous wonderland of a park, sitting right in the middle of Manhattan, provides both metaphorical and spiritual oxygen to its residents. Tens of thousands of people lounge and play on its vast lawns on warm weekends, while others stroll along its meandering paths past forested groves and picturesque ponds.

❧ OUR DON'T MISS LIST

❶ GREAT LAWN

Located between 79th and 86th Sts, this massive emerald carpet hosts outdoor concerts each summer. It's also home to eight softball fields, basketball courts and a canopy of London plane trees. Not far from the actual lawn are several other big sites: the Delacorte Theater, home to the annual Shakespeare in the Park festival, and the panoramic Belvedere Castle.

❷ STRAWBERRY FIELDS

Standing inside the park near 72nd St, this poignant, tear-shaped garden is a memorial to John Lennon, who was murdered nearby in 1980. Strawberry Fields is the most visited spot in Central Park, and is maintained with some help from a $1 million grant from Lennon's widow Yoko Ono (who still resides at the Dakota, the apartment building where Lennon was shot). The peaceful spot contains a grove of stately elms and a tiled mosaic that's often strewn

Clockwise from top: Ice-skating rink (p240); Romeo & Juliet statue; Central Park Wildlife Center (p233); 'Imagine' mosaic, Strawberry Fields; Central Park South at night

CLOCKWISE FROM TOP: GAVIN GOUGH; DONALD C & PRISCILLA ALEXANDER EASTMAN (ROMEO & JULIET, MILTON HEBALD, 1977); ALLAN MONTAINE; BRUCE BI; JEAN-PIERRE LESCOURRET

with rose petals and other offerings from visitors. It says, simply, 'Imagine.'

❸ CENTRAL PARK WILDLIFE CENTER

The penguins are the main attraction at this zoo (p233), though you'll find more than two dozen other species to visit, including polar bears, snow leopards, tamarin monkeys and red pandas. Feeding times are especially rowdy and fun to stroll through: watch the sea lions chow down at 11:30am, 2pm and 4pm, and see the penguins gobble fish at 10:30am and 2:30pm. The attached Tisch Children's Zoo (btwn 65th & 66th Sts) is perfect for smaller children.

❹ STATUARY IN THE PARK

Central Park is home to some wonderful, freestanding works of art.

While almost everyone is familiar with Angel of the Waters atop Bethesda Fountain, even New Yorkers may have overlooked the Falconer Statue, on a rise overlooking the 72nd St Transverse nearby. Literary Walk is lined with statues. East and north is the Conservatory Water, where model sailboats drift by and kids crawl over the giant toadstools of the Alice in Wonderland statue.

⤴ THINGS YOU NEED TO KNOW

Survival tip Look out for speeding cyclists when walking the park loop Hard facts The full loop is 6 miles; the north end has some tough hills Best photo op Bow Bridge, stretching over the lake from Cheery Hill to the Ramble For more on Central Park, see p232. For Central Park WalkingTour, see p226.

HIGHLIGHTS

2

⌖ AMERICAN MUSEUM OF NATURAL HISTORY

Kids of all ages will find something intriguing at the American Museum of Natural History (p229), whether it's the stuffed Alaskan brown bear, the Star of India sapphire in the Hall of Minerals and Gems, the IMAX film on jungle life, or the skullcap of a pachycephalosaurus. Step inside the Rose Center for Earth & Space, a high-tech planetarium that traces the origins of the planets.

3

⌖ RIVERSIDE PARK

Riverside Park (p229) stretches for 4 miles between W 72nd St and W 158th St along the Hudson River, and is a great place for strolling, running, cycling or simply gazing at the sun as it sets over the Hudson River. There are well-placed benches and a dog run, the seasonal Boat Basin Café at 79th St, and various works of public art, including a statue of Eleanor Roosevelt at the 72nd St entrance.

↘ JAZZ AT LINCOLN CENTER

Back in 2004 Jazz at Lincoln Center (www.jazzatlincolncenter.com) left its old home for its grand new digs at the Frederick P Rose Hall in the Time Warner Center, a 100,000-sq-ft, $128-million facility built specifically for jazz music. The multiroom space hosts opera, dance, theater and symphony shows, but its main theme is jazz.

↘ BROADWAY

While it's a far cry from the bad ol' days of the 1970s and even '80s – when there was an unsavory feel in the air – today's stretch of Broadway on the Upper West Side has been colonized by banks, pharmacies and retail chains. However, it's still the spine of the neighborhood, lined with prewar apartments, used-book dealers, and traditional diners.

↘ MORNINGSIDE HEIGHTS

The Upper West Side bleeds into this neighborhood, where Columbia University (p232) dominates the architectural and social milieu. Overlooking Morningside Park is the restored Cathedral of St John the Divine (p232). Grab a croissant with the students and professors at the Hungarian Pastry Shop across the street.

2 DENNIS JOHNSON; 3 DAN HERRICK; 4 DAN HERRICK; 5 COREY WISE; 6 DAN HERRICK

2 Allosaurus skeleton, American Museum of Natural History (p229); 3 Riverside Park (p229); 4 Jazz at Lincoln Center; 5 Apartments in Upper West Side; 6 Cathedral of St John the Divine (p232)

A WALK IN THE PARK WALKING TOUR

This walk begins at Strawberry Fields just inside the park at 72nd St and ends at Columbus Circle at Central Park South (59th St) and Central Park West. The itinerary covers around 2 miles and should take around two hours.

❶ STRAWBERRY FIELDS

Fittingly, **Strawberry Fields** (p222), the memorial garden for John Lennon, is located in the area of Central Park that's just across the street from the **Dakota**, the building where he lived – and died. Head in and hang for a while; you'll most likely find yourself in the company of guitar players, flower bearers and other assorted mourners and fans.

❷ SHEEP MEADOW

Continue a bit deeper into the park and head south; you'll soon come to this vast open lawn where, on warm days, there's nary an inch of grass not occupied by sunbathers and picnickers.

❸ THE CAROUSEL

Just south of here around midpark at 64th St is one of the more photographed sights – an old-fashioned, calliope-tooting carousel that looks like it belongs in a state fair. Grab a seat or simply watch the joy on the faces of youngsters spinning around on one of the country's largest merry-go-rounds.

❹ THE MALL

From here, follow the roadway east until you come to the formal, tree-lined promenade called the **Mall**, which culminates at the elegant **Bethesda Fountain**, with the uplifting *Angel of the Waters* sculpture at the center. In warm weather, you'll find a vendor near here doling out warm, fresh crepes and empanadas, providing the perfect opportunity for a snack break.

❺ CONSERVATORY WATER

Find a path east to the loop roadway and walk a little way north until you see this American version of a Parisian model-boat pond. Rest on one of the surrounding benches as elaborately designed radio-powered boats ply the waters.

❻ RAMBLE

After so much civilized elegance you'll want to head back into the wilds. To the west of the boathouse is the **Ramble**, a lush, wooded expanse that serves as a decent bird-watching pocket. Be sure to note your surroundings so you don't get hopelessly turned around in your hike.

❼ BELVEDERE CASTLE
Try to exit somewhere north or follow the roadway on the west side until you see the lovely 19th-century **Belvedere Castle**, which rises up out of Vista Rock and provides breezy, beautiful views of the surrounding parkland. It's one of the best perches for park photos.

❽ DELACORTE THEATER
Just on the other side of Turtle Pond is the **Delacorte Theater** (p233), home to summertime Shakespeare in the Park productions, where the main scenery is the verdant park itself.

❾ GREAT LAWN
North of here is the grand (and appropriately named) **Great Lawn** (p233), where free concerts are occasionally held. Pick a corner, spread out and enjoy.

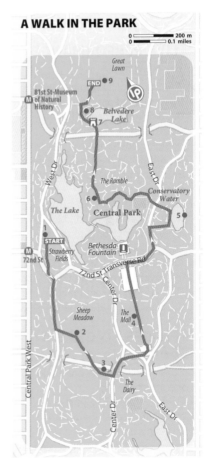

A WALK IN THE PARK

BEST...

⇘ LIVE PERFORMANCE SPACES

- **Theater** Magical summer evening performances of Shakespeare at the Delacorte Theater (p233).
- **Opera** Top stars and mind-boggling costumes and sets from September to May; visiting operas from around the world from June to August (p239).
- **Classical Music** The acoustics at Avery Fisher Hall (p230) have been improved; it's home to the New York Philharmonic.
- **Jazz** Jazz lounge Smoke (p238) offers inventive and traditional jazz.
- **Dance** Premieres and revivals at the New York State Theater (p238).

⇘ PLACES TO GRAB A BAGEL

- **Zabar's** (p240) Take one to go at the attached cafe.
- **Fairway** (p240) The upstairs restaurant serves them with lox, eggs and onions.

- **Barney Greengrass** (p235) Get a sturgeon sandwich on your choice of eight varieties.

⇘ OLD-SCHOOL APARTMENT BUILDINGS

- **Ansonia** Grand and sophisticated building at Broadway between 73rd and 74th.
- **Dakota** On Central Park West & 72nd St; where *Rosemary's Baby* was filmed and John Lennon was fatally shot.
- **Dorilton** An enormous arched entryway and Beaux Arts magnificence at W 71st at Broadway.

⇘ FESTIVALS

- **Lincoln Center Out of Doors Festivals** (p230) A series of dance and music concerts.
- **New York Film Festival** (p238) Each September at Lincoln Center's Walter Reade Theater.

ANGUS OBORN

Zabar's (p240)

DISCOVER UPPER WEST SIDE & CENTRAL PARK

Home to aging liberals, wealthy young families and an eclectic mix of actors and musicians, the Upper West Side stretches up along the western side of Central Park to Riverside Park, which runs along the Hudson River. Quaint residential blocks and bustling sections of Broadway have been hyperdeveloped into strips of high-rise condos, drugstore chains and banks. Much of the area is still an architectural wonderland, though, with everything from opulent apartment buildings to the newly designed Lincoln Center.

Designed as a leisure space for all New Yorkers, the vast and majestic Central Park is an oasis from the urban insanity. The lush lawns, cool forests, flowering gardens, glassy bodies of water, and meandering, wooded paths provide the dose of serene nature that New Yorkers crave. That such a large expanse of prime real estate has survived intact for so long again proves that nothing eclipses the heart, soul and pride that forms the foundation of New York City's greatness.

SIGHTS

UPPER WEST SIDE

AMERICAN MUSEUM OF NATURAL HISTORY

☎ 212-769-5100; www.amnh.org; Central Park West at 79th St; suggested donation adult/child/senior & student $16/9/12, last hr free; ⏰ 10am-5:45pm (Rose Center to 8:45pm 1st Fri of the month); ◉ B, C to 81st St-Museum of Natural History, 1 to 79th St

Founded in 1869, this classic museum for kids of all ages contains halls of fascinating wonderlands holding more than 30 million artifacts; its interactive exhibits, both in the original museum and its newest section, the Rose Center for Earth & Space, are also out of this world. The most famous attractions are its three large dinosaur halls, with various skeletons for ogling, and the enormous (fake) blue whale that hangs from the ceiling of the Hall of Ocean Life.

It's the Rose Center for Earth & Space, though, that has really been the star attraction since its much-heralded opening over a decade ago. Just gazing at its facade – a massive glass box that contains a silver globe, home to space-show theaters and the planetarium – is mesmerizing, especially at night when all of its otherworldly features are aglow. Another, smaller theater explores the Big Bang Theory with Maya Angelou's voice as your guide – and a virtual adventure lets you experience a 'Field Trip to the Moon,' with all of the requisite shaking and spectacular views.

RIVERSIDE PARK

www.riversideparkfund.org; from 59th to 158th Sts along Hudson River; ◉ 1, 2, 3 to 72nd St or higher

This skinny, lively green space is a great place to stroll, bike, run or sit back and watch all those active types pass by. It's lined with cherry trees that blossom into

Lincoln Center

RICHARD CUMMINS

↘ LINCOLN CENTER

The 16-acre Lincoln Center complex includes a dozen large performance spaces built in the 1960s, which controversially replaced a group of tenements called San Juan Hill, where exterior shots for the movie *West Side Story* were filmed. The latest controversy has been a massive redesign, by New York 'starchitects' Diller Scofidio + Renfro, which began in 2007 as a way to usher in Lincoln Center's 50th anniversary celebration. One of the most exciting new additions has been that of the David Rubenstein Atrium, a modern public space offering a lounge area, a cafe, a ticket vendor offering on-the-day discount tickets to Lincoln Center performances and a roster of Thursday-eve free performances.

New buildings aside, though, if you have just a shred of culture vulture in you, Lincoln Center is a must-see, since it contains the Metropolitan Opera House, its lobby adorned by murals by Marc Chagall, and the New York State Theater, home to the New York City Ballet and the New York City Opera. The New York Philharmonic holds its season in Avery Fisher Hall, and you'll find high-quality theatrical productions at the Mitzi E Newhouse and Vivian Beaumont Theaters.

To the right stands the New York Public Library for the Performing Arts, which houses the city's largest collection of recorded sound, video and books on film and theater. Then there's the Walter Reade Theater, the city's most comfortable film-revival space and the major screening site for the New York Film Festival. On any given night there are at least 10 performances happening throughout Lincoln Center, and even more in summer when Lincoln Center Out of Doors (a series of dance and music concerts) and Midsummer Night Swing (ballroom dancing under the stars) lure those who love parks *and* culture.

Things you need to know: David Rubenstein Atrium (Broadway btwn 62nd & 63rd Sts); Lincoln Center (☎ 212-875-5456; www.lincolncenter.org; Columbus Ave at 64th St; ◉ 1 to 66th St-Lincoln Center); New York Public Library for the Performing Arts (☎ 212-870-1630) puffs of pink in the spring; community gardens that are lovingly tended by volunteers; 14 playgrounds that are popular with the local eight-and-under set; basketball courts and baseball fields. It's a gem worth trekking to, especially at sunset, when the Hudson River is bathed in soft gold tones and the city seems like a peaceful place at last.

NEW-YORK HISTORICAL SOCIETY
☎ 212-873-3400; www.nyhistory.org; 2 W 77th St at Central Park West; suggested donation adult/student/senior $12/7/9, Fri 6-8pm pay what you wish; 🕙 10am-6pm Tue, Thu & Sat, to 8pm Fri, 11am-5:45pm Sun; 🚇 B, C to 81st St-Museum of Natural History, 1 to 79th St

As the antiquated hyphenated name implies, the New-York Historical Society is the city's oldest museum, founded in 1804 to preserve the city's historical and cultural artifacts. Only here can you see 17th-century cowbells and baby rattles and the mounted wooden leg of colonial-era statesman Gouverneur Morris. The Henry Luce III Center for the Study of American Culture, which opened in 2000, is a 21,000-sq-ft showcase of more than 40,000 objects from the museum's permanent collection, and features items such as fine portraits, Tiffany lamps and model ships.

CHILDREN'S MUSEUM OF MANHATTAN
☎ 212-721-1234; www.cmom.org; 212 W 83rd St btwn Amsterdam Ave & Broadway; adult & child/senior/child under 1yr $10/7/free, 5-8pm 1st Fri of the month free; 🕙 10am-5pm Tue-Sun; 🚇 1 to 86th St, B, C to 81st St-Museum of Natural History

Always crowded and a perpetual rainy-day saver for neighborhood parents (and, often, nannies), this is a play center where interactive exhibits are scaled down for little people. It features discovery centers for toddlers, a postmodern media center where technologically savvy kids can work in a TV studio, and the Inventor Center, where all the latest, cool tech stuff such as digital imaging and scanners is made available.

RICHARD I'ANSON

Children's Museum of Manhattan

UPPER WEST SIDE & CENTRAL PARK

SIGHTS

Low Library, Columbia University

MICHELLE BENNETT

⤵ IF YOU LIKE...

If you enjoy marveling at the architecture of the **Lincoln Center** (p230), we think you'll enjoy these other sights:

- **Cathedral of St John the Divine** (☎ 212-316-7540; www.stjohndivine.org; Amsterdam Ave at 112th St; public tours $5, vertical tours including stair climb $15; ⏰ 7am-6pm Mon-Sat, to 7pm Sun; ⊕ B, C, 1 to 110th St-Cathedral Pkwy) The largest place of worship in the USA, this recently restored masterpiece truly inspires awe. High Mass held at 11am Sunday often features sermons by well-known intellectuals.

- **Cloisters** (☎ 212-923-3700; www.metmuseum.org/cloisters/; Fort Tryon Park; suggested donation adult/child/senior & student $20/free/10; ⏰ 9:30am-4:45pm Tue-Sun Nov-Feb, to 5:15pm Mar-Oct; ⊕ A to 190th St) Located far north of the UWS in Washington Heights, this branch of the Met – with commanding views of the Hudson – was constructed from stones and fragments of several French and Spanish medieval monasteries.

- **Columbia University** (☎ 212-854-1754; www.columbia.edu; Broadway at 116th St; ⊕ 1 to 116th St-Columbia University) The centerpiece of this Ivy league college campus is a grassy quadrangle that's dominated by the 1895 neoclassical Low Library.

- **Riverside Church** (☎ 212-870-6700; www.theriversidechurchny.org; 490 Riverside Dr at 120th St; ⏰ 7am-10pm; ⊕ 1 to 116th St-Columbia University) A 1930 Gothic-style marvel, famous for its 74 carillon bells that are rung every Sunday at noon and 3pm, as well as for its diverse and activist congregation.

CENTRAL PARK

Like the city's subway system, the vast and majestic **Central Park** (www.centralparknyc. org), an 843-acre rectangle of open space in the middle of Manhattan, is a great class leveler – which is exactly what it was envisioned to be. Created in the 1860s and '70s by Frederick Law Olmsted and Calvert

Vaux on the marshy northern fringe of the city, the immense park was designed as a leisure space for all New Yorkers, regardless of color, class or creed.

Today, this 'people's park' is still one of the city's most popular attractions, beckoning throngs of New Yorkers with free outdoor concerts at the **Great Lawn**, animals at the **Central Park Wildlife Center** (☎ 212-861-6030; www.centralpark zoo.com; 64th St at Fifth Ave; adult/child/under 3yr $10/5/free; ✆ 10am-5pm Mon-Fri, to 5:30pm weekends & holidays Apr-Oct, 10am-4:30pm daily Nov-Mar; ◉ N, Q, R to 5th Ave-59th St) and top-notch drama at the annual Shakespeare in the Park productions, held each summer at the open-air **Delacorte Theater**.

Some other recommended stops include the **Bethesda Fountain** (midpark at 72nd St), which edges the **Lake** and its **Loeb Boathouse**, where you can rent rowboats; the **Shakespeare Garden** (west side btwn 79th & 80th Sts), which has lush plantings and skyline views; and the **Ramble** (midpark from 73rd to 79th Sts), a wooded thicket that's popular with bird-watchers. While parts of the park swarm with joggers, in-line skaters, musicians and tourists on warm weekends, it's quieter on weekday afternoons – but especially in less well-trodden spots above 72nd St such as the **Harlem Meer** (at 110th St) and the **North Meadow** (north of 97th St). Folks flock to the park even in winter, when snowstorms can inspire cross-country skiing and sledding or a simple stroll through the white wonderland, and crowds turn out every New Year's Eve for a midnight run.

SLEEPING

INN NEW YORK CITY
B&B $$$

☎ 212-580-1900, 800-660-7051; www.innnew yorkcity.com; 266 W 71st St at West End Ave; ste $475-645; ◉ 1, 2, 3 to 72nd St; ✵

Four massive, quirky suites occupy a whole floor in this 1900 town house, which allows you to feel as if you're living in a mansion. It's far west, close to Riverside Park (and near Central Park), and its rooms feature antique chestnut furnishings, feather beds topped in down comforters, jacuzzis and stained-glass panels – if just a bit too much flowered carpeting.

COUNTRY INN THE CITY
B&B $$

☎ 212-580-4183; www.countryinnthecity.com; 270 W 77th St btwn Broadway & West End Aves; apt $250-350; ◉ 1 to 79th St; ✵ ▭

Just like staying with your big-city friend: this 1891 limestone town house sits on a stellar, tree-lined street, and the four popular, self-contained apartments are

DAN HERRICK

Playing music, Central Park

cool and sophisticated, with four-poster beds, glossed wooden floors, warm color schemes and lots of light. There's a three-night minimum.

EMPIRE HOTEL · Hotel $$

☎ 212-265-7400; www.empirehotelnyc.com; 44 W 63rd St at Broadway; r $229-750; ⊕ 1 to 66th St; ⊠ ☐

An old hotel remade, complete with canopied pool deck and rooftop bar, the new and improved Empire's making quite a splash on the staid Upper West Side (it even made it into a few episodes of *Gossip Girl*). The extra-large (for NYC) rooms are in either a beachy orange or basic black, and both have plush dark leather furnishings, with zebra stripe accents.

ON THE AVE · Boutique Hotel $$

☎ 212-362-1100, 800-497-6028; www.ontheave. com; 2178 Broadway at W 77th St; r $179-309; ⊕ 1 to 79th St, 2, 3 to 72nd St; ⊠ ☐

An excellent uptown hotel, the stylish and cool 16-floor On the Ave boasts 266 rooms done up in warm earthy tones and

brimming with extras (eg fudge-colored suede headboards backing new featherbeds, flat-screen TVs and bedside CD players). There's a super glassed-in top-floor balcony with seats facing the north.

HOTEL NEWTON · Traveler Hotel $

☎ 212-678-6500; www.newyorkhotel.com/ newton; 2528 Broadway btwn 94th & 95th Sts; r from $130; ⊕ 1, 2, 3 to 96th St; ⊠ ☐

This 109-room hotel has all-new furnishings and caters to a mix of international visitors and academic folk wanting a base for Columbia University, 20 blocks north. All rooms have refrigerators, microwaves, internet access and double-paned windows, but are nothing if not nondescript.

EATING
UPPER WEST SIDE

OUEST · Traditional French-American $$$

☎ 212-580-8700; 2315 Broadway at 84th St; ☾ dinner; ⊕ 1 to 86th St

Behind the deco facade you'll find sumptuous red leather banquettes, huge mir-

Empire Hotel

DAN HERRICK

rors and low lighting that casts a romantic amber glow. But it's the heavy-hitting, expertly prepared classics – shellfish ragout, grilled rack of lamb, pan-roasted squab, seared tuna – that people trudge here for.

CAFÉ LUXEMBOURG
French Brasserie $$$

☎ 212-580-8700; 200 W 70th St btwn Broadway & West End Ave; breakfast, lunch & dinner daily, brunch Sun; 1, 2, 3 to 72nd St
The quintessential city eatery, this neighborhood stalwart has it all: an elegant setting, friendly staff, a crowd of locals and flattering lighting – with an outstanding menu to boot. Its execution of standards, including salmon tartare, cassoulet and steak *frites*, is consistently excellent, as is its approach to a range of other options, from salads and fresh pasta dishes to fabulous and eggy brunch options.

SALUMERIA ROSI PARMACOTTO
Italian Small Plates $$

☎ 212-877-4800; 284 Amsterdam Ave at 73rd St; 11am-11pm; 1, 2, 3 to 72nd St
One of the newest buzzed-about spots in the neighborhood is this intimate little meat-loving nook, where you can begin with small platters of sliced cheeses and meats like salamis, slow-roasted pork loins, sausages, cured hams and all other manner of pig imaginable, and then move on to sharing plates of various tasty treats.

PEACEFOOD CAFE
Vegan Cafe & Bakery $$

☎ 212-362-2266; 460 Amsterdam Ave at 82nd St; lunch & dinner; 1 to 79th St
You'll be hard pressed to find an undelicious item on this creative menu, which has several standouts including the seitan sandwich, served on homemade focaccia and topped with creamy 'goat cheese' and arugula, and the fresh quinoa salad,

On the Ave
DAN HERRICK

studded with fresh corn kernals and avocado.

BARNEY GREENGRASS
Jewish Deli $$

☎ 212-724-4707; 541 Amsterdam Ave at 86th St; breakfast & lunch; 1 to 86th St
Step back in time at this century-old 'sturgeon king' gourmet shop and eatery serving a long list of traditional Jewish delicacies, including bagels and lox, a kippered salmon and whitefish platter, pastrami on rye, and sturgeon scrambled with eggs and onions.

KEFI
Greek $$

☎ 212-873-0200; 505 Columbus Ave btwn 84th & 85th Sts; dinner; B, C to 86th St
When it opened in 2007, this taverna-style spot became an instant classic thanks to

BRUCE ESBIN

Afternoon tea in Central Park

its elegant take on hearty, traditional Greek food and its intimate dining room decked out with billowy wall hangings. Settle into plates of moussaka, spanakopita, grilled octopus, lamb, and rich, raisin-studded meatballs.

BOUCHON BAKERY   Eclectic Cafe $
☎ 212-823-9366; 50 Columbus Circle, Time Warner Center; ☾ lunch & dinner; ◉ A, C, B, D to 59th St-Columbus Circle
The most accessible of the bevy of high-end restaurants in the Time Warner Center, this one, from Per Se owner Thomas Keller, brings new meaning to 'food court.' An open-air (well, mall-air) cafe, its fare is outstanding: beet and mâche salad, three-bean soup, turkey, tuna and veggie sandwiches that soar to new gourmet heights.

CENTRAL PARK
CENTRAL PARK BOATHOUSE
RESTAURANT   Upscale American $$$
☎ 212-517-2233; Central Park Lake, enter Fifth Ave at 72nd St; ☾ lunch daily, brunch Sat & Sun year-round, dinner daily Apr-Nov; ◉ 6 to 77th St

Escape the city and enter this magical lakeside setting, just by taking a 10-minute walk off Central Park West. The historic **Loeb Boathouse**, perched on the shores of the park's lake, is one of the city's most incredible settings for a serene and romantic meal – and the food is top-notch, too.

Reserve early and aim for an outdoor table – or simply slip up to the bar and enjoy a lakeside cocktail.

SHEEP MEADOW CAFE
Casual American $
☎ 212-396-4100; Central Park W at 69th St; ☾ breakfast & lunch daily Sep-May, breakfast, lunch & dinner Jun-Aug; ◉ B, C to 72nd St
Another above-foodcart option within the park is the alfresco Sheep Meadow Cafe, which functions as a typical snack bar by day – burgers, fries, ice cream – but which lights some candles and doles out surprisingly good mains, including grilled swordfish and steak platters, on balmy nights.

DRINKING

EMERALD INN   Irish Pub
☎ 212-874-8840; 205 Columbus Ave btwn 69th & 70th Sts; ◉ 1, 2, 3 to 72nd St
Elderly men and postwork suits cloister in this pocket-sized, ever-inviting pub with a (real) Irish accent. There's plenty of good food (burgers and shepherd's pie, naturally). Seating's a bit cramped if you can't get the sofa by the front.

'CESCA   Wine Bar
☎ 212-787-6300; 164 W 75th St btwn Amsterdam & Columbus Aves; ◉ 1, 2, 3 to 72nd St
With lots of dark wood, some romantic tables and a large free-floating bar in the center of the room, the front area of 'Cesca is handsome in a gentlemen's smoking lounge sort of way. There's an impressive list of wines by the glass, plus great bar food.

ENTERTAINMENT & ACTIVITIES
UPPER WEST SIDE
TOGA BIKE SHOP   Bicycle Rental
☎ 212-799-9625; www.togabikes.com; 110 West End Ave btwn 64th & 65th Sts; rentals per 24hr $35; ◷ 11am-7pm Mon-Fri, 10am-6pm Sat, 11am-6pm Sun; ◉ 1 to 66th St-Lincoln Center
Located between Central Park and the Hudson River path, this friendly and long-standing bike shop rents bikes in good weather (typically April through October).

MERKIN CONCERT HALL
                                              Classical Music
☎ 212-501-3330; www.kaufman-center. org/merkin-concert-hall; 129 W 67th St btwn Amsterdam Ave & Broadway; ◉ 1 to 66th St-Lincoln Center

The 450-seat Merkin Concert Hall, part of the Kaufman Center, which also runs a public arts school and public school for musically gifted kids, is one of the city's more intimate venues to hear classical music.

SYMPHONY SPACE   Classical Music
☎ 212-864-1414; www.symphonyspace.org; 2537 Broadway at 95th St; ◉ 1, 2, 3 to 96th St
A multigenre space with several facilities in one, this Upper West Side performance space turns out some impressive classical music along with theater, opera, jazz and readings.

Peacefood Cafe (p235)

DAN HERRICK

DAN HERRICK

Shopping at Fairway (p240)

METROPOLITAN OPERA HOUSE

Dance

☎ 212-362-6000; www.metopera.org; Lincoln Center, 64th St at Columbus Ave; ⓔ 1 to 66th St-Lincoln Center

The **American Ballet Theatre** (www.abt. org) presents its largely classical season of full-length ballets each spring at this grand and massive theater at **Lincoln Center** (p230), also the place to catch visiting ballets from around the world. Be sure to get as close as you can afford, as high-up seats remove you greatly from the pomp and circumstance onstage.

NEW YORK STATE THEATER　Dance

☎ 212-870-5570; www.nycopera.com; Lincoln Center, 64th St at Columbus Ave; ⓔ 1 to 66th St-Lincoln Center

Established by Lincoln Kirstein and George Balanchine in 1948, the **New York City Ballet** (www.nycballet.com) features a varied season of premieres and revivals, including a production of George Balanchine's *The Nutcracker* during the Christmas holidays. All performances are held at this 2755-seat Lincoln Center theater, designed by Philip Johnson and featuring a grand terrace, where you can gaze into the center courtyard during intermissions.

WALTER READE THEATER　Film & TV

☎ 212-875-5600; www.filmlinc.com; Lincoln Center, 165 W 65th St; ⓔ 1 to 66th St-Lincoln Center

The Walter Reade boasts some wonderfully wide, screening-room-style seats and hosts, every September, the New York Film Festival, featuring plenty of New York and world premieres. At other times of the year you can catch independent films, career retrospectives and themed series.

SMOKE　Jazz & Experimental

☎ 212-864-6662; www.smokejazz.com; 2751 Broadway btwn 105th & 106th Sts; ⓔ 1 to 103rd St

The 1999 incarnation of Augie's, this swank but laid-back lounge – with good stage views from plush sofas – brings out some old-timers, with many New York faves such as George Coleman, Hank Jones and local Lea Delaria, who scatted here for her 2007 live album. Most nights there's a $10 cover, plus $20 to $30 food and drink minimum.

BEACON THEATRE　Live Music

☎ 212-465-6500; www.beacontheatre.com; 2124 Broadway btwn 74th & 75th Sts; ⓔ 1, 2, 3 to 72nd St

This historic 1929 theater is a perfect in-between-sized venue, with 2000 seats (not a terrible one in the house) and a constant flow of national acts, though many tend to be on the geriatric side (Dave Matthews band, Allman Brothers). Following a $16 million restoration completed in 2009, the theater looks snazzier than ever.

METROPOLITAN OPERA HOUSE

Opera

☎ 212-362-6000; www.metopera.org; Lincoln Center, 64th St at Columbus Ave; ⊕ 1 to 66th St-Lincoln Center

New York's premier opera company, the Metropolitan Opera offers a spectacular mixture of classics and premieres. The season runs from September to April. Though ticket prices start at $70 and can get close to $300, the standing-room tickets ($15 to $20) are one of NYC's best bargains.

NEW YORK STATE THEATER   Opera

☎ 212-870-5630; www.nycopera.com; Lincoln Center, 64th St at Columbus Ave; ⊕ 1 to 66th St-Lincoln Center

This is the home of the **New York City Opera**, a more daring and lower-cost company than the Metropolitan Opera. It performs new works, neglected operas and revitalized old standards in the recently and marvelously renovated Philip Johnson–designed space.

CENTRAL PARK

LOEB BOATHOUSE

Bicycle Rental, Boating & Kayaking

☎ 212-517-2233; www.thecentralparkboathouse.com; Central Park btwn 74th & 75th Sts; ⊕ B, C to 72nd St, 6 to 77th St

Central Park's boathouse has a fleet of 100 **rowboats**, plus three **kayaks** for rent (per hour $12; open 10am to dusk from April to November, weather permitting). In the summer you can also hire a Venetian-style **gondola** that seats up to six (per 30 minutes $30).

Various types of **bikes** are available (per hour $9 to $15; open 10am to 6pm weekdays, 9am to 6pm weekends, weather permitting), roughly April to November.

DAN HERRICK

Metropolitan Opera House

You'll need an ID and credit card to rent one. Helmets provided.

WOLLMAN SKATING RINK Ice Skating
☎ 212-439-6900; www.wollmanskatingrink.com; Central Park, near 59th St & Sixth Ave entrance; adult/child/senior $10.25/5.50/4.75 Mon-Thu, $14.75/5.75/8.25 Fri-Sun, skate rental $6.25; ⏲ 10am-2:30pm Mon & Tue, to 10pm Wed & Thu, to 11pm Fri & Sat, to 9pm Sun Oct-Apr; ⊕ F to 57 St, N, Q, R to 5th Ave-59th St
Larger than Rockefeller's, and allowing all-day skating (as if…), this rink is at the southern edge of Central Park, and has nice views. It's open mid-October through April.

SHOPPING
The traditionally Jewish neighborhood still has places true to its roots, such as fabled sturgeon king Barney Greengrass, plus delis, bagelries, gourmet shops and such. Three main avenues (Broadway, Amsterdam and Columbus) run through the neighborhood. You'll find endless chain stores including Barnes & Noble, Banana Republic and Gap on Broadway between about 80th and 90th Sts.

FAIRWAY Gourmet Food
☎ 212-595-1888; 2127 Broadway at 75th St; ⏲ 6am-1am; ⊕ 1, 2, 3 to 72nd St
Like a museum of good eats, this landmark grocery spills its lovely mounds of produce into its sidewalk bins, seducing you inside to its aisles of international goodies, fine cooking oils, nuts, cheeses, prepared foods and, upstairs, an organic market and chichi cafe.

ZABAR'S Gourmet Food, Kitchenware
☎ 212-787-2000; 2245 Broadway; ⏲ 8:30am-7:30pm Mon-Fri, 8am-8pm Sat, 9am-6pm Sun; ⊕ 1 to 79th St
A New York classic gourmet emporium, Zabar's is famous not only for its food – especially the amazing array of cheeses, olives, jams, coffee, caviar and smoked fish – but also its large 2nd-floor kitchenware department.

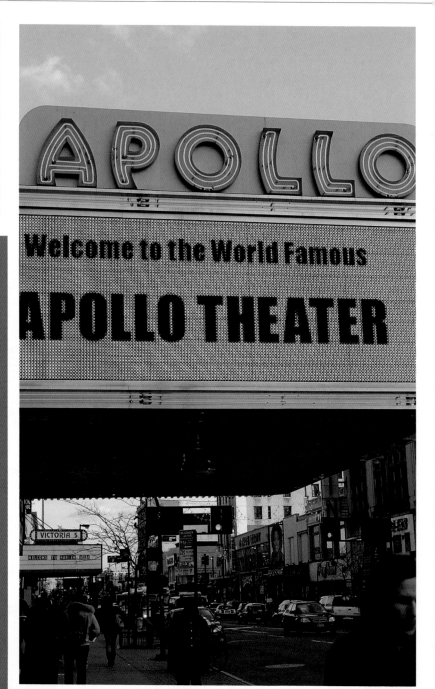

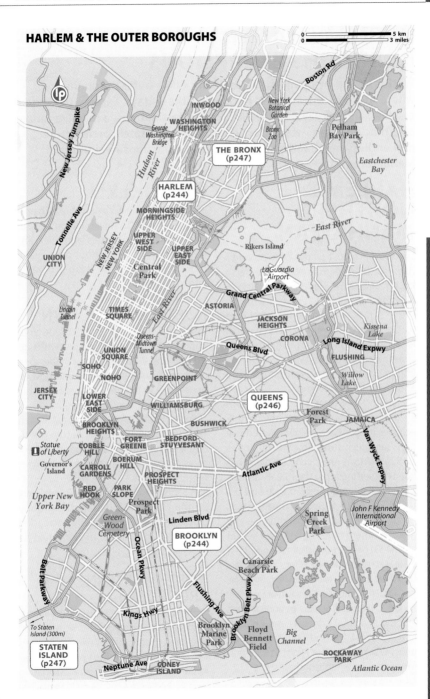

HARLEM & THE OUTER BOROUGHS

0 ——— 5 km
0 ——— 3 miles

Boston Rd

New Jersey Turnpike

INWOOD

New York
Botanical
Garden

WASHINGTON
HEIGHTS

George
Washington
Bridge

Bronx
Zoo

Pelham
Bay Park

**THE BRONX
(p247)**

Eastchester
Bay

Hudson River

**HARLEM
(p244)**

Tonnelle Ave

MORNINGSIDE
HEIGHTS

East River

Rikers Island

UPPER
WEST
SIDE

UPPER
EAST
SIDE

NEW JERSEY
NEW YORK

LaGuardia
Airport

UNION
CITY

Central
Park

Grand Central Parkway

Lincoln
Tunnel

ASTORIA

East River

JACKSON
HEIGHTS

Kissena
Lake

TIMES
SQUARE

CORONA

Long Island Expwy

Queens-
Midtown
Tunnel

Queens Blvd

FLUSHING

UNION
SQUARE

Willow
Lake

SOHO

NOHO

GREENPOINT

JERSEY
CITY

LOWER
EAST
SIDE

WILLIAMSBURG

**QUEENS
(p246)**

Forest
Park

JAMAICA

BROOKLYN
HEIGHTS

BUSHWICK

Statue
of Liberty

COBBLE
HILL

FORT
GREENE

BEDFORD-
STUYVESANT

Van Wyck Expwy

Governor's
Island

BOERUM
HILL

CARROLL
GARDENS

PROSPECT
HEIGHTS

Atlantic Ave

RED
HOOK

PARK
SLOPE

John F Kennedy
International
Airport

Upper New
York Bay

Green-
Wood
Cemetery

Prospect
Park

Linden Blvd

Spring
Creek
Park

Ocean Pkwy

**BROOKLYN
(p244)**

Belt Parkway

Canarsie
Beach Park

Flushing Ave

Brooklyn Belt Pkwy

Big
Channel

Kings Hwy

To Staten
Island (300m)

Brooklyn
Marine
Park

Floyd
Bennett
Field

ROCKAWAY
PARK

**STATEN
ISLAND
(p247)**

Neptune Ave

CONEY
ISLAND

Atlantic Ocean

HARLEM & OUTER BOROUGHS EXCURSIONS

Worlds in and of themselves, New York City's outer boroughs are where much of the action is happening these days. Explore the sandy beaches and breezy boardwalks, foodie destinations, a massive range of ethnic enclaves, world-class entertainment, stately architecture and endless neighborhood streets – the attractions rival those of Manhattan.

HARLEM & NORTHERN MANHATTAN

The southernmost swatch of the island's top end is **Harlem**; East Harlem, also known as Spanish Harlem or El Barrio, is filled primarily with Latino residents. To the west is **Morningside Heights**, home to **Columbia University**; to the north is **Washington Heights**, with its large Dominican community, and **Inwood**, edged by attractive waterfront parkland and home to the **Cloisters**.

Harlem – bordered roughly by 125th St to the south and 155th to the north – eclipses its northern neighbors because of its famous history. From its origins as a 1920s African American enclave, it has been the setting for extraordinary accomplishments in art, music, dance and letters. A visit offers museums, theaters, jazz, historic architecture, gospel churches and great Southern fare. The **Apollo Theater** (☎ 212-531-5337; www.apollotheater.com; 253 W 125th St at Frederick Douglass Blvd; tours $16 Mon-Fri, $18 Sat & Sun; ⏱ tours 11am, 1pm, 3pm Mon, Tue, Thu, Fri, 11am Wed, 11am & 1pm Sat & Sun; ◉ A, B, C, D to 125th St) has been Harlem's leading space for concerts and political rallies since 1914 and continues its famous weekly Amateur Night as well as performances by established artists.

BROOKLYN

Brooklyn is New York's most buzzing borough. Owing to its new buildings, parks, bars, restaurants, hotels and live venues popping up at a furious pace, many Brooklynites find little reason to travel into Manhattan.

NORTHERN BROOKLYN

New York's 'it' neighborhood for 20-somethings with tousled hair and just-woke-up expressions, **Williamsburg** is made up of old warehouses and unassuming town houses, but its bars, restaurants and music venues light up the area at night.

Follow Bedford Ave north past McCarren Park until it turns into Manhattan Ave to find **Greenpoint**, a Polish 'hood with increasing numbers of spillover apartment renters and bars.

A couple more stops past Williamsburg on the L from Manhattan, the grubby blocks of **Bushwick** are seeing increasing spillover from Williamsburg for would-be musicians seeking cheap rent.

NORTHWESTERN BROOKLYN

In the Brooklyn Heights Historic District, 19th-century brownstones sit on quiet, tree-lined streets. All east–west lanes head to the **Brooklyn Heights Promenade**, offering amazing views of Lower Manhattan

RACHEL LEWIS

Manhattan Bridge, Brooklyn

and New York Harbor, as well as Brooklyn Bridge Park below.

South of Brooklyn Heights and Downtown Brooklyn is a cluster of tree-lined brownstone neighborhoods – **Boerum Hill**, **Cobble Hill** and **Carroll Gardens**. Its main thoroughfares – Court and Smith Street – are lined with boutiques, restaurants, bars and bookshops.

In recent years, charming cafes and restaurants, as well as a Fairway supermarket and IKEA, have opened in **Red Hook**, which remains mostly a district of warehouses and project buildings. Many of the long-time residents remain linked with the area's gritty dock-worker reputation, which inspired the film *On the Waterfront* (1954).

A bit Berkeley, a bit Upper West Side, **Park Slope** is the 'hood of choice for newbie New Yorkers or Manhattan-expats seeking 19th-century brownstone homes and leafy sidewalks on which to push their baby strollers. Restaurants, cafes and shops line Fifth and Seventh Avenues.

Frederick Law Olmsted and Calvert Vaux, creators of the 585-acre **Prospect Park** (☎ 718-965-8951; www.prospectpark.org; ◉ B, Q to Prospect Park, 2, 3 to Grand Army Plaza, F to 15th St-Prospect Park), considered this an improvement over their other New York project, Central Park. Prospect Park attracts visitors to its long meadow, hilly forests, and running and cycling paths.

Just across Flatbush Ave from Park Slope is **Prospect Heights**, bypassed by scruffy Washington Ave to the east and the ever-changing Vanderbilt Ave in the center, with a handful of restaurants, bars, cafes and wine shops.

Facing Grand Army Plaza at the southern boundary of Prospect Heights is the **Brooklyn Public Library** (☎ 718-230-2100; www.brooklynpubliclibrary.org; Grand Army Plaza), an art-deco masterpiece from 1941.

Fort Greene has brownstone blocks, cafes and restaurants spreading east and south from the Brooklyn side of the Manhattan Bridge.

Past the north–south Clinton Ave is **Clinton Hill**, with remarkable, century-old

WHAT'S IN A NABE?

Brooklyn is a little of everything. Here are who and what you're likely to find in the various 'hoods:

Bedford-Stuyvesant Historic African American neighborhood

Brooklyn Heights Brooklyn's big-money types, coming-of-age trust-fund kids

Cobble Hill, Boerum Hill & Carroll Gardens Budding yupsters, Italian long-termers, Arab community, characters from Jonathan Lethem novels

Coney Island & Brighton Beach Latin Americans, Italians, Ukrainian Jews, Woody Guthrie's ashes

Dumbo Smattering of artists, furniture sellers, architects, dot-com millionaires seeking river views

Fort Greene African Americans and 20-something students

Park Slope New Brooklynites pushing strollers back to brownstones, 20-somethings along Fifth Ave

Prospect Heights Caribbean Americans

Red Hook Latin Americans, Italians, dock workers, entrepreneurs ahead of the curve

Williamsburg Hipsters, Polish old-timers, Dominicans, Puerto Ricans, Hasidic Jews

mansions along Clinton and Washington Aves, as well as the **Pratt Institute**, a noted art and design school.

SOUTHERN & CENTRAL BROOKLYN

Some 50 minutes by subway from Midtown, Coney Island and Brighton Beach sit on the calm Atlantic tides, well connected by a boardwalk. Quieter Brighton Beach caters to locals born in the former Soviet Union, while Coney Island is an amusement park district. Gems of **Coney Island** include the 1920 Wonder Wheel and the 1927 Cyclone roller coaster. Other attractions include the Mermaid Parade, new carnival rides, a minor-league baseball team and an aquarium.

Bedford-Stuyvesant, NYC's largest African American neighborhood, gets a bad rap from its 'Bed-Stuy: Do or Die' rep. But the neighborhood – which sprawls between Flushing and Atlantic Aves beside Williamsburg and Clinton Hill – defies its infamy. Past blocks of boarded-up town houses and bleak housing projects are stunning historic districts.

QUEENS

With elevated train lines and busy streets, Queens' signature is its diversity. Some 46% of its 2.3 million residents were born out of the country, representing some 150 nations and making it the most ethnically diverse neighborhood in the world. A ride on the 'International Express' (the 7 subway line) flies past a bewildering mix of neighborhoods – Indian, Filipino, Irish, Italian, Colombian, Korean. Home to two of NYC's airports, the **Mets** and the **US Open** tennis tournament, Queens' other attractions include **P.S.1 Contemporary Art Center** (www.ps1.org) and the **Museum of the Moving Image**.

Just a subway stop from Manhattan, **Long Island City** is a mix of elevated trains rattling by graffiti-covered warehouses and new condo towers hugging the waterfront.

Astoria, the northwestern edge of Queens, is home to the largest Greek community in NYC. Bakeries, diners and delis line the streets, particularly along

Broadway and around 31st St and Ditmars Blvd. An influx of Eastern Europeans, Brazilians, Middle Eastern folk and hip kids have added to the scene.

Jackson Heights, the international whirlwind found off the 7 train's 74th St-Broadway stop, is home to many Indians – with curry and Bollywood DVD shops to suit – but you can also find Bangladeshi, Vietnamese, Korean, Mexican, Colombian, Ecuadorian and other ethnic groups.

Aside from the Mets' new stadium and the US Open, **Flushing** and **Corona** are two otherwise little-known neighborhoods. However, Flushing – at the end of the 7 subway line – has a flourishing **Chinatown** that's bigger than Manhattan's. In between the two areas is Flushing Meadows Corona Park, built for the 1939 and 1964 World's Fairs.

Jamaica, where 50 Cent and LL Cool J first penned their rhymes, is home to many West Indian immigrants and Latinos. It's getting attention from travelers, specifically those interested in superb 'hip-hop' shopping.

The **Rockaways** – the country's largest urban beach and New York's best – is just a $2.25 trip on the A train. The Rockaways are home to some surprisingly natural scenery and surf spots. Much of the area is part of the 26,000-acre **Gateway National Recreation Area** (www.nps.gov/gate). The boardwalk, beach and picnic areas are popular in summer.

THE BRONX

Sitting on the mainland above Manhattan, the Bronx has a diverse array of neighborhoods and topography – parkland, beaches, hilly greenspaces, residential enclaves, crumbling ghettos and the largest concentration of Irish immigrants in the city. It's given us the the

MICHELLE BENNETT

P.S.1 Contemporary Art Center

Yankees, hip-hop, plus Jennifer Lopez, Colin Powell and, uh, Billy Joel.

Like Queens, the Bronx is home to an ethnically diverse population. Nearly a quarter of the population is Puerto Rican and another quarter is black, with growing numbers of Jamaicans, Indians, Vietnamese, Cambodians and Eastern Europeans.

STATEN ISLAND

If not for its namesake ferry, New York's 'forgotten borough' might be a complete unknown. Most visitors here exit the ferry (see p62) – which docks in downtown St George, on the northern tip of the 58-sq-mile island – then re-board right away, but there are a few interesting things to see within walking distance of the pier.

ARTS

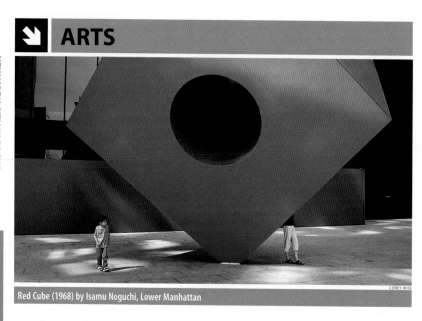

Red Cube (1968) by Isamu Noguchi, Lower Manhattan

COREY WISE

The sheer number of performance venues and companies is testament to how in love with culture this city's residents and tourists are. You could pick your favorite medium – classical music, jazz or ballet, for example – and find all of the options, or skim through everything: a poetry reading one night, followed by an indie film matinee and a night at the opera, with an off-off-Broadway show thrown in for good measure.

PAINTING & VISUAL ARTS

The center of the gallery scene lies in Chelsea (see www.chelseaartgalleries.com for a definitive list of what's there), with close to 250 art spaces. But pockets of edgier galleries are popping up in other neighborhoods, mainly the Lower East Side, Williamsburg, Greenpoint and Dumbo in Brooklyn, and Long Island City in Queens.

Art museums have also seen some excitement recently. El Museo del Barrio, the city's leading Latino art center, reopened at the end of 2009 after a sparkling renovation. Folks are still buzzing about the New Museum of Contemporary Art (p100), which hit the Bowery a few years back, as well as renovations of the Brooklyn Museum, and various galleries at the Metropolitan Museum of Art (Met; p204) which, along with the Museum of Modern Art (MoMA; p182) and the Whitney (p209), generate the biggest crowds.

MUSIC

NYC remains *the* destination for musicians of all forms. This is where vaudeville exploded; it's the home of Broadway and an endless roster of greats such as Louis

Armstrong and Billie Holiday. Folk musicians such as Bob Dylan and Woody Guthrie played downtown venues here; rockers from Elvis to Janis Joplin snagged coveted spots on the NYC-based *Ed Sullivan Show* while others reigned at downtown hot spots. Then came disco culture and the legendary Studio 54. Even rap originated here, through ad-hoc DJ soirees in the Bronx and Queens that gave rise to stars including the Sugar Hill Gang and Run-DMC.

You can still find the best of the best when it comes to nostalic genres – jazz at clubs such as the Village Vanguard (p149) and Birdland (p195), dance music at parties such as the 718 Sessions, and vaudeville-inspired burlesque at trendy spots including Joe's Pub (p88) and Galapagos Art Space. Broadway and classical sounds abound at established venues all over town.

An endless stream of new musicians has gained attention both nationally and internationally. Brooklyn is the site of several purveyors of indie cool – venues include Warsaw, Galapagos Art Space, and intimate rock shops including Southpaw and Union Hall. There are hip Manhattan venues aplenty, including the Delancey (p107) and Le Poisson Rouge (p148).

THEATER

Big, splashy Broadway shows are probably what are best associated with NYC's entertainment scene. But Broadway shows refer strictly to productions staged in the 40 official Broadway theaters – lavish early-20th-century jewels surrounding Times Sq.

Off-Broadway (more adventurous, less costly theater played to smaller houses) and off-off-Broadway (even edgier, more affordable performances housed in theaters for crowds of less than 100) are both big businesses here.

Experimental theater fans should watch for the Fringe Festival (p48), held in various downtown venues every August. Also in summer is the acclaimed Shakespeare in the Park festival (p222). Tickets are free, but you need to line up bright and early to claim yours.

COMEDY, CABARET & PERFORMANCE ART

The comedy scene is divided between the big-name, big-ticket clubs and the more experimental and obscure places. Check out the Upright Citizens Brigade Theatre (p149), the Magnet Theater (www.magnettheater.com) and the PIT (People's Improv Theater; www.thepit -nyc.com).

When it comes to cabaret, styles differ depending on the pricing and on whether

↘THE BEST

DAN HERRICK

Drawing Center (p81)

NYC ART SPACES

- **New Museum of Contemporary Art** (p100)
- **Drawing Center** (p81)
- **Frick Collection** (p211)
- **International Center of Photography** (p185)
- **Neue Galerie** (p210)

the venue is considered 'classic,' such as Feinstein's (p217) and Café Carlyle (p217). Though most cabaret has a gay bent by its very nature, the queer feel is more evident at places like the Duplex (p148); gay bars and lounges such as Therapy (p192) often become ad-hoc cabaret venues.

CLASSICAL MUSIC & OPERA

With fountains, reflecting pools and wide-open spaces, Lincoln Center houses the main halls of Alice Tully, Avery Fisher, the Metropolitan Opera House (the most opulent of all the venues here) and the New York State Theater, as well as the Juilliard School, the Fiorello LaGuardia High School for the Performing Arts, and the Vivian Beaumont and Mitzi Newhouse Theaters. Resident companies include the Metropolitan Opera and the New York City Opera, the New York Philharmonic, the New York City Ballet and the Chamber Music Society of Lincoln Center.

MICHELLE BENNETT

Billboards for Broadway shows, Times Sq

The smaller Carnegie Hall is just as beloved a venue, offering piano concerts as well as eclectic alt-folk and world music. A similarly solid classical lineup can be found at the Merkin Concert Hall (p237), known for top-notch piano and chamber music shows.

At the Brooklyn Academy of Music (BAM), the country's oldest academy for the performing arts, you'll find opera seasons and concerts from its resident Brooklyn Philharmonic.

DANCE

The NYC dance scene is comprised of both the classical and the modern, and is one of the most renowned dance capitals on the globe. It started here in the 1930s, when American classical ballet took off and laid the foundation for what would soon become the world-class American Ballet Theatre (ABT) and New York City Ballet.

Martha Graham, among others, sowed the seeds of the modern movement, which continued after WWII by masters including Merce Cunningham, Paul Taylor, Alvin Ailey and Twyla Tharp.

Today's up-and-coming dancers continue to bring their own interpretations to downtown theaters including the Kitchen, the Joyce Theater (p149) and Dance Theater Workshop (p145).

LITERATURE

New York's lit scene goes beyond a great selection of bookstores. Take all the top-notch writers and the still-unknowns that reside here, throw in the fact that New York is the capital of the publishing industry, and you've got quite a bookish city indeed. That should come as no surprise, considering the city's long and storied literary history.

DOWNTOWN INSPIRATION

Greenwich Village has perhaps the most glorified such history. Literary figures including Henry James, Herman Melville and Mark Twain lived near Washington Sq at the turn of the 19th century, where tight-knit clans of playwrights and poets wrote about bohemian life and gathered at cafes for literary salons and liquor-fueled tête-à-têtes. They were later followed by novelists and poets such as Ralph Ellison, ee cummings, Edna St Vincent Millay and Dylan Thomas, who is said to have died at the local White Horse Tavern in 1953 after downing one too many drinks.

The area is closely associated with the late 1950s and '60s, when the Beat movement was led by Allen Ginsberg, Jack Kerouac and their gang. In 1966 Ginsberg helped found the Poetry Project at St Mark's Church-in-the-Bowery in the East Village, which is still an active literary forum and resource for writers.

Harlem has a long literary history as well. James Baldwin, whose novels include *Go Tell It on the Mountain* and *Giovanni's Room*, was born here. Audre Lorde, a Caribbean American lesbian, activist and writer, was raised in Harlem and attended Columbia University. In the 1920s, Dorothy Parker held court at the famous Algonquin Round Table – a private clique of writers who talked endlessly about culture, politics and literature.

In the 1980s novelists such as Bret Easton Ellis *(American Psycho)* expounded upon the greedy, coke-fueled era, while East Village writers took readers into the rebellious downtown art world.

NEW YORK CITY IN FOCUS

ARTS

FILM FESTIVALS

With more than 30 film festivals in NYC every year, chances are you'll be able to hit one no matter when you visit. Many credit the highly publicized and quickly growing **Tribeca Film Festival** for upping the ante when it comes to the quality of films and screening locations. Festival topics are about as varied as the city itself, with options ranging from **Dance on Camera** (January), a celebration of movies about dance, to the **New York International Children's Film Festival** (February), the largest such fest in North America. The old fave **New York Film Festival** (September) highlights up-and-coming directors every year, and the **African American Women in Cinema Festival** (March) is a self-explanatory and finely focused showcase. The **Williamsburg Film Festival** (March) has brought the fun to that artsy-trendy Brooklyn neighborhood, screening work by local filmmakers. The **Human Rights Watch Film Festival** (June) enlightens locals to the evils of society around the globe, while the **Asian American International Film Festival** (July) and the **Israeli Film Festival** (June) focus on those varied cultures.

BROOKLYN VOICES

Before any of this, Walt Whitman wrote *Leaves of Grass* (1855) from his home in Brooklyn, later followed by contemporary Brooklyn authors including Betty Smith, who wrote *A Tree Grows in Brooklyn* in 1943; Jonathan Lethem, whose *Motherless Brooklyn* (1999) sparked new interest in the Cobble Hill and Brooklyn Heights area; and Colson Whitehead *(Sag Harbor*, 2009*)*, who chided, 'As you may have heard, all the writers are in Brooklyn these days…You're simply not a writer if you don't live here,' in a recent *New York Times* essay on the phenomenon.

FILM & TELEVISION

New York has a long and storied life in TV and film. Many shows are regularly filmed and produced here. An endless array of TV stations and some major film companies have homes here.

Though New York is home to some of the top film schools in the country, you don't have to be a student to learn, as plenty of museums – namely the Museum of the Moving Image (p246) in Astoria, Queens, and the Paley Center for Media (p178) – serve as showcases for screenings and seminars about productions both past and present.

Companies such as On Location Tours (p274) will take you to spots where your favorite films and TV shows were filmed. Or you can do it yourself after visiting the Mayors Office of Film, Theater & Broadcasting (MOFTB) website (www.nyc.gov/film) and downloading 'Made in NY: Walking Tours of Film and TV Locations in New York City' podcasts.

BUYING TICKETS

To purchase tickets for shows, you can head directly to the venue's box office, or use one of several ticket-service agencies to order by phone or online. Many of the websites listed here have some added perks, from reviews to entertainment news.

Playbill (**www.playbill.com**) Offering theater news, listings and ticket purchases.

SmartTix.com (☎ **212-868-4444; www.smarttix.com**) Info on comedy, cabaret, performance art, music, dance and downtown theater.

Telecharge (☎ **212-239-6200; www.telecharge.com**) Selling tickets for Broadway and off-Broadway shows.

Theatermania (☎ **212-352-3101; www.theatermania.com**) For any form of theater; provides listings, reviews and ticketing.

Ticketmaster (**www.ticketmaster.com**) Tickets for every conceivable form of big-time entertainment.

FAMILY TRAVEL

CHRISTOPHER GROENHOUT

Wonder Wheel, Coney Island (p246)

Contrary to popular belief, New York can be a child-friendly city – it just takes a bit of guidance to find all the little creature comforts that you're accustomed to having back home. Visiting during warm weather tends to make things easier, as you can always resort to the many parks, playgrounds and zoos to let your kids expel some pent-up energy.

ACCOMMODATIONS

When seeking accommodations, steer clear of the supertrendy boutique hotels that tend to have tiny rooms and single-person party-monster vibes (and, often, no-children policies); there are plenty of other options that welcome kids with open arms. At the Crosby Street Hotel (p83), kids are welcomed with robes and slippers, and parents can depend on babysitting services and planned kids' activities run by staff. The Four Seasons (p186) offers free cribs, high chairs and strollers. As a rule, the larger hotel chains – Sheraton, Hilton, Doubletree – are kid friendly, offering babysitting services and other amenities.

For more child-friendly accommodations options, visit www.gocitykids.com.

SIGHTS & ACTIVITIES

Museums, especially those geared toward kids such as the Children's Museum of Manhattan (p231) and the American Museum of Natural History (p229), are always great places to hit, as are children's theaters, movie theaters, book and toy stores, aquariums and kid-friendly restaurants.

NITTY GRITTY

- **Change Facilities** Not common in bars and restaurants
- **Cots** Available in midrange and top-end hotels, but reserve in advance
- **Health** The city has high health-care standards
- **High chairs** Many restaurants have at least one
- **Nappies (diapers)** Widely available
- **Strollers** Bring your own; not allowed on buses unless folded up
- **Transport** Subway stairs can be challenging with strollers; taxis are exempt from car seat laws

For more details, pick up Lonely Planet's *Travel with Children*. When you get to town, get your hands on a copy of the weekly *Time Out New York Kids* magazine, available at newsstands.

TRANSPORTATION

The biggest pitfalls tend to revolve around public transportation, as a startling lack of subway-station elevators will have you lugging strollers up and down flights of stairs (though you can avoid the turnstile by getting buzzed through an easy-access gate); visit www.mta.info/mta/ada to find a guide to subway stations with elevators and escalators. Strollers are not allowed on public buses (unless they're folded up, sans child). Taxis are often the easiest option.

BABYSITTING

While most major hotels (and a handful of boutique-style places) offer on-site babysitting services, or can at least provide you with referrals, you could also turn to a local childcare organization. **Baby Sitters' Guild** (☎ 212-682-0227; www.babysittersguild.com), established in 1940 specifically to serve travelers staying in hotels with children, has a stable of sitters who speak a range of 16 languages. All are carefully screened, most are CPR-certified and many have nursing backgrounds; they'll come to your hotel room and even bring games and arts-and-crafts projects. Another good option is **Pinch Sitters** (☎ 212-260-6005). Both will set you back about $20 per hour.

FOOD & DRINK

MICHELLE BENNETT

Perusing the menu in a NYC diner

Chowing down in New York City is not your standard affair. That's no surprise in a far-from-typical city but, still, lining up for an hour to consume a bowl of homemade soba noodles or a sugary cupcake? Forking out more than $20 for a Kobe-beef burger? Trolling the greenmarkets on a 90-degree summer day just to find local organic gooseberries and artisanal tofu? Getting exactly what you want in your belly is what the foodie scene is all about here, folks. And approaching the task with a sense of adventure is what makes it an utterly dazzling journey.

GOING GLOBAL

The range of global cuisine you'll find in NYC is staggering. Get ready to dive your chopsticks into some authentic Cantonese or Korean; sop up Ethiopian with a spongy shred of *injera* bread; pull apart a fresh lobster with your bare hands; chase Turkish mezes, Spanish tapas or Mexican *torta* sandwiches with a glass of raki, sherry or *mezcal*, respectively.

TRENDS

Just so you're prepared, here's a rundown of the current NYC dining trends (but keep in mind that the restaurant scene and its trends are constantly shifting): authentic BBQ, heavy on the smoked meats; global small plates (paired with the perfect pour of wine); Korean fried chicken, served in whimsically designed to-go boxes; frozen yogurt joints; Israeli cafes; authentic Mexican, which has been in short supply for years; creative takes on *bánh mì* (Vietnamese sandwiches); and eating locally, with an emphasis on

NEW YORK CITY IN FOCUS

FOOD & DRINK

THE BEST

Momofuku Noodle Bar (p120)

RESTAURANTS

- **Peasant** (p83)
- **WD 50** (p103)
- **Blue Hill** (p142)
- **Momofuku Noodle Bar** (p120)
- **Gramercy Tavern** (p163)
- **Ouest** (p234)

veggies and cheeses that are grown within a 50-mile radius, thus making chic diners feel very good about themselves and their reduced carbon footprint.

SPECIALTIES

Unlike California, the South or the Southwest, New York is never really referred to as having one defining cuisine. Try asking for some 'New York food,' for example, and you could wind up getting anything from a hot dog, a South Indian feast or a $500 Japanese prix fixe at the Time Warner Center's Masa. Cuisine in this multicultural town is global by definition, and constantly evolving by its very nature.

That said, it's the food items with the longest histories that folks usually have in mind when they refer to New York City specialties. Those at the top of the list – bagels and slices of pizza – were introduced by Eastern European Jews and Italians, because those groups were among the earliest wave of immigrants. But egg creams, cheesecake and hot dogs (just to name a few) are also uncontested staples of New York eats.

VEGETARIANS & VEGANS

Herbivore oases dot the entire landscape. Downtown and Brooklyn are home to many veggie places and, while many come and go, a few delicious stalwarts include **Counter** (☎ 212-982-5870; 105 First Ave btwn 6th & 7th Sts, East Village; ☽ dinner; ⊕ F to Lower East Side-2nd Ave), **Blossom** (☎ 212-627-1144; 187 Ninth Ave btwn 21st & 22nd Sts; ☽ lunch & dinner; ⊕ C, E to 23rd St), the **Wild Ginger Pan-Asian Café** (☎ 212-966-1883; 380 Broome St btwn Mulberry & Mott Sts; ☽ lunch & dinner; ⊕ 6 to Spring St), **Pure Food & Wine** (p163) and **Soy Luck Club** (p143).

Uptown standouts include **Candle Café** (p216) and the new **Peacefood Cafe** (p235).

PRICE GUIDE

The following is a guide to the pricing system in this book. Prices are per meal per person, excluding taxes:

$	under $15
$$	$15 to $30
$$$	over $30

GAY & LESBIAN NEW YORK CITY

NEW YORK CITY IN FOCUS

GAY & LESBIAN NEW YORK CITY

ANGUS OBORN

Balloon float, Gay Pride Parade

New York doesn't differentiate much between heterosexual and homosexual – at least, not when it comes to dancing, drinking and eating. Chelsea, Greenwich Village, Jackson Heights and Park Slope are famously gay-friendly communities, but there's hardly any establishment in town where gays and lesbians wouldn't feel welcome. The one rule to remember is that the age of consent in New York for sex (of any kind) is 17.

GAY PRIDE

Gay Pride is a month-long celebration in June of the city's long-standing and diverse queer communities, and an apt description of New York's gay and lesbian lifestyle, unabashedly out and empowered in a city noted for its overachievers. For more details on Gay Pride, check out nycpride.org.

FURTHER INFORMATION

The magazines *HX* and *Next* are available at restaurants and bars, or pick up *LGNY* and *NY Blade* from street-corner boxes and the lifestyle magazine *Metrosource* at shops and the LGBT Community Center. *Time Out New York* features a good events section.

Useful counseling, referral and information centers include the **Gay & Lesbian Hotline** (☎ 212-989-0999; glnh@glnh.org) and the **LGBT Community Center** (☎ 212-620-7310; www.gaycenter.org; 208 W 13th St at Seventh Ave; ☺ 9am-11pm).

HISTORY

MICHAEL TAYLOR

New York Public Library (p178)

Long before land-grabbing settlers or property-obsessed residents took hold of this area, great numbers of Algonquin-speaking people had made the Manhattan area their home. Ever since the arrival of European settlers, wave upon wave of immigrants have shaped the city's history as their stories of trial and perseverance have mirrored the city's own.

ENCOUNTERS

Around 11,000 years before the first Europeans arrived, the Lenape ('original people') foraged, hunted and fished the regional bounty. European explorers muscled in, touching off decades of raids on Lenape villages. Dutch West India Company employee Henry Hudson arrived in 1609, and in 1624 the Company sent 110 settlers to begin a trading post. They settled in Lower Manhattan and called their colony New Amsterdam. In 1626 the colony's first governor, Peter Minuit, offered to buy Manhattan's 14,000 acres from the Lenape for 60 guilders ($24). The Lenape agreed, probably thinking the exchange was about rent, and permission to hunt, fish and trade. By the time peg-legged Peter Stuyvesant arrived in 1647, the Lenape population had dwindled to around 700.

c AD 1500	1625-26	1646
About 15,000 Native Americans live in 80 different sites around the island.	The Dutch West India Company imports slaves from Africa for the fur trade and to work in construction.	The Dutch found the village of Breuckelen on the eastern shore of Long Island.

Governor Stuyvesant set about remaking the colony into an orderly and prosperous trading port. By the 1650s, warehouses, workshops and gabled houses spread back from the dense establishments at the river's edge on Pearl St.

In 1664 the English arrived in battleships. Stuyvesant avoided bloodshed by surrendering without a shot. King Charles II renamed the colony after his brother the Duke of York. New York was becoming a prosperous British port and the population rose to 11,000 by the mid-1700s; however, colonists were becoming resentful over British taxation.

REVOLUTION & THE CITY

By the 18th century the economy was so robust that the locals were improvising ways to avoid sharing the wealth with London, and New York became the stage for the fatal confrontation with King George III. Revolutionary battle began in August of 1776, when General George Washington's army lost about a quarter of its men in just a few days. He retreated, and fire encompassed much of the colony. But soon the British left and Washington's army reclaimed their city.

In 1789 the retired general found himself addressing crowds at Federal Hall, gathered to witness his presidential inauguration. Alexander Hamilton began rebuilding New York as Washington's secretary of the treasury, working to establish the New York Stock Exchange. But people distrusted a capitol located adjacent to the financial power of Wall St, and New Yorkers lost the seat of the presidency to Philadelphia.

POPULATION BUST, INFRASTRUCTURE BOOM

There were setbacks at the start of the 19th century: the bloody Draft Riots of 1863, cholera epidemics, tensions among 'old' and new immigrants, and poverty

RICHARD CUMMINS
George Washington Statue, Federal Hall (p64)

1754	1784	1811
King's College is founded by George II; later, it's reborn as Columbia University.	Alexander Hamilton founds America's first bank, the Bank of New York, with holdings of $500,000.	Manhattan's grid plan is developed by Mayor DeWitt Clinton, which leads to the reshaping of the city.

and crime in Five Points, the city's first slum. But the city prospered and found resources for mighty public works. Begun in 1855, Central Park was a vision of green reform and a boon to real-estate speculation, and offered work relief when the Panic of 1857 shattered the nation's finance system. Another vision was realized by German-born engineer John Roebling who designed the Brooklyn Bridge, spanning the East River and connecting lower Manhattan and Brooklyn.

19TH-CENTURY CORRUPTION & IMMIGRATION

Out of such growth and prosperity came the infamous William 'Boss' Tweed – a powerful, charming politician and leader of the political organization Tammany Hall. He took charge of the city treasury and spent years embezzling funds, putting the city in debt and contributing to citizens' growing poverty.

By the turn of the 20th century, elevated trains carried a million people a day in and out of the city. Rapid transit opened up areas of the Bronx and Upper Manhattan. Tenements were overflowing with immigrants arriving from southern Italy and Eastern Europe, who boosted the metropolis to around three million.

Newly wealthy folks – boosted by an economy jump-started by financier JP Morgan – built splendid mansions on Fifth Ave. Reporter and photographer Jacob Riis illumi-

ALLAN MONTAINE

Exhibits, Ellis Island Immigration Museum (p54)

1825	1853	1863
The Erie Canal, an engineering feat, is completed, influencing trade and commerce in New York.	The State Legislature authorizes the allotment of public lands for what will later become Central Park.	Civil War Draft Riots erupt; order restored by the Federal Army.

nated the widening gap between the classes, leading the city to pass much-needed housing reforms.

1898: BOROUGHS JOIN MANHATTAN

After years of governmental chaos caused by the 40 independent municipalities around the area, 1898 saw the ratification of the Charter of New York, which joined the five boroughs of Brooklyn, Staten Island, Queens, the Bronx and Manhattan into the largest city in America.

Wretched factory conditions in the early 20th century were illuminated when the 1911 Triangle Shirtwaist Company fire killed 146 women workers trapped behind locked doors. The event led to sweeping labor reforms. Nurse and midwife Margaret Sanger opened the first birth-control clinic in Brooklyn and suffragists held rallies to obtain the vote for women.

THE JAZZ AGE

James Walker was elected mayor in 1925 – a time when jazz ruled; Babe Ruth reigned at Yankee Stadium; and the Great Migration from the South led to the Harlem Renaissance, when the neighborhood became the center of African American culture and society, producing poetry, music, art and an innovative attitude that continues to influence and inspire. Harlem's nightlife attracted the flappers and gin-soaked revelers that marked the complete failure of Prohibition.

HARD TIMES

The stock market crashed in 1929 and the city dealt with the Great Depression through grit, endurance, rent parties, militancy and public works projects. Texas-born, Yiddish-speaking Mayor Fiorello LaGuardia worked to bring relief in the form of New Deal-funded projects.

WWII brought troops to the city, ready to party in Times Sq before shipping off to Europe. Converted to war industries, factories hummed, staffed by women and African Americans who had rarely before had access to good, unionized jobs. With few evident controls on business, Midtown bulked up with skyscrapers after the war. The financial center marched north, while banker David Rockefeller and his brother Governor Nelson Rockefeller dreamed up the Twin Towers to revitalize downtown.

ENTER ROBERT MOSES

Working with LaGuardia to usher the city into the modern age was Robert Moses, an urban planner who influenced the physical shape of the city more than anyone else in the 20th century. He was the mastermind behind the Triborough and

1886	1919	1931
The Statue of Liberty's pedestal is completed and a dedication ceremony held.	The Yankees acquire slugger Babe Ruth from Boston, leading to their first championship.	The Empire State Building becomes the world's tallest skyscraper.

NEW YORK CITY IN FOCUS

HISTORY

Verrazano-Narrows Bridges, Jones Beach State Park, the West Side Hwy and the Long Island parkway system – plus endless highways, tunnels and bridges, which shifted this mass-transit area into one largely dependent on the automobile.

BEATS & GAYS

The 1960s ushered in an era of legendary creativity and anti-establishment expression, with many of its creators centered in Greenwich Village. Writers such as Beat poets Allen Ginsberg and Jack Kerouac gathered in coffeehouses to exchange ideas and find inspiration, often in the form of folk music from burgeoning stars, like Bob Dylan. The environment was ripe for rebellion – a task gay revelers took on with gusto, finding their political strength and voice in fighting a police raid at the Stonewall Inn in 1969.

'DROP DEAD'

By the early 1970s deficits had created a fiscal crisis. President Ford refused to lend federal aid – summed up by the *Daily News* headline 'Ford to City, Drop Dead!' Massive layoffs decimated the working class; untended bridges, roads and parks reeked of hard times.

The traumatic '70s – which reached a low point in 1977 with a citywide blackout and the existence of serial killer Son of Sam – drove down rents, helping to nourish an alternative culture that transformed the former industrial precincts of SoHo and Tribeca into energized nightlife districts.

OUT OF THE ASHES

While the stock market boomed for much of the 1980s, neighborhoods struggled with the spread of crack cocaine; the city reeled from the impact of addiction, crime, and AIDS. Squatters in the East Village fought back when police tried to clear a big homeless encampment, leading to the Tompkins Sq Park riots of 1988. In South Bronx, a wave of arson reduced blocks of apartments to cinders. But amid the smoke, an influential hip-hop culture was born there and in Brooklyn.

Still convalescing from the real-estate crash of the late 1980s, the city faced crumbling infrastructure, jobs leaking south, and Fortune 500 companies leaving for suburbia. Then the dot-com market roared in, turning the New York Stock Exchange into a specu-lator's fun park and the city launched a frenzy of building and partying unparalleled since the 1920s.

With pro-business, law-and-order Rudy Giuliani as mayor, the dingy and destitute were swept from Manhattan's yuppified streets to the outer boroughs, leaving room for Generation X to live the high life. Giuliani grabbed headlines with his campaign to stamp out crime, even kicking the sex shops off notoriously seedy 42nd St.

1945	1961	1977
The UN, headquartered on Manhattan's east side, is established.	Nineteen-year-old folk singer Bob Dylan arrives in NYC.	A 24-hour blackout leads to rioting around the city.

↘ THE BEST

LEE FOSTER

Ellis Island Immigration Museum (p54)

PLACES TO LEARN ABOUT NYC'S HISTORY

- **Ellis Island** (p54, p62)
- **Lower East Side Tenement Museum** (p99)
- **Museum of City of New York** (p212)
- **New York Historical Society** (p231)

Real-estate prices sizzled, setting off a construction spree of high-rises. Though no new housing for ordinary people was built, the city's population grew, as ambitious graduates flocked to the financial center.

SEPTEMBER 11

On September 11, 2001, terrorists flew two hijacked planes into the World Trade Center's Twin Towers, turning the complex into dust and rubble and killing nearly 2800 people. Downtown Manhattan took months to recover from the fumes wafting from the ruins, as forlorn missing-person posters grew ragged on brick walls. While recovery crews coughed their way through the debris, the city mourned the dead amid constant terrorist alerts and an anthrax scare. Shock and grief drew people together in a determined effort not to succumb to despair.

THE UNSINKABLE MAYOR MIKE

In 2002 Mayor Michael Bloomberg began the unenviable task of picking up the pieces of a shattered city. The boom in NYC probably didn't hurt his bid for re-election four years later and by the latter part of Bloomberg's second term, the entire city seemed to be under construction. But developers found themselves paralyzed by the troubled economy. Financially savvy Bloomberg, nearing the end of his second and final term, altered the term-limits law to allow for a third term. He won, but with much less of an edge than he had expected.

1988	2001	2010
Crowds of squatters riot when cops attempt to forcibly remove them from East Village's Tompkins Sq Park.	On September 11, terrorist hijackers fly two planes into the Twin Towers, killing nearly 2800 people.	Mayor Mike Bloomberg is sworn into a third term.

SHOPPING

JEAN-PIERRE LESCOURRET

Shop window, SoHo

New Yorkers live in a city of temptation. Candy-colored fashion boutiques, cutting-edge music shops, atmospheric antique stores, tea parlors – no matter what your weakness, you'll come face to face with all the objects your heart desires and plenty of curiosities you never knew existed.

SHOPPING NYC-STYLE

Shopping here isn't just about collecting pretty, fanciful things. It's also about experiencing the city in all its variety and connecting to New York's many subcultures. Vinyl heads bond over the seemingly endless bins of jazz and soul albums at one of many LP shops in the East Village. Old-school hip-hop fans flock to well-hidden stores in the Lower East Side, while fashion insiders elbow-joust over rare denim at lesser-known SoHo boutiques. There are shops for lovers of chess (with pick-up games for browsers), street art (the tagger might be working the cash register), cuddly robots, artist monographs, Danish things, handmade jewelry, Ukrainian handicrafts, old-fashioned toys, vintage boots, New York State wine and mosaics made by you. This is just the beginning and there really is no end.

Shopping can also give you a taste of local history, whether you're stopping by the mom-and-pop shops still left in the Lower East Side, exploring the storefronts in Harlem or browsing the rare titles of a longtime antiquarian bookseller. There are also the many antique sellers and excellent flea markets where you can put your hands on those little fragments from New York's past.

While New York can seem like pure quicklime to the budget, insiders know where to find the deals. In addition to great thrift shops there are many discount stores that sell top

WHERE TO SHOP

- **E 9th St** (Map p110) More pleasant than chaotic St Marks Pl one block south, East 9th between Second Ave and Ave A is a good intro to the vintage stores and curio shops of the East Village.
- **Bleecker St** (Map p128) Running south from Abingdon Sq, tree-lined Bleecker (between Bank and W 10th Sts) is sprinkled with eye-catching storefronts and boutiques selling trendy apparel.
- **Christopher St** (Map p128) Proudly flying the rainbow colors, Christopher St between Greenwich and W 4th Sts has its fair share of leather and sex shops, with some friendly bars and cafes along the way.
- **Fifth Ave** (Map p168) Between Central Park and Rockefeller Center, this commercial strip is the El Dorado of shopping. Stepping into Tiffany's, Bergdorf's and Takashimaya is just the beginning…
- **Madison Ave** (Map p202) To get 'the treatment' (which can be good or bad depending on the size of your expense account), head to Madison and 72nd, gateway to the bejeweled storefronts of the Upper East Side.
- **Mott St** (Map p74) Less touristy than SoHo, Nolita (Mott St between Houston and Broome Sts) has lovely little clothing, shoe and accessory shops carrying up-and-coming designers.
- **Orchard St** (Map p92) For edgier fashions and urban style, begin your Lower East Side explorations on Orchard between Houston and Grand Sts.
- **West Broadway** (Map p74) These days, SoHo is one big shopping mall, with high-end fashion well represented along West Broadway between Houston and Grand Sts.

fashion labels at excellent prices – though you'll have to dig. There are also superb sample sales, where you can walk away looking like a million bucks without having to spend it.

DOWNTOWN

Downtown neighborhoods are the stomping grounds of fashion-forward folk. You'll find across-the-board bargains, as well as more of the small, stylish boutiques. Downtown's coolest offerings are in Nolita (just east of SoHo), the East Village and the Lower East Side. SoHo has more expensive though no less fashionable stores while Broadway from Union Sq to Canal St is lined with big retailers like H&M and Urban Outfitters, as well as dozens of jeans and shoe stores. The museum-like Prada NYC flagship is also here.

The streets of Chinatown are filled with knockoff designer handbags, jewelry, perfume and watches. The West Village has tiny, well-known boutiques, while the Meatpacking District is home to designer havens including Jeffrey and Stella McCartney. Chelsea has more unique boutiques, though it too has been colonized by banks, drug stores and big-box retailers.

MIDTOWN & UPTOWN

Well-funded shoppers head to Midtown's Fifth Ave and the Upper East Side's Madison Ave, where high-end fashion is served in the glittering front windows of Bergdorf-style

⌦ THE BEST

COREY WISE

Macy's (p200)

STORES

- **Century 21** (p21)
- **Zabar's** (p240)
- **Strand Book Store** (p165)
- **J&R Music & Computer World** (p72)
- **Macy's** (p200)
- **FAO Schwarz** (p199)

department stores and famous shops such as Cartier. Midtown is the place for big-box retailers including Macy's, multi-storied H&M and other chain stores, along with overflowing tourist shops selling tacky but essential souvenirs such as Big Apple snow globes. For unique gifts, hit the museum shops.

OPENING HOURS

With the exception of Lower Manhattan and shops run by Orthodox Jews (who close their doors on Saturday), nearly all stores, boutiques and megastores are open daily. Few stores open before 10am, though many stay open until 7pm or 8pm. Things open a little later (at 11am or noon) in more residential pockets (such as the East Village, Lower East Side and Brooklyn).

⌄ DIRECTORY & TRANSPORTATION

DIRECTORY

DIRECTORY
ACCOMMODATIONS

You need a good place to recharge your batteries in high-octane New York. The changing economy is a boon to travelers, who can often find great, last-minute deals online (even the fanciest hotels will sometimes slash prices to try and fill empty rooms). But during peak seasons, when space is at a premium (such as the December holidays and much of the summer), it pays to book in advance.

ROOM RATES

The average room costs $340 a night, with some seasonal fluctuations (lowest in January and February, highest in September and October), and there are plenty of options both below and above this rate. When you get your bill, the hotel will also tack on a 14.75% room tax and a $3.50 per night occupancy tax.

BUSINESS HOURS

Most offices are open from 9am to 5pm Monday to Friday. Most shops are on a later clock, typically opening at 10am or 11am, or even noon in downtown neighborhoods, and closing between 7pm and 9pm – often later on weekends (or not at all on Sunday). Restaurants serve breakfast

ACCOMMODATIONS

PRICE RANGES

	Sleeping	Eating
Budget	<$150	<$15
Midrange	$150-350	$15-30
Top end	>$350	>$30

Accommodation prices are for a double per night during peak season. Eating prices are per meal per person, excluding taxes.

---

from about 6am to noon, and then lunch till 3pm or 4pm, with just enough time to start serving dinner by 5pm – although prime dinner hour is more like 8pm (9pm on weekends). Most stores are open on public holidays (except Christmas Day) but banks, schools and offices are usually closed. Though most banks are open from 9am to 4:30pm or 5pm Monday to Friday, a few in Chinatown have limited Saturday hours, and the Commerce Bank chain, with locations all over Manhattan, has daily hours that vary, with most open on Sundays from 11am to 4pm.

CLIMATE

While global warming has brought recent oddities like 70°F January evenings, there is still a basic framework you can usually count on. Spring in New York is lovely – blossoming trees pop into reds and pinks, sunny days glimmer and even rainy days have a lovely, cleansing feel to them. The temperatures can still dip down to a chilly 40°F in early April evenings, but average temperatures hover at around 60°F, creating days that are perfect for strolling in the city.

Summers can be beastly, as temperatures in July and August can climb to the 100°F mark; usually it's between 70°F and 80°F, with occasional thunderstorms that light up the sky and cool everything down until the sun comes out again.

Autumn in New York: why does it seem so inviting? Probably because of its pleasantly cool days (averaging in the 50s) and gorgeously colored leaves, on full display in Central Park and other green spaces.

Winters, of course, are cold. It can be gray for days, with sleet and snow showers that quickly turn into a mucky brown film at your feet and temperatures that can easily dip down into the single digits come January. But a good snowstorm is a

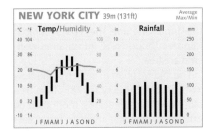

NEW YORK CITY 39m (131ft)

beautiful thing in these parts, and a cold night inspires cuddling, which can make for a damn romantic visit.

CUSTOMS REGULATIONS

US customs allows each person over the age of 21 to bring 1L of liquor and 200 cigarettes duty free into the USA (smokers take note: cigarettes cost around $8 a pack here in the big city, so take advantage of those duty-free shops). Agricultural items including meat, fruits, vegetables, plants and soil are prohibited. US citizens are allowed to import, duty free, up to $800 worth of gifts from abroad, while non-US citizens are allowed to import $100 worth. If you're carrying more than $10,000 in US and foreign cash, traveler's checks, money orders etc, you need to declare the excess amount. There is no legal restriction on the amount that may be imported, but undeclared sums in excess of $10,000 will probably be subject to investigation. If you're bringing prescription drugs, make sure they're in clearly marked containers; and leave the illegal narcotics at home. For updates, check www.cbp.gov.

DISCOUNT CARDS

The New York City Pass (www.citypass.com), which you can purchase either online or at any major city attraction (museums, historic sites etc), buys you admission into six major attractions – the Empire State Building, the Metropolitan Museum of Art, the Museum of Modern Art, the Guggenheim Museum, the American Museum of Natural History and a Circle Line cruise or a Liberty Island/Ellis Island visit, with an overall saving of 44% – for just $79 ($59 for ages six to 17). New York Pass (www.newyorkpass.com), meanwhile, sells online cards for $75 ($55 for kids) and gives you day-long access to 40 top attractions (the UN, the Statue of Liberty, the Guggenheim etc), as well as discounts at 25 stores and restaurants. Two-, three- and seven-day passes are also available.

EMBASSIES

The presence of the UN in New York City means that nearly every country in the world maintains diplomatic offices in Manhattan. Some foreign consulates, all in Manhattan, include the following:

Australia (Map p168; ☎ 212-351-6500; www.australianyc.org; 34th fl, 150 E 42nd St; ⏲ 8:30am-5pm Mon-Fri; ⓜ 4, 5, 6 to Grand Central-42nd St)

Canada (Map p180; ☎ 212-596-1628; www.canada-ny.org; 1251 Sixth Ave; ⏲ 8:45am-5pm Mon-Fri; ⓜ B, D, F, M to 47th-50th Sts–Rockefeller Ctr)

France (Map p202; ☎ 212-606-3680; www.consulfrance-newyork.org; 934 Fifth Ave; ⏲ 9am-1pm Mon-Fri; ⓜ 6 to 77th St)

⚓ BOOK YOUR STAY ONLINE

For more accommodation reviews and recommendations by Lonely Planet authors, check out the online booking service at www.lonelyplanet.com. You'll find the true, insider lowdown on the best places to stay. Reviews are thorough and independent. Best of all, you can book online.

Germany (Map p168; ☎ 212-610-9700; www.
germany.info; 871 UN Plaza at 49th St & First
Ave; ⏱ 9am-noon Mon-Fri; ◉ 4, 5, 6 to Grand
Central-42nd St)

UK (Map p168; ☎ 212-745-0200; 845 Third Ave
btwn 51st & 52nd Sts; ⏱ 9am-5pm Mon-Fri; ◉ 6
to 51st St, E, M to Lexington Ave-53rd St)

HOLIDAYS

Following is a list of major NYC holidays
and special events. These holidays may
force closure of many businesses or attract crowds, making dining and accommodations reservations difficult. See p46
for a list of more specific dates.

New Year's Day January 1
Martin Luther King Day Third Monday
in January
Presidents' Day Third Monday in
February
Easter March/April
Memorial Day Late May
Gay Pride Last Sunday in June
Independence Day July 4
Labor Day Early September
Rosh Hashanah and **Yom Kippur** Mid-
September to mid-October
Halloween October 31
Thanksgiving Fourth Thursday in
November
Christmas Day December 25
New Year's Eve December 31

INTERNET ACCESS

Hotels all provide some sort of online access these days. For laptop toters, in-room
services include either DSL hookups or
wireless access, often for fees averaging
$10 a day. Travelers without laptops can
almost always find monitors available for
use in a hotel's lobby or business center.
Around the city, you can find service on
street corners in the form of more than
100 TCC Internet Phones, found mostly
in Midtown but also sprinkled throughout

the East Village, SoHo, Chinatown and on
the Upper East Side. They cost $1 for four
minutes, though NYC information websites are free.

The mid-Manhattan branch of the **New
York Public Library** (p178) offers free
half-hour internet access; more than 80
other local branches also have free access
and usually with no wait; for locations,
visit www.nypl.org/branch/local. There
are many wi-fi access hot spots around
the city.

LEGAL MATTERS

If you're arrested, you have the right to
remain silent. There is no legal reason
to speak to a police officer if you don't
wish to – especially since anything you
say 'can and will be used against you' –
but never walk away from an officer until
given permission. All persons who are arrested have the legal right to make one
phone call. If you don't have a lawyer
or family member to help you, call your
consulate. The police will give you the
number upon request.

MONEY

The US dollar (familiarly called a 'buck') is
divided into 100 cents (¢). Notes come in
$1, $2 (extremely rare), $5, $10, $20, $50
and $100 denominations. Coins come in
denominations of 1¢ (penny), 5¢ (nickel),
10¢ (dime), 25¢ (quarter), the practically
extinct 50¢ (half-dollar), and the not-oft-
seen golden dollar coin.

CHANGING MONEY

Banks and moneychangers, found all over
New York City (and right in the airports
where you'll land), will give you US currency based on the current exchange rate.
See p270 for information on bank opening hours.

TRAVELER'S CHECKS

Checks issued by American Express and Thomas Cook are widely accepted, and both offer efficient replacement policies. Keeping a record of the check numbers and the checks you've used is vital when it comes to replacing lost checks. Keep this record in a separate place from the checks themselves.

NEWSPAPERS & MAGAZINES

Newspapers include the following:

New York Daily News (www.nydaily news.com) One of two sensationalistic tabloids, this is slightly more staid in tone than the *Post*.

New York Post (www.newyorkpost.com) The *Post* is known for screaming headlines, conservative political views and its popular Page Six gossip column.

New York Times (www.nytimes.com) 'The gray lady' has gotten hip in recent years, adding sections on technology, arts and dining out.

Village Voice (www.villagevoice.com) Owned by national alternative-newspaper chain New Times, the legendary *Voice* has less bite but still plenty of bark.

Wall Street Journal (www.wallstreet journal.com) This intellectual daily has a focus on finance – though its new owner, media mogul Rupert Murdoch, has ratcheted up the general coverage to rival that of the *Times*.

Magazines that give a good sense of the local flavor include the following:

New York magazine (www.nymag.com) This weekly magazine has feature stories and great listings about anything and everything in NYC, with an indispensable website.

New Yorker (www.newyorker.com) The highbrow weekly covers politics and culture through its famously lengthy works of reportage, and also publishes fiction and poetry.

Time Out New York (http://newyork.time out.com) A weekly magazine, its focus is on being complete (as you'll see from its bible-like listings on everything cultural) plus articles and interviews on arts and entertainment.

ORGANIZED TOURS

Big Onion Walking Tours (☎ 212-439-1090; www.bigonion.com; tours $15) Choose from nearly 30 tours, including Brooklyn Bridge and Brooklyn Heights; the 'Official' Gangs of New York Tour; A Gay and Lesbian History Tour – Before Stonewall; and Chelsea and the High Line.

Bike the Big Apple (☎ 877-865-0078; www.bikethebigapple.com; tours incl bike & helmet $70-80) Biking tours let you cover more ground than walking tours – and give you a healthy dose of exercise to boot.

Circle Line Boat Tours (Map p168; ☎ 212-563-3200; www.circleline42.com; 42nd St at Twelfth Ave, Midtown West; tours $20-29.50; ⊙ A, C, E to 42nd-Port Authority) The classic Circle Line – whose local 1970s TV-commercial song is now the stuff of kitschy nostalgia – guides you through all the big sights from the safe distance of a boat that circumnavigates the five boroughs.

Foods of New York (☎ 212-239-1124; www.foodsofny.com; tours $40-75) The official foodie tour of **NYC & Company** (Map p180) offers various three-hour tours that help you eat your way through gourmet shops in either Chelsea or the West Village.

Gray Line (☎ 212-397-2620; www.newyork sightseeing.com; tours $50-75) The most ubiquitous guided tour in the city, Gray Line is responsible for bombarding New

DIRECTORY

NEWSPAPERS & MAGAZINES

York streets with the red double-decker buses that locals love to hate. Really, though, for a comprehensive tour of the big sights, it's a great way to go.

On Location Tours (☎ 212-209-3370; www. screentours.com; tours $18-42) This company offers four tours – covering *Sex and the City, The Sopranos,* general TV and movie locations, and Central Park movie locations – that allow you to live out your entertainment-obsessed fantasies.

TAXES

Restaurants and retailers never include the sales tax – 8.875% – in their prices, so beware of ordering the $4.99 lunch special when you only have $5 to your name. Several categories of so-called 'luxury items,' including rental cars and dry-cleaning, carry an additional city surcharge of 5%, so you wind up paying an extra 13.875% in total for these services. Clothing and footwear purchases under $110 are tax-free; anything over that amount has a state sales tax of 4.375%. Hotel rooms in New York City are subject to a 14.75% tax, plus a flat $3.50 occupancy tax per night. Since the US has no nationwide value-added tax (VAT), there is no opportunity for foreign visitors to make 'tax-free' purchases.

TELEPHONE

Phone numbers within the USA consist of a three-digit area code followed by a seven-digit local number. If you're calling long distance, dial ☎ 1 + the three-digit area code + the seven-digit number.

For local and national directory assistance, dial ☎ 1-212-555-1212. As part of a miraculous citywide system, you can dial ☎ 311 for any issues that are city-related – whether you have a noise complaint, have a question about parking regulations or simply want to find the nearest dog run. Operators are available 24 hours and will quickly connect you to the government office that'll best be able to serve you.

If you're calling NYC from abroad, the international country code for the USA is 1. To dial an international number directly from NYC, dial ☎ 011, then the country code, followed by the area code (without any leading '0') and phone number. (To find country codes, check the phone book or dial ☎ 411 and ask for an international operator.) International rates vary depending on the time of day and the destination.

In New York City, Manhattan phone numbers are in the 212 or 646 area code (although cell phones and some businesses use 917) and the four outer boroughs are in the 718 or 347 zone. No matter where you're calling within New York City, even if it's just across the street in the same area code, you must *always* dial ☎ 1 + the area code first.

PAY PHONES

Though they seem outmoded, pay phones still exist on NYC streets and are almost always available.

To use a pay phone, you can pump in quarters, use a phone credit or debit card or make collect calls. There are thousands of pay phones on the New York City streets, seemingly all with a different price scheme, though most (especially the Verizon phones, which have yellow handles) are 50¢ for untimed local calls.

You can also make long-distance calls at global calling stations, which have low by-the-minute rates; you'll find them all over the city, but especially in and around Times Sq.

PHONECARDS

An excellent long-distance alternative is phone debit cards, which allow you to pay in advance, with access through a toll-free 800 number. These are available in amounts of $5, $10, $20 and $50 from Western Union, machines in airports and train stations, some supermarkets and nearly every corner deli.

TIME

New York City is in the Eastern Standard Time (EST) zone – five hours behind Greenwich Mean Time, two hours ahead of Mountain Standard Time (including Denver, Colorado) and three hours ahead of Pacific Standard Time (San Francisco and Los Angeles, California). Almost all of the USA observes daylight-saving time: clocks go forward one hour from the second Sunday in March to the first Sunday in November, when the clocks are turned back one hour. (It's easy to remember by the phrase 'spring ahead, fall back.')

TRAVELERS WITH DISABILITIES

Federal laws guarantee that all government offices and facilities are accessible to the disabled. For information on specific places, you can contact the mayor's **Office for People with Disabilities** (☎ 212-788-2830; � 9am-5pm Mon-Fri), which will send you a free copy of its *Access New York* guide if you call and request it. Another excellent resource is the **Society for Accessible Travel & Hospitality** (SATH; Map p168; ☎ 212-447-7284; www.sath.org; 347 Fifth Ave at 34th St; � 9am-5pm; ☉ 6 to 33rd St, ☐ M34 to Fifth Ave, M1 to 34th St), which gives advice on how to travel with a wheelchair, kidney disease, sight impairment or deafness.

Though New York is congested and difficult to navigate, things are improving slowly but surely; buses, which all have wheelchair elevation systems and ride space, are definitely the way to go. Subways, on the other hand, are either on elevated tracks or deep below ground and there are very few elevators to access them. For detailed information on subway and bus wheelchair accessibility, call the **Accessible Line** (☎ 718-596-8585) or visit www.mta.info/mta/ada for a list of subway stations with elevators or escalators.

VISAS

Because of the ever-lingering fear of terrorism, foreigners needing visas to travel to the US should plan ahead. However, there is a reciprocal visa-waiver program in which citizens of certain countries may enter the USA for stays of 90 days or less with a passport but without first obtaining a US visa. There are 27 countries included in this scheme, including Australia, France, Germany, Italy, Japan, the Netherlands, Switzerland and the UK (for a complete list, visit www.cbp.gov). Under this program you must have a round-trip ticket that is nonrefundable in the USA, and you will not be allowed to extend your stay beyond 90 days.

Other travelers will need to obtain a visa from a US consulate or embassy. In most countries, the process can be done by mail. Visa applicants may be required to 'demonstrate binding obligations' that will ensure their return home. Because of this requirement, those planning to travel through other countries before arriving in the USA are generally better off applying for their US visa while they are still in their home country – rather than after they're already on the road.

The Non-Immigrant Visitors Visa is the most common visa. It is available in two forms, B1 for business purposes and B2 for tourism or visiting friends and relatives. The validity period for US visitor visas depends on which country you're from. The length of time you'll be allowed to stay in the USA is ultimately determined by US immigration authorities at the port of entry.

For updates on visas and other security issues, you can visit the US Department of State (www.travel.state.gov/visa) and the Travel Security Administration (www.tsa.gov). Check out our website, lonelyplanet.com, for updates as well.

TRANSPORTATION

With its three bustling airports, two train stations and a monolithic bus terminal, New York rolls out the mat for the 47-odd million visitors who come here each year.

AIR

When booking tickets, note that high season in New York City runs from mid-June to mid-September (summer), and one week before and after Christmas. February and March, and from October to Thanksgiving (the fourth Thursday in November) serve as shoulder seasons, when prices drop slightly.

JFK INTERNATIONAL AIRPORT

This busy airport (JFK; ☎ 718-244-4444; www.panynj.gov, www.kennedyairport.com; Jamaica, Queens), 15 miles from Midtown in southeastern Queens, has eight terminals, serves 45 million passengers annually and hosts flights coming and going from all corners of the globe. Major renovations have been in progress for several years, including the AirTrain link with the subway (and free service between terminals).

LAGUARDIA AIRPORT

Used mainly for domestic flights, LaGuardia (LGA; ☎ 718-533-3400; www.panynj.gov, www.laguardiaairport.com; Flushing, Queens) is smaller than JFK but only eight miles from midtown Manhattan; it sees about 26 million passengers per year. US Airways and Delta have their own terminals there.

NEWARK LIBERTY INTERNATIONAL AIRPORT

The same distance from Midtown as JFK, Newark's airport (EWR; ☎ 973-961-6000; www.panynj.gov, www.newarkairport.com; Newark, NJ), 16 miles from Midtown, brings many New Yorkers out for flights (there's some 36 million passengers annually).

BICYCLE

It's not the most bike-friendly city, but New Yorkers are getting better at tolerating cyclists, thanks in part to improved road conditions, new bike paths and the efforts of bike clubs.

⬏ CLIMATE CHANGE & TRAVEL

Every form of transport that relies on carbon-based fuel generates CO_2, the main cause of human-induced climate change. Modern travel is dependent on aeroplanes, which might use less fuel per kilometer per person than most cars but travel much greater distances. The altitude at which aircraft emit gases (including CO2) and particles also contributes to their climate change impact. Many websites offer 'carbon calculators' that allow people to estimate the carbon emissions generated by their journey and, for those who wish to do so, to offset the impact of the greenhouse gases emitted with contributions to portfolios of climate-friendly initiatives throughout the world. Lonely Planet offsets the carbon footprint of all staff and author travel.

For maps of bike paths and a clearinghouse of tips, check the website of **Transportation Alternatives** (Map p168; ☎ 212-629-8080; www.transalt.org; Suite 1002, 127 W 26th St). Key Manhattan bike lanes are along Ninth Ave, Eighth Ave, Broadway, Grand and 20th, 21st, 9th and 10th Sts. Free NYC bike maps, updated annually, are available at most bike shops.

If you get on a bike, always wear a helmet, choose a solid frame with wide tires to help you handle potholes and other bits of street debris and be alert so you don't get 'doored' by a passenger exiting a taxi. Unless your urban skills are well honed, stick to the pastoral paths in Central and Prospect Parks and along the Hudson River. And don't even think of pedaling on the sidewalks – it's illegal. If you must lock a bike up somewhere in the city, forgo anything that's not the most top-of-the-line U-lock you can find – or, better yet, stick to the $100 coated chains that weigh a ton.

BOAT

The zippy yellow boats that make up the fleet of **New York Water Taxi** (Map p168; ☎ 212-742-1969; www.nywatertaxi.com; commuter 1-way tickets $3.50-6, 1-day pass adult/child $20/15, 2-day pass $25/15) provide an interesting, alternative way of getting around. Boats run along several different routes, including a hop-on, hop-off weekend service around Manhattan that starts at W 44th St on the Hudson River, with stops at W 26th St, Christopher St, World Financial Center, Battery Park, South Street Seaport, Fulton Ferry Landing (near Dumbo in Brooklyn) and E 34th St. This service runs from mid-April to mid-October. NY Water Taxi also runs year-round commuter service connecting the following locations: Hunters Point (Long Island City, Queens), E 34th St (Manhattan), Schaefer Landing (Williamsburg, Brooklyn), Fulton Ferry Landing (Dumbo, Brooklyn) and Pier 11 (near Wall Street in Manhattan). There's also year-round service between Pier 11 and the IKEA store in Red Hook, Brooklyn.

Another bigger, brighter ferry (this one's orange) is the commuter-oriented Staten Island Ferry (p62), which makes constant free journeys across the New York Harbor.

For information on boat tours, see p273.

BUS

Many New York buses aren't too bad, and they've certainly improved in the past decade or so. They run 24 hours a day and the routes are easily navigable, going crosstown at all the major street byways – 14th, 23rd, 34th, 42nd and 72nd Sts, and all the others that are two-way roads – and uptown and downtown, depending on which avenue they serve. Stops, many with shelters, are every few blocks and all have maps and marked schedules, which are rough guides as to how often you can expect a bus to pass. That said, buses do get overcrowded at rush hour, and slow to a crawl in heavy traffic. So when you're in a hurry, stay underground.

The cost of a bus ride is the same as the subway, $2.25, though express bus routes cost $5.50 (running during rush hours; best for long journeys from the boroughs). You can pay with a MetroCard or *exact* change but *not* dollar bills. Transfers from one line to another bus within two hours are free, as are transfers to or from the subway.

For long-distance bus trips, you'll leave and depart from the world's busiest bus station, the **Port Authority Bus Terminal** (Map p180; ☎ 212-564-8484; www.panynj.gov; 41st St at Eighth Ave), which sees nearly 60 million passengers pass through each year.

SUBWAY

The New York subway's 660-mile system, run by the Metropolitan Transportation Authority (MTA), is iconic, cheap ($2.25 per ride), round-the-clock and easily the fastest and most reliable way to get around the city. It's also safer and (a bit) cleaner than it used to be (and now with overly cheerful automated announcements on some lines).

For subway updates and information, call ☎ 718-330-1234 or visit www.mta. info. It's a good idea to grab a free map, available from any attendant. When in doubt, ask someone who looks like they know what they're doing.

TAXI

Hailing and riding in a cab are rites of passage in New York – especially when you get a driver who's a neurotic speed demon, which is often.

The **Taxi & Limousine Commission** (TLC; ☎ 311), the taxis' governing body, has set fares for rides (which can be paid with credit or debit card). It's $2.50 for the initial charge (first one-fifth of a mile), 40¢ each additional one-fifth mile as well as per 60 seconds of being stopped in traffic, $1 peak surcharge (weekdays 4pm to 8pm), and a 50¢ night surcharge (8pm to 6am), plus a new NY State surcharge of 50¢ per ride. Tips are expected to be 10% to 15%, but give less if you feel in any way mistreated – and be sure to ask for a receipt and use it to note the driver's license number.

To hail a cab, look for one with a lit (center) light on its roof. It's particularly difficult to score a taxi in the rain, at rush hour and around 4pm, when many drivers end their shifts.

TRAIN

Penn Station (Map p168; 33rd St btwn Seventh & Eighth Aves) is the departure point for all **Amtrak** (☎ 800-872-7245; www.amtrak.com) trains. There is no baggage-storage facility at Penn Station.

Long Island Rail Road (☎ 718-217-5477; www.mta.nyc.ny.us/lirr/) serves some 280,000 commuters each day, with services from Penn Station to points in Brooklyn, Queens and to Long Island. **New Jersey Transit** (☎ 800-772-2287; www.njtransit.com) also operates trains from Penn Station, with services to the suburbs and the Jersey Shore.

Another option for getting into NJ's northern points, such as Hoboken and Newark, is the **New Jersey PATH** (☎ 800-234-7284; www.panynj.gov/path), which runs trains ($1.75) along the length of Sixth Ave, with stops at 33rd, 23rd, 14th, 9th and Christopher Sts, as well as at the re-opened World Trade Center site.

The last line departing from Grand Central Terminal (42nd St at Park Ave), the **Metro-North Railroad** (☎ 212-532-4900; www.mta.info/mnr) serves Connecticut, Westchester County and the Hudson Valley.

⬊ BEHIND THE SCENES

THE AUTHORS
MICHAEL GROSBERG
Coordinating author

Growing up, Michael spent holidays with his large New York City family and grew to know their neighborhoods as if they were his own. After several long overseas trips and many careers, some abroad, Michael returned to New York City for graduate school in comparative literature and taught literature and writing in several New York City colleges. He's lived in Manhattan, Queens and Brooklyn and taught in the Bronx, and claims to know much of the city like the back of his hand.

Author thanks To the memory of my love Rebecca Tessler, who is always in my heart; who I carry along wherever I go, in our home, and in the streets of our neighborhood in Brooklyn and the entire city. Thanks also to Carly Neidorf for her invaluable feedback, support and help on this book. Of course, a huge acknowledgment to Ginger Adams Otis, Beth Greenfield and Regis St Louis for their work on Lonely Planet New York City books, and to the waiters and baristas at Le Petit Café and Ted & Honey's, where much of this work was done. Thanks also to my cousin Adam Gauthier and my uncle Larry Grosberg for their input.

GINGER ADAMS OTIS
Although not a native daughter, Ginger is proud to call New York City home. A country girl from New Hampshire, she starting living in the city fast lane in the late 1990s. Ginger now considers herself a New Yorker except during baseball season, when she reverts to being a die-hard member of the Red Sox nation. Ginger's done extensive reporting for radio outlets, newspapers and magazines in Central and South America, and worked on Lonely Planet guides to Brazil, South America, Puerto Rico and the Caribbean. When not working for Lonely Planet she's an intrepid beat reporter for one of New York's daily newspapers.

LONELY PLANET AUTHORS
Why is our travel information the best in the world? It's simple: our authors are passionate, dedicated travelers. They don't take freebies in exchange for positive coverage so you can be sure the advice you're given is impartial. They travel widely to all the popular spots, and off the beaten track. They don't research using just the internet or phone. They discover new places not included in any other guidebook. They personally visit thousands of hotels, restaurants, palaces, trails, galleries, temples and more. They speak with dozens of locals every day to make sure you get the kind of insider knowledge only a local could tell you. They take pride in getting all the details right, and in telling it how it is. Think you can do it? Find out how at lonelyplanet.com.

BETH GREENFIELD

A New Jersey native, Beth spent her teenage years yearning to someday live on the other side of the river. She began living the dream in 1993, right after college, and has been a New Yorker ever since. She's currently a staff editor at *Time Out New York* magazine, and has written about travel, entertainment, gay culture and parenting for publications including the *New York Times, Time Out New York Kids* and *Out*. Her memoir, *Ten Minutes From Home*, was recently published by Random House. For Lonely Planet, Beth contributed to the previous three editions of *New York City* as well as to *Miami & the Keys, Mexico* and *USA*.

REGIS ST LOUIS

A Hoosier by birth, Regis grew up in a sleepy town where he dreamed of big-city intrigue and small, expensive apartments. He settled in New York, which had all that and more, in 2001. Based in Boerum Hill, Brooklyn, Regis is a full-time travel writer and has contributed to more than two dozen Lonely Planet titles.

THE PHOTOGRAPHER

Dan Herrick has been based in New York City for a number of years after having lived and studied in Latin America and Europe. He enjoys documenting the city's changes and its frenetic way of life. On occasion he is able to pull himself away from it all to travel abroad, or more often to travel to one of the many different worlds that exist within the city's boundaries.

THIS BOOK

This 1st edition of *Discover New York City* was coordinated by Michael Grosberg, and researched and written by Michael, Ginger Adams Otis, Beth Greenfield and Regis St Louis. This guidebook was commissioned in Lonely Planet's Oakland office, and produced by the following:

Commissioning Editor Jennye Garibaldi
Coordinating Editor Dianne Schallmeiner
Coordinating Cartographer Diana Duggan
Coordinating Layout Designer Nicholas Colicchia
Managing Editor Sasha Baskett
Managing Cartographers Alison Lyall, Amanda Sierp
Managing Layout Designers Indra Kilfoyle, Celia Wood
Assisting Editor Susan Paterson
Cover Research Naomi Parker

Thanks to Glenn Beanland, Barbara Delissen, Joshua Geoghegan, Michelle Glynn, Brice Gosnell, Wayne Murphy, Darren O'Connell, Raphael Richards, Rebecca Skinner, Gerard Walker, Juan Winata

Internal photographs p4 Brooklyn Bridge, Glenn van der Knijff; p10 Brooklyn Bridge, Brent Winebrenner; p3, p12 Taxis at Times Sq, Christopher Groenhout; p29 Interior rotunda of The Solomon R. Guggenheim Museum, New York © The Solomon R.

Guggenheim Foundation, New York; Jean-Pierre Lescourret; p31 Horse and cart ride, Central Park, Christopher Groenhout; p39 Waldorf-Astoria, Angus Oburn; p3, p50 Tourists taking photos of Statue of Liberty, Gavin Gough; p3, p73 Billboard and water tower, SoHo, Bruce Bi; p3, p91 Chinese New Year celebrations, Chinatown, Angus Oburn; p3, p109 St Mark's-in-the-Bowery, Angus Oborn; p3, p127 Basketball game, Greenwich Village, Ionas Kaltenbach; p3, p153 Flatiron Building, Dan Herrick; p3, p167 Chrysler Building, Bruce Esbin; p3, p201 Park Ave, Manhattan, Jean-Pierre Lescourret; p206 Skylight rotunda in The Solomon R. Guggenheim Museum, New York © The Solomon R. Guggenheim Foundation, New York; Gavin Gough; p212 Exterior view of The Solomon R. Guggenheim Museum, New York © The Solomon R. Guggenheim Foundation, New York; Rob Blakers; p3, p219 Central Park, Christopher Groenhout; p3, p241 Roller coaster at Coney Island, Brooklyn, Steven Greave; p242 Apollo Theater, Harlem, Dan Herrick; p3, p248 View of Manhattan, taken from the Empire State Building, Richard I'Anson; p269 NYC yellow taxis, Huw Jones

ACKNOWLEDGMENTS

Many thanks to the following for the use of their content:
New York City Subway Map © 2010 Metropolitan Transportation Authority. Used with permission.
New York City Bus Map © 2010 Metropolitan Transportation Authority. Used with permission.

BEHIND THE SCENES

ACKNOWLEDGMENTS

SEND US YOUR FEEDBACK

We love to hear from travelers – your comments keep us on our toes and help make our books better. Our well-traveled team reads every word on what you loved or loathed about this book. Although we cannot reply individually to postal submissions, we always guarantee that your feedback goes straight to the appropriate authors, in time for the next edition. Each person who sends us information is thanked in the next edition, and the most useful submissions are rewarded with a free book.

Visit lonelyplanet.com to submit your updates and suggestions or to ask for help. Our award-winning website also features inspirational travel stories, news and discussions.

Note: We may edit, reproduce and incorporate your comments in Lonely Planet products such as guidebooks, websites and digital products, so let us know if you don't want your comments reproduced or your name acknowledged. For a copy of our privacy policy visit lonelyplanet.com/privacy.

See also separate subindexes for Activities (p288), Drinking (p288), Eating (p289), Entertainment (p290), Shopping (p291), Sights (p292) and Sleeping (p295).

INDEX

C-F

INDEX

F-J

INDEX

N-S

000 Map pages
000 Photograph pages

INDEX

S-Y

INDEX

EATING

INDEX

SIGHTS

INDEX

SIGHTS

MAP LEGEND

ROUTES
Tollway
Freeway
Primary
Secondary
Tertiary
Lane
Under Construction
Unsealed Road

One-Way Street
Mall/Steps
Tunnel
Pedestrian Overpass
Walking Tour
Walking Tour Detour
Walking Path
Track

TRANSPORT
Ferry
Metro
Monorail

Rail/Underground
Tram
Cable Car, Funicular

HYDROGRAPHY
River, Creek
Intermittent River
Swamp/Mangrove
Reef

Canal
Water
Dry Lake/Salt Lake
Glacier

BOUNDARIES
International
State, Provincial
Disputed

Regional, Suburb
Marine Park
Cliff/Ancient Wall

AREA FEATURES
Area of Interest
Beach, Desert
Building/Urban Area
Cemetery, Christian
Cemetery, Other

Forest
Mall/Market
Park
Restricted Area
Sports

POPULATION
○ **CAPITAL (NATIONAL)**
● LARGE CITY
● Small City

◉ **CAPITAL (STATE)**
● Medium City
○ Town, Village

SYMBOLS

Sights/Activities
Buddhist
Canoeing, Kayaking
Castle, Fortress
Christian
Confucian
Diving
Hindu
Islamic
Jain
Jewish
Monument
Museum, Gallery
Point of Interest
Pool
Ruin
Sento (Public Hot Baths)
Shinto
Sikh
Skiing
Surfing, Surf Beach
Taoist
Trail Head
Winery, Vineyard
Zoo, Bird Sanctuary

Information
Bank, ATM
Embassy/Consulate
Hospital, Medical
Information
Internet Facilities
Police Station
Post Office, GPO
Telephone
Toilets
Wheelchair Access

Eating
Eating

Drinking
Cafe
Drinking

Entertainment
Entertainment

Shopping
Shopping

Sleeping
Camping
Sleeping

Transport
Airport, Airfield
Border Crossing
Bus Station
Bicycle Path/Cycling
FFCC (Barcelona)
Metro (Barcelona)
Parking Area
Petrol Station
S-Bahn
Taxi Rank
Tube Station
U-Bahn

Geographic
Beach
Lighthouse
Lookout
Mountain, Volcano
National Park
Pass, Canyon
Picnic Area
River Flow
Shelter, Hut
Waterfall

LONELY PLANET OFFICES

Australia
Head Office
Locked Bag 1, Footscray, Victoria 3011
☎ 03 8379 8000, fax 03 8379 8111

USA
150 Linden St, Oakland, CA 94607
☎ 510 250 6400, toll free 800 275 8555,
fax 510 893 8572

UK
2nd fl, 186 City Rd,
London EC1V 2NT
☎ 020 7106 2100, fax 020 7106 2101

Contact
talk2us@lonelyplanet.com
lonelyplanet.com/contact

Published by Lonely Planet Publications Pty Ltd
ABN 36 005 607 983

MIX
Paper from
responsible sources
FSC™ C021741
www.fsc.org